T4-AQM-891

A Descriptive Catalogue of the Bibliographies of Twentieth Century British Poets, Novelists, and Dramatists

A Descriptive Catalogue of the Bibliographies of Twentieth Century British Poets, Novelists, and Dramatists

by

Elgin W. Mellown

Second Edition,

Revised and Enlarged

The Whitston Publishing Company
Troy, New York
1978

Library of Congress Catalog Card Number 79-183301

ISBN 0-87875-137-8

Printed in the United States of America

PREFACE

The favorable response to *A Descriptive Catalogue of the Bibliographies of Twentieth-Century British Writers,* which I published in 1972, encouraged me to bring out a second edition so that the bibliographies published between 1971 and 1977 would be more easily accessible to students. But the number of these recent publications demanded that, if this catalogue were to be kept to a reasonable length, I would have to revise my rules for selecting authors to be included. These standards are reflected in the new title, *A Descriptive Catalogue of the Bibliographies of Twentieth-Century British Poets, Novelists, and Dramatists.*

The scope of this new book has also been influenced by the publication of the *New Cambridge Bibliography of English Literature, 1900-1950* (1972) which provides bibliographies of writers in all genres. I have attempted to add to its listings the most up-to-date bibliographical information for a specific group of authors. I have retained the format of my earlier work, although I have attempted to incorporate the helpful--and gratefully received--suggestions made by reviewers of that book, particularly the anonymous reviewer of the *Times Literary Supplement;* Professor William White (in the *Library Journal);* and Professor Peter Davison (in *The Library*). I have been much encouraged by the American Library Association's recommending the earlier work as one of the "outstanding reference books" of 1972.

My original purpose in compiling this *Catalogue* remains unchanged: to assist the student and the general reader of twentieth-century British literature in finding the most reliable bibliographical information for the imaginative writers of the period. To this end I have listed (in alphabetical order and with birth and death years and pseudonyms) all the British poets, dramatists, and novelists who, born after 1840, published the larger part of their work in England after 1890 or thereabouts and who have been the subject of bibliographical study. I include both Scottish and Welsh authors, as well as Irish, if the latter were born before 1920 (or thereabouts), or if they published primarily in England or had some significant relationship to British literature. I have stepped over these national boundaries from time to time by including writers from other parts of the Commonwealth; and I pass by my limitations as to genre when I look at the members of certain literary groups or coteries. In short, I try to include all those writers whom the student may encounter in his *literary* studies and reasonably expect to find listed here.

The bibliographical information is given in two forms. For those writers who have only been included in one or more of the General Bibliographies which are listed and described below (pp. ix-xiv), the author-entries contain the appropriate abbreviations of these general bibliographies. For those writers who have been the subjects of more intensive bibliographical study, the author-entry is subdivided into three main sections. Under PRIMARY are bibliographies of writings *by* the author, while under SECONDARY are lists of writings, either critical or biographical, *about* the author. Under GENERAL are those bibliographies listed below. The entries within these three sections are chronologically arranged, the aim being to list the most inclusive, informative, and authoritative bibliographies, and the inclusion of several seemingly similar items indicating that each one provides information not found in the others. I have also tried to find both a British and an American publication for each category.

I have described these PRIMARY and SECONDARY bibliographies in reference to the four main areas listed below. Since the GENERAL bibliographies give the same type of information for each author, they are described here, along with the abbreviations which refer to them in the *Catalogue*.

INFORMATION GIVEN

ABOUT EACH BIBLIOGRAPHY

I. The scope of the work in question.

Primary signifies that all writings and all editions are included. *Primary first editions* shows that all first editions or first publications are included, but not reprints or later editions. *Primary books* indicates that no other form is included. *Secondary* means that the compiler has attempted to list all writings about the author, while *secondary selected* shows that the compiler has consciously omitted some writings.

II. The arrangement of each bibliography.

The arrangement is described as either *Chronological,* indicating one year-by-year list; or *Form,* meaning that it is divided according to the form of publication—book, periodical, part of a book, etc.—and is generally chronological within each section; or *Genre,* indicating a division according to literary genre—poetry, drama, fiction, etc.—and generally a chronological arrangement within each section; or some special arrangement which is described.

III. The details provided by each bibliography.

The description may include:

Transcribed title page;

Full collation: information concerning the format (the binder's term—quarto, octavo, etc.—is given), the signatures, the total number of pages, and the size of the volume in inches or centimeters;

Partial collation: information about two of the points listed above;

Pagination: description of each page;

Binding: description of physical appearance of volume;

Date of publication;

Price;

Number of copies;

Variants: an account of textual variants;

Reprints;

Contents: a list of titles or parts within the volume;

Notes: either bibliographical or textual.

IV. Evaluation of the bibliography.

When possible, I quote some authority; if the bibliography is the only one available, or if one should consult all of the bibliographies listed, there is generally no comment.

GENERAL BIBLIOGRAPHIES

Adelman & Dworkin.

Irving Adelman and Rita Dworkin. *Modern Drama. A Checklist of Critical Literature on 20th Century Plays.* Metuchen, N. J.: Scarecrow Press, 1967. Pp. 370.

Alphabetical list of authors with titles of plays under each name; relevant studies under each title. Books: place, publisher, date. Periodicals: volume, date, pages.

Adelman & Dworkin (Novel).

Irving Adelman and Rita Dworkin. *The Contemporary Novel. A Checklist of Critical Literature on the British and American Novel since 1945.* Metuchen, N. J.: Scarecrow Press, Inc., 1972. Pp. 614.

Alphabetical list of authors with critical studies of each listed under either the title of the novel studied or "General." Books: place, publisher, date. Periodicals: volume, date, pages.

Batho & Dobrée.

Edith Clara Batho and Bonamy Dobrée. *The Victorians and After, 1830-1914.* Volume IV, *Introductions to English Literature,* General Editor, Bonamy Dobrée. New York: R. M. McBride and Co.; London: Cresset Press, 1938. Pp. 370.

Authors arranged by genre and chronology; for each author, titles and dates of primary books arranged by genre; selected secondary books. A British guide for the beginning student.

Breed & Sniderman.

Paul F. Breed and Florence M. Sniderman. *Dramatic Criticism Index. A Bibliography of Commentaries on Playwrights from Ibsen to the Avant-Garde.* Detroit: Gale Research Co., 1972. Pp. [x], 1022.

Alphabetical list of authors with critical studies of each listed under either title of play studied or "General." Indices of play-titles, of critics, and of books indexed. Books: place, publisher, date. Periods: volume, date, pages.

Bufkin.

E. C. Bufkin. *The Twentieth-Century Novel in English: A Checklist.* Athens: University of Georgia Press, 1967. Pp. vi, 138.

Alphabetical list of authors with titles of their novels (no other genre included). Title, place, publisher, date, of first English edition.

Coleman & Tyler.

Arthur Coleman and Gary R. Tyler. *Drama Criticism. Volume One. A Checklist of Interpretation since 1940 of English and American Plays.* Denver: Alan Swallow, 1966. Pp. 457.

Alphabetical list of authors with titles of plays under each name; relevant studies under each title. Includes criticism written between 1940 and 1964. Books: place, publisher, date. Periodicals: volume, date, pages.

Daiches.

David Daiches. *The Present Age. After 1920.* Volume V, *Introductions to English Literature.* General Editor, Bonamy Dobrée. London: Cresset Press; Bloomington: Indiana University Press, 1958. Pp. x, 376.

Authors arranged by genre and chronology; for each author, titles and dates of primary books arranged by genre; selected secondary books. A British guide for the beginning student.

Drescher & Kahrmann.

Horst W. Drescher and Bernd Kahrmann. *The Contemporary English Novel. An Annotated Bibliography of Secondary Sources.* Frankfurt: Athenäum-Verlag, 1973. Pp. [xviii], 204.

Alphabetical list of authors; for each, selected list of primary works with dates and with an alphabetical-by-author list of reviews and critical studies:

very brief annotations for each entry. Books: place, publisher, date. Periodicals: volume, date, pages. Pp. 5-38, titles of general studies of the novel.

Hogan.

Robert Hogan. *After the Irish Renaissance. A Critical History of the Irish Drama since 'The Plough and the Stars.'* Minneapolis: University of Minnesota Press, 1967. Pp. xii, 282.

Pp. 260-271, alphabetically arranged list of authors; for each, published plays, non-dramatic works, and secondary criticism. Books: place, publisher, date. Periodicals: volume, date, pages.

Longaker & Bolles.

Mark Longaker and Edwin C. Bolles. *Contemporary English Literature.* New York: Appleton-Century Crofts, Inc., 1953. Pp. [xviii] 526.

Information as in Millett (below); in addition short discussions of each author, the whole arranged under headings determined by genre and chronology. For the beginning student.

Millett.

Fred B. Millett. *Contemporary British Literature. A Critical Survey and 232 Author Bibliographies.* Third revised and enlarged edition, based on the second revised and enlarged edition by John M. Manly and Edith Rickert. New York: Harcourt, Brace and Co., 1935, 1950. Pp. [xii], 556.

One alphabetical list of authors. For each author, titles and dates of primary books arranged by genre; short secondary selected bibliography of books (author, title, date) and periodicals (volume, date, pages). Ends at 1934. Obviously restricted in scope but very useful for the beginning student.

NCBEL, III, *and* NCBEL, IV.

George Watson, ed. *New Cambridge Bibliography of English Literature. Volume III. 1800-1900.* Cambridge University Press, 1969. Pp. xxiv; columns 1-1948; Index, pp. 1949-[1956]. I. R. Willison, ed.

New Cambridge Bibliography of English Literature. Volume IV. 1900-1950. Cambridge University Press, 1972. Pp. [xx]; columns 1-1408; Index, pp. 1409-[1414].

Authors arranged by genre of work. For each author, primary books with date, sub-divided by genre. Selected secondary bibliography. Authoritative lists of primary writings.

Palmer & Dyson.

Helen E. Palmer and Anne Jane Dyson. *European Drama Criticism.* Hamden, Conn.: Shoe String Press, Inc., 1968. Pp. [viii], 460; *European Drama Criticism. Supplement I.* Hamden, Conn.: Shoe String Press, Inc., 1970. Pp. [viii], 243.

Alphabetical list of authors with titles of plays and date of performance under each name; relevant studies under each title. Books: publisher, date, pages. Periodicals: volume, date, pages.

Salem.

James M. Salem. *A Guide to Critical Reviews. Part III. British and Continental Drama from Ibsen to Pinter.* Metuchen, N. J.: Scarecrow Press, Inc., 1968. Pp. 309.

Alphabetical list of authors with titles of plays under each name; date of first American performance (1909-1966) of each play and reviews of this performance. Periodicals: volume, pages, date. Various appendices and Index.

Stratford.

Jenny Stratford. *The Arts Council Collection of Modern Literary Manuscripts 1963-1972. A Catalogue . . . with a Preface by Philip Larkin.* London: Turret Books, 1974. Pp. [xxiv], 168.

Detailed descriptions of manuscripts and printed materials listed under the author's name. Information varies, but in addition to the descriptions, there are almost always notes on other collections of manuscripts and the available bibliographies, as well as extensive annotations. Books: place, publisher, date. Periods: volume, date, pages. The more extensive collections are cited in the primary entry for the author.

Temple & Tucker.

Ruth Z. Temple and Martin Tucker. *Twentieth Century British Literature: A Reference Guide and Bibliography.* New York: Frederick Ungar Publishing Co., 1968. Pp. x, 261.

Alphabetical list of authors; for each author, titles, dates, and genre of primary books; title of one or two critical or bibliographical studies. Various appendices and indices. Additional material published 1965-1975, as well as new authors who came into notice during this period, are listed by Martin Tucker and Rita Stein. *Modern British Literature. A Library of Literary Criticism. Volume IV. Supplement.* New York: Frederick Ungar Publishing Co., 1975. Pp. [xiv], 650. Bibliographical information, in the same format as the 1968 work, is provided on pp. 587-615.

Vinson-Dramatists.

James Vinson, ed. *Contemporary Dramatists.* London: St. James Press; New York: St. Martin's Press, 1973. Pp. [xvi], 926.

Alphabetical list of authors, each entry providing biographical information, bibliography of primary books (place, publisher, date), comment by the dramatist, and a signed, critical comment. Some entries include a brief list of secondary items. An enlarged, second edition was published in 1977, after this Catalogue was completed.

Vinson-Novelists.

James Vinson, ed. *Contemporary Novelists.* London: St. James Press; New York: St. Martin's Press, 1972. Pp. [xviii], [1442].

Alphabetical list of novelists, each entry providing biographical information, brief critical essay on the novelist, bibliography of primary books (genre, place, publisher, date), brief list of critical studies, including bibliographies and location of manuscript collections.

Vinson-Poets.

James Vinson, ed. *Contemporary Poets.* Second edition. London: St. James Press; New York: St. Martin's Press, 1975. Pp. [xvi], 1849.

Alphabetical list of poets, each entry providing a biography, primary bibliography of books (place, publisher, date, genre), a comment by the poet, and a signed, critical essay. Some entries include brief secondary bibliographies and details of manuscript collections.

ABBREVIATIONS

AWTW. *Australian Writers and Their Work*

TEAS. *Twayne's English Authors Series*

TP. Title page

TUSAS. *Twayne's United States Authors Series*

TWAS. *Twayne's World Authors Series*

WTW. *Writers and Their Work*

Periods. Periodicals

ACKNOWLEDGEMENTS

During the four and a half years that I worked on the first edition of the *Catalogue* I was assisted by various persons, and it gives me pleasure to thank them here. I am grateful to the Duke Research Council for financial assistance that enabled me to spend the summer, 1967, at the British Museum Reading Room, and to the Duke Endowment for subsequent financial assistance. I appreciate both the personal and professional kindnesses shown to me by Ian R. Willison, formerly Assistant Keeper and Superintendent of the North Library of the British Museum Reading Room; but indeed I am indebted to the entire staff of the Reading Room for assistance over a number of years: my work on this particular project confirmed once again what all students privileged to use the Reading Room know: that helpfulness, courtesy, and efficiency are unfailing at the British Museum. I have also been greatly helped by the Acquisitions Department of the William R. Perkins Library, Duke University, and by members of the Reference Department, especially Miss Florence Blakely and Miss Mary Canada; and also by the staff of the East Campus Library, particularly Miss Evelyn Harrison and Mrs. Betty Young.

My research for this new edition has been conducted mainly in the William R. Perkins Library, Duke University, and I am most grateful to the many librarians there who have helped me. I have also worked in the University of London Library and in the British Museum (now the British Library): again I give my thanks to the staff members of these institutions for their assistance.

April, 1977.

Elgin W. Mellown
Duke University

A DESCRIPTIVE CATALOGUE

A.E.: see RUSSELL, GEORGE WILLIAM

ABERCROMBIE, LASCELLES (1881-1938)

PRIMARY

Jeffrey Cooper. *A Bibliography and Notes on the Works of Lascelles Abercrombie.* London: Kaye and Ward, Ltd., 1968; Hamden, Conn.: Archon Books, 1969. Pp. 166.

Primary complete. Form arrangement. Books: transcribed TP, full collation, pagination, binding, date, price, contents, extensive notes on textual history and bibliography of each piece of writing. Periods (arranged alphabetically by title of periodical): volume, pages, date, extensive notes on Abercrombie's association with each periodical. Reviews by Abercrombie include author and title of book reviewed. Each section begins with list of books or periodical titles described in the section. Pp. 150-152, Table of Item Numbers in Chronological Order. Pp. 155-166, Index. An authoritative and extremely helpful work.

GENERAL

Millett; Longaker & Bolles; Daiches; Batho and Dobrée; Temple & Tucker.

ABLEMAN, PAUL (1927-)

Vinson-Dramatists; Vinson-Novelists

ABSE, DANNIE (1923-)

Vinson-Dramatists; Vinson-Novelists; Vinson-Poets; Temple & Tucker.

ACKERLEY, JOE RANDOLPH (1896-1967)

PRIMARY

J. R. Ackerley. *My Father and Myself.* London: Bodley Head, 1968. Pp. 219.

Although there is no bibliography in this autobiography, there are many references to Ackerley's writings, with his books being listed on p. [2].

GENERAL

Bufkin; NCBEL, IV, 905.

ACKLAND, RODNEY (1908-)

Vinson-Dramatists; NCBEL, IV, 905-906.

ACTON, SIR HAROLD MARIO MITCHELL (1904-)

NCBEL, IV, 229.

AGATE, JAMES EVERSHED (1877-1947)

PRIMARY

James Agate. *An Anthology.* Herbert Van Thal, ed. Introduction by Alan Dent. London: Rupert Hart-Davis, 1961. Pp. [xxiv], 288.

P. ii, list of primary books, 1917-1949. Chronological arrangement. Date. Pp. ix-xxiii, bibliographical information, *passim.*

Additional information can be gained from Agate's autobiography, *Ego* (Vols. 1-9), London, 1935-1948.

GENERAL

Temple & Tucher.

ALDINGTON, RICHARD (1892-1962)

PRIMARY

Alistair Kershaw. *A Bibliography of the Works of Richard Aldington from 1915 to 1948.* London: Quadrant Press, 1950. Pp. [xii], 57.

Primary books. Genre arrangement. Transcribed TP, part collation, date, occasionally contents, printer. Includes translations by Aldington.

Kershaw modestly describes his work as "an extended checklist," but it it quite complete.

–and Frédéric-Jacques Temple, eds. *Richard Aldington An Intimate Portrait.* Carbondale: Southern Illinois University Press, 1965. Pp. [xxii], 186. Pp. 175-186, "A Chronological Checklist of the Books of Richard Aldington," by Paul Schlueter. Primary British and American first editions. Genre arrangement. Place, publisher, year, bibliographical notes by Kershaw. Includes translations and books edited or introduced by Aldington.

A convenient checklist which adds to Kershaw's bibliography.

SECONDARY

V. M. Parchevskaia. *Richard Aldington.* Moscow: Kniga Publishing House (Writers of Foreign Countries Series), 1965, Pp. [60].

Pp. 21-29, primary bibliography. Pp. 30-47, secondary bibliography. Arranged: General Criticism; English and American Reviews, Russian Reviews (listed under titles by Aldington being reviewed). Books: place, publisher, date, pages. Periods: volume, pages, date. (In Russian)

GENERAL

Millett; Longaker & Bolles; Daiches; Temple & Tucker; NCBEL,

IV, 511-514; Bufkin.

ALDISS, BRIAN WILSON (1925-)

PRIMARY

Margaret Manson. *Item Forty-Three. Brian W. Aldiss: A Bibliography 1954-1962.* With Annotations by Brian Aldiss. Wisbech: Fantast (Medway) Ltd., [1963]. Pp. [24]. 500 copies.

Primary. Four lists (each arranged alphabetically by title): primary fiction, journals to which Aldiss contributed, miscellaneous primary writings, volumes edited by Aldiss. Books: publisher, date, pages. Periods: volume, date, number of words. Contents listed of books edited by Aldiss. Miscellaneous bibliographical notes. Includes translations of primary writings.

GENERAL

Vinson-Novelists.

ALLEN, WALTER ERNEST (1911-)

Temple & Tucker; Vinson-Novelists; NCBEL, IV, 514.

ALLISON, DRUMMOND (1921-1943)

Stratford.

ALLOTT, KENNETH (1912-)

NCBEL, IV, 230.

ALVAREZ, ALFRED (1929-)

Vinson-Poets; Temple & Tucker.

AMBLER, ERIC (1909-)

PRIMARY

[? Paxton Davis]. "Books by Eric Ambler." *Hollins Critic* 8

(February 1971): 6-7.

Primary books, all English-language editions. Chronological arrangement. Place, publisher, date, price, British and American titles. Filmscripts by Ambler listed on p. 5 with suggestion of other primary writings.

GENERAL

Bufkin; Vinson-Novelists.

AMIS, KINGSLEY WILLIAM (1922-)

PRIMARY

Jack G. Gohn. *Kingsley Amis: A Checklist.* Kent, Ohio: Kent State University Press (Serif Series: No. 34), 1976. Pp. xviii, 230.

Pp. 1-78, primary bibliography. Arranged by genre under Unpublished Materials and Published materials. Books (all editions and translations): place, publisher, date, genre, serialization if any, translator; cross-references to reviews of the book in the second part. Periods: volume, date, pages, annotations. Reviews by Amis include author and title of work reviewed and summary of Amis's judgment of the work. Pp. 78-167, secondary bibliography, including reviews of Amis's work listed under title of the work. Pp. 169-230, indices of names and of titles. Each item is numbered.

One of the most elaborate bibliographies published for a living and still producing author.

SECONDARY

Above, Gohn, pp. 78-167.

J. Don Vann and James T. F. Tanner. "Kingsley Amis. A Checklist of Recent Criticism." *Bulletin of Bibliography* 26 (1969): 115-117, 105, 111.

Alphabetical by author arrangement. Books: place, publisher, date. Periods: volume, date, pages.

A comprehensive list including reviews.

GENERAL

Temple & Tucker; Bufkin; Adelman & Dworkin (Novelists); Vinson-Poets; Vinson-Novelists; Drescher & Kahrmann.

ANDERSON, PATRICK (1915-)

Vinson-Poets.

ANSTEY, F. (1856-1934)

Pseudonym of Thomas Anstey Guthrie.

PRIMARY

Martin John Turner. *Bibliography of the Works of F. Anstey [Thomas Anstey Guthrie].* London: Privately Published, 1931, Pp. 44. 150 copies.

Primary. Form arrangement. Transcribed TP, full collation, binding, date, variants, reprints, contents. Contributions to periodicals other than *Punch* listed. Index.

Lord Esher, *Book Collector's Quarterly*, No. 5 (January-March 1932), p. 36: "an almost perfect example of bibliographical work."

F. Anstey. *A Long Retrospect.* London and New York: Oxford University Press, 1936. Pp. 424.

Pp. 415-416, primary books, 1882-1936. Title, date. Occasional references to periodical contributions in text, *passim.*

GENERAL

Batho & Dobrée; Temple & Tucker; NCBEL, III, 1034.

ANTHONY, C. L.: *see* SMITH, DODIE

ANTROBUS, JOHN (1933-)

Vinson-Dramatists.

ARCHER, WILLIAM (1856-1924)

PRIMARY

Lt. Col. Charles Archer. *William Archer: Life, Work and Friendships.* London: George Allen and Unwin, 1931. Pp. 451.

Pp. 421-434, "Bibliographic Appendix." Primary. Chronological arrangement. Books: publisher, pages. Periods: date. English works edited by Archer listed alphabetically by main author with publisher, date. Translations or books edited by Archer listed alphabetically by main author with publisher, date.

GENERAL

Batho & Dobrée, Temple & Tucker; Salem; Palmer & Dyson; NCBEL, III, 1417-1418.

ARDEN, JOHN (1930-)

PRIMARY

Simon Trussler. *John Arden.* New York: Columbia University Press (Columbia Essays on Modern Writers, 65), 1973. Pp. 48.

P. 47, primary books, British and American editions. Chronological arrangement. Place, publisher, dates of production and of publication. P. 48, secondary bibliography.

Glenda Leeming. *John Arden.* Harlow: Longman Group Ltd. (WTW 238), 1974. Pp. 34.

P. 33, select primary books: place, date, collaborators. P. 34, select secondary titles: volume, date, pages.

GENERAL

Coleman & Tyler; Adelman & Dworkin; Vinson-Dramatists; Temple & Tucker; Breed & Sniderman.

ARLEN, MICHAEL (1895-1956)

Formerly Dikran Kouyoumdjian.

PRIMARY

Harry Keyishian. *Michael Arlen.* Boston: Twayne Publishers, G. K. Hall and Co. (TEAS 174), 1975. Pp. 150.

Pp. 133-142, primary bibliography. Arranged by form and genre, including unpublished plays, screenplays, films based upon Arlen's novels and stories, translations of Arlen's novels, reprintings of stories in anthologies. Books (British and American first editions): place, publisher, date, contents of collections. Period: volume, date, pages. Pp. 142-145, selected secondary bibliography, annotated. Additional secondary material is given in the Notes, pp. 123-132. One of the best primary bibliographies in all of the TEAS books.

SECONDARY

Above, Keyishian.

GENERAL

Daiches; Temple & Tucker; NCBEL, IV, 514-515.

ARMSTRONG, MARTIN DONISTHORPE (1882-1974)

PRIMARY

R. L. Mégroz. *Five Novelist Poets.* London: Joiner and Steele, 1933.

Pp. 245-246, primary books, first editions, 1912-1932. Chronological arrangement. Publisher, place, pages, date.

Martin Armstrong. Poet and Novelist: A Bibliography. Bristol: Public Libraries, 1937. Pp. [4].

Primary books. Genre arrangement. Publisher, date.

GENERAL

Millett; Temple & Tucker.

ARMSTRONG, TERENCE: *see* GAWSWORTH, JOHN

ARNIM, GRÄFIN VON: *see* ELIZABETH

ASCHE, OSCAR: *see* HEISS, JOHN STANGER

ASHTON, WINIFRED: *see* DANE, CLEMENCE

AUDEN, WYSTAN HUGH (1907-1973)

PRIMARY

B[arry] C[ambray] Bloomfield and Edward Mendelson. *W. H. Auden. A Bibliography 1924-1969.* Second Edition. Charlottesville: University of Virginia Press for the Bibliographical Society of the University of Virginia, 1972. Pp. [xviii], 420.

Primary complete (to 1969); secondary selected. Form arrangement. Books: transcribed TP, full collation, pagination, binding, type of paper, date, price, contents, number of copies; textual, bibliographical, and publishing-history notes. Reviews of primary books listed under book title. Periods: volume, date, pages. Reviews by Auden include title and author of book reviewed. Auden's writings in forms other than books and periodicals listed under thirteen different headings, including Unpublished Work, MSS, Anthologies, Musical Settings, Translations [of Auden]. Pp. 325-366, secondary bibliography, including on p. 326 a list of earlier bibliographies. Appendices. Index (one alphabetical list including titles of works by Auden).

The standard bibliography. Peter Davison, *Library* 28 (1973): 361-363: "splendid piece of scholarship. . . this second edition replaces its predecessor but it is much more than an updating of a work of reference. This is that rare contribution to scholarship, a bibliography we can enjoy as well as use." There does not appear to be any listing of the writings of Auden's last four years, nor of posthumous publications.

SECONDARY

Above, Bloomfield and Mendelson: reviews of books by Auden, *passim;* other secondary studies, pp. 325-366.

Joseph P. Clancy. "A. W. H. Auden Bibliography 1924-1955." *Thought* 30 (Summer 1955): 260-270.

Pp. 266-270, secondary bibliography arranged alphabetically by author.

George T. Wright. *W. H. Auden.* New York: Twayne Publishers, Inc. (TUSAS 144), 1969. Pp. 180.

Pp. 170-173, secondary bibliography. Form arrangement. Annotated.

John E. Stoll. *W. H. Auden: A Reading.* Muncie: Ball State University (Monograph No. 18; Publication in English No. 12), 1970. Pp. [iv], 40.

Pp. 38-40, secondary bibliography arranged alphabetically by author. "Especially relevant" items marked with an asterisk.

GENERAL

Longaker & Bolles; Daiches; Temple & Tucker; Coleman & Tyler; Adelman & Dworkin; Salem; Palmer & Dyson; Breed & Sniderman; Vinson-Poets; Vinson-Dramatists; NCBEL, IV, 207-220; Stratford.

AUSTIN, ALFRED (1835-1913)

PRIMARY

Norton B. Crowell. *Alfred Austin, Victorian.* Albuquerque: University of New Mexico Press; London: Weidenfeld and Nicolson, 1955. Pp. [x], 296.

Pp. 268-273, primary bibliography. Form arrangement. Books: place, publisher, date. Periods: volume, pages, date. Pp. 273-291, secondary bibliography.

SECONDARY

Above, Crowell, pp. 273-291.

GENERAL

NCBEL, III, 608-609.

BAGNOLD, ENID (1889-)

(Lady Jones)
Coleman & Tyler; Adelman & Dworkin; Salem; Palmer & Dyson; Vinson-Dramatists; NCBEL, IV, 908-909.

BAILEY, HENRY CHRISTOPHER (1878-1961)

NCBEL, IV, 515-516.

BAKER, ELIZABETH (1876-1962)

NCBEL, IV, 909.

BALCHIN, NIGEL MARLIN (1908-1970)

Pseudonym used: Mark Spade.

Bufkin; Temple & Tucker; NCBEL, IV, 516-517.

BALLARD, JAMES GRAHAM (1930-)

Vinson-Novelists.

BANTOCK, GAVIN MARCUS AUGUST (1939-)

Vinson-Poets.

BARBELLION, W. N. P. (1889-1919)

Pseudonym of Bruce Frederick Cummings.

Dictionary of National Biography, 1912-1921.

BARING, MAURICE (1874-1945)

PRIMARY

"Bibliographies of Modern Authors. The Hon. Maurice Baring." *London Mercury 2* (1920): 346.

Primary books, 1899-1920. Genre arrangement. Publisher, date.

Leslie Chaundy. *A Bibliography of the First Editions of the Works of Maurice Baring.* Introduction by Desmond McCarthy. London: Dulau, 1925. Pp. 48. 250 copies.

Primary books, first editions. Chronological arrangement. Transcribed TP, part collation, binding, date, brief notes.

Louis Chaigne. *Maurice Baring. Biographie.* Paris: J. de Gigord, 1935. Pp. 72.

Pp. 67-70, primary books. Chronological arrangement. Dates. French translations listed separately: translator, publisher, date. Pp. 71-72, secondary bibliography.

Paul Horgan, ed. *Maurice Baring Restored: Selections from his Work.* New York: Farrar, Strauss, and Giroux, 1970. Pp. [x], [444].

Pp. 439-440, primary books. Dates.

SECONDARY

Above, Chaigne, pp. 71-72.

GENERAL

Millett; Batho & Dobrée; Daiches; Temple & Tucker.

BARKER, AUDREY LILLIAN (1918-)

Vinson-Novelists; Drescher & Kahrmann.

BARKER, GEORGE GRANVILLE (1913-)

PRIMARY

Martha Fodaski. *George Barker.* New York: Twayne Publishers, Inc. (TEAS 90), 1969. Pp. 190.

Pp. 181-184, primary bibliography. Genre arrangement. Books: place, publisher, date. Periods: volume, date, pages. Includes book reviews by Barker with author and title of book reviewed. Pp. 184-185, Secondary bibliography, annotated. Information as for primary; see notes, pp. 175-181, for additional secondary criticism.

Not a complete record of Barker's extensive writings, but at least a start toward it.

SECONDARY

Above, Fodaski, pp. 175-181, 184-185.

GENERAL

Longaker & Bolles; Daiches; Temple & Tucker; Vinson-Poets.

BARKER, H. GRANVILLE: *see* GRANVILLE-BARKER, H.

BARLOW, JANE (1857-1917)

NCBEL, III, 1908.

BARNSLEY, ALAN GABRIEL: *see* FIELDING, GABRIEL

BARON, JOSEPH ALEXANDER (1917-)

NCBEL, IV, 519.

BARRIE, SIR JAMES MATTHEW (1860-1937)

PRIMARY

Herbert Garland. *A Bibliography of the Writings of Sir James M.*

Barrie. London: Bookman's Journal, 1928. Pp. 146.

Primary complete, secondary selected, 1887-1924. Form arrangement. Books: transcribed TP, full collation, binding, date, contents, notes. Periods: dates; includes unsigned writings. Pp. 139-141, secondary books.

Bradley D. Cutler. *Sir James M. Barrie. A Bibliography, with Full Collations of the American Unauthorized Editions.* New York: Greenberg, 1931. Pp. 242. 1000 copies.

Primary books, secondary selected. Transcribed TP, part collation, pagination, binding, date, variants, notes. Pp. 223-233, prices and price trends of first editions. Pp. 215-220, secondary books.

Supplements Garland with the American edns. Additional prices are given in Andrew Block. *Sir James M. Barrie His First Editions: Points and Values.* London: W. and G. Foyle Ltd., 1933. Pp. 48. 500 copies. Alphabetical list of primary books: publisher, date, size, binding, value in sterling.

Roger Lancelyn Green. *James M. Barrie.* London: Bodley Head (Bodley Head Monograph), 1960, Pp. 64.

Pp. 59-64, "Book List." Genre, form arrangement. Publisher, date. Selected secondary bibliography.

Together these three works include most of the primary books; there is no complete list of Barrie's periodical contributions.

SECONDARY

Above, Garland, pp. 139-141; Cutler, pp. 215-220; Green, p. 64.

Katharine G. Shields. "Sir James M. Barrie, Bart., Being a Partial Bibliography." *Bulletin of Bibliography* 16 (1937): 44-46, 68-69, 97, 119, 140-141, 162.

Arranged under six topical divisions. Books: publisher, place, year, annotations. Periods: volume, pages, date, annotations.

Harry M. Geduld. *Sir James Barrie.* New York: Twayne Publishers, Inc. (TEAS 105), 1971. Pp. 187.

Pp. 180-184, bibliography. Books: place, publisher, date. Period: volume, pages, date. Annotated. Additional items in notes, pp. 173-177.

GENERAL

Millett; Longaker & Bolles; Daiches; Temple & Tucker; Coleman & Tyler; Adelman & Dworkin; Salem; Palmer & Dyson; NCBEL, III, 1188-1192.

BARSTOW, STANLEY (1928-)

Vinson-Novelists; Drescher & Kahrmann; Temple & Tucker.

BATES, HERBERT ERNEST (1905-1974)

PRIMARY

John Gawsworth. *Ten Contemporaries. Notes Toward their Definitive Bibliography (Second Series).* London: Joiner & Steele Ltd., 1933. Pp. 240. 1000 copies.

Pp. 23-34, primary books, first editions, 1926-1932. Chronological arrangement. Transcribed TP, full collation, pagination, binding, date, bibliographical notes.

H. E. Bates. *The Vanished World. An Autobiography. Volume One.* London: Michael Joseph, 1969; Columbia: University of Missouri Press, 1971. Pp. [189].

Autobiography of childhood and adolescent years with little information concerning literary career; see p. [2] for list of primary books, arranged by genre.

GENERAL

Millett; Longaker & Bolles; Daiches; Temple & Tucker; Vinson-Novelists; NCBEL, IV, 520-521; Bufkin.

BATES, RALPH (1899-)

Daiches; Bufkin; Temple & Tucker; NCBEL, IV, 521-522.

BAWDEN, NINA (1925-)

(Mrs. A. S. Kark)

Vinson-Novelists.

BAX, CLIFFORD (1886-1962)

Temple & Tucker; NCBEL, IV, 910-911.

BEACHCROFT, THOMAS OWEN (1902-)

Daiches; NCBEL, IV, 522.

BEARDSLEY, AUBREY VINCENT (1872-1898

PRIMARY

A. E. Gallatin. *Aubrey Beardsley. Catalogue of Drawings and Bibliography.* New York: Grolier Club, 1945. Pp. 162. 300 copies.

Pp. 17-70, catalogue of drawings (1096 entries). Pp. 73-128, primary and secondary bibliography. Information arranged under these headings: Albums of Drawings, Monographs on Beardsley, Studies on Beardsley in Books and Periodicals, Beardsley's Literary Work, Collections of Beardsley's Letters, Catalogues of Beardsley Exhibitions. Appendices.

Additional information is provided by R. A. Walker. *Le Morte Darthur with Beardsley Illustrations. A Bibliographical Essay.* Bedford: Published by the Author, 1945. Pp. 24. 350 copies; and by A. E. Gallatin and Alexander D. Wainright, *The Gallatin Beardsley Collection in the Princeton University Library, A Catalogue.* Princeton University Press, 1952. Pp. 43. First published in the *Princeton University Library Chronicle* 10 (1949): 81-84; 12 (1951): 67-82; 126-147.

SECONDARY

Above, Gallatin (1945).

GENERAL

NCBEL, III, 610-611.

BEATY, ARTHUR DAVID (1919-)

Vinson-Novelists.

BECKETT, SAMUEL BARCLAY (1906-)

PRIMARY

Raymond Federman and John Fletcher. *Samuel Beckett. His Works and His Critics. An Essay in Bibliography.* Berkeley: University of California Press, 1970. Pp. [xiv], 383.

Pp. 1-109, primary complete. Pp. 113-319, secondary complete (described below). Arranged by language in which written, or by genre; chronological in each section. Books: transcribed TP, part collation, pagination, binding, date, price, number of copies, variants, reprints and subsequent editions, extensive bibliographical notes and annotations. Periods: volume, pages, date, reprintings, notes. Extensive appendices and indices. Pp. ix-xiii, explanation of arrangement.

The basic primary bibliography, which James Mays reviews, providing detailed corrections and additions, in "Samuel Beckett Bibliography: Comments and Corrections." *Irish University Review* 2 (1972): 189-208. Additional information about the primary works and details of the post-1970 publications are given by R. J. Davis, *Calepins de Bibliographie. No. 2. Samuel Beckett,* Peter C. Hoy, general editor. Paris: Minard (Lettres Modernes), 1972 [2nd printing of the 2nd edition]. Unnumbered pages. Later editions of this primary bibliography appear separately as *Essai de bibliographie des œuvres de Samuel Beckett* in the Minard "BIBLIOthèque" series [not seen].

SECONDARY

Federman and Fletcher, described above.

Pp. 113-319, secondary complete. Form arrangement. Books: place, publisher, date, pages, contents, critical résumé, reviews. Periods: volume, date, pages, reprints, annotations. Additional primary and secondary bibliographies listed on pp. 317-319.

This authoritative bibliography of primary writings, the starting point for all study of Beckett, is supplemented by J. R. Bryer, M. J. Friedman, and Peter C. Hoy in the continuing editions of the *Beckett Calepins de Bibliographie* described above.

James T. F. Tanner and J. Don Vann. *Samuel Beckett. A Checklist of Criticism.* Kent: Kent State University Press (Serif Series No. 8), 1969. Pp. [vi] , 85.

Secondary selected. Form arrangement with reviews of books about Beckett listed under book title; pp. 73-85, reviews of Beckett's books listed under title of book reviewed. Books: place, publisher, date, pages. Periods: volume, date, pages.

A useful checklist, particularly in its isolation of the book reviews of Beckett's writings.

GENERAL

Temple & Tucker; Coleman & Tyler; Adelman & Dworkin; Salem; Palmer & Dyson; Breed & Sniderman; Adelman & Dworkin (Novel); Vinson-Poets; Vinson-Dramatists; Vinson-Novelists; NCBEL, IV, 885-906.

The *Journal of Beckett Studies,* ed. James Knowlson, published by John Calder Ltd. and the Beckett Archive, University of Reading, appeared for the first time in the winter, 1976. It will hopefully prove as valuable to Beckett studies as the other single author journals are to the study of their respective subjects.

BEDFORD, SYBILLE (1911-)

(Mrs. Walter Bedford)

Temple & Tucker; Bufkin; Vinson-Novelists.

BEECHING, HENRY CHARLES (1859-1919)

PRIMARY

George Arthur Stephen. "An Annotated Bibliography of the Writings of Dean Beeching and the Works Edited by Him." *Norwich Public Library Reader's Guide* 7 (April 1919): 82-90.

Primary. Form and genre arrangement. Books: place, publisher, date, part collation, contents. Periods: volume, date, pages. Miscellaneous notes. Reviews by Beeching include title and author of book reviewed. Names of periodicals including unsigned contributions by Beeching. List of obituary notices.

GENERAL

NCBEL, III, 611.

BEEDING, FRANCIS: see PALMER, JOHN LESLIE.

BEER, PATRICIA (1924-)

Vinson-Poets.

BEERBOHM, SIR HENRY MAXIMILIAN (1872-1956)

PRIMARY

A. E. Gallatin. *Sir Max Beerbohm: Bibliographical Notes.* Cambridge, Mass.: Harvard University Press, 1944. Pp. 121. 400 copies.

Primary complete, secondary selected. Form arrangement. Transcribed TP, part collation, binding, date, contents.

–and L. M. Oliver. *A Bibliography of the Works of Max Beerbohm.* London: Rupert Hart-Davis (Soho Bibliography No. 3), 1952. Pp. 60.

Primary books. Chronological arrangement. Transcribed TP, full collation, pagination, binding, date. Full account of subsequent editions; limits of publication. Full bibliographical notes. Pp. 57-60, description of MSS in the Gallatin and Harvard collections.

J. G. Riewald. *Sir Max Beerbohm, Man and Writer. A Critical Analysis with a Brief Life and a Bibliography.* Hague: Martinus Nijhoff, 1953. Pp. 369.

Pp. 213-333, bibliography. Primary complete, secondary complete. Form arrangement. Transcribed TP, full collation, pagination, binding, date, price, number of copies. Subsequent editions and reprints described briefly; extensive notes; for each title a list of early reviews. Pp. 306-333, secondary bibliography. Pp. 333-343, subject index to Beerbohm's dramatic criticism.

P. 213: Riewald describes his work as a "reasonably complete list of the published works, both collected and uncollected. . .and of the secondary studies and notes." An overwhelmingly inclusive list--yet the differences between Riewald, Gallatin (1944), and Gallatin and Oliver are so great that the three books must be used together, no one being complete in itself.

Roy Huss. "Max Beerbohm's Drawings of Theatrical Figures." *Theatre Notebook* 21 (1966-1967): 75-86, 102-119, 169-180.

Described by Huss as a "*catalogue raisonné* of Max's drawings of theatrical figures. . . designed as the pictorial counterpart of J. G. Riewald's index. . ." (p. 75). A comprehensive catalogue giving all required information.

Rupert Hart-Davis. *A Catalogue of the Caricatures of Max Beerbohm.* London: Macmillan, 1972. Pp. 258.

Alphabetical arrangement of subjects under headings "Real People" and "Imaginary People and Allegorical Subjects." For each entry, title, description of drawing, reproduction of all written matter, exhibitions, reproductions, and owner; other notes. Indices of titles, books and periodicals, and owners. The principles of selection are described in the "Introduction," pp. 9-15.

SECONDARY

Above, Gallatin (1944), pp. 93-100; Riewald, pp. 306-333.

GENERAL

Millett; Longaker & Bolles; Batho & Dobrée; Temple & Tucker; NCBEL, IV, 1000-1003.

BEHAN, BRENDAN (1922-1964)

PRIMARY

Raymond J. Porter. *Brendan Behan.* New York: Columbia University Press (Columbia Essays on Modern Writers, 66), 1973. Pp. 48.

P. 48, selected primary and secondary books, British and American editions. Place, publisher, date.

SECONDARY

Above, Porter, p. 48.

GENERAL

Temple & Tucker; Coleman & Tyler; Adelman & Dworkin; Palmer & Dyson; Breed & Sniderman; Hogan.

BEITH, MAJOR GENERAL JOHN HAY: *see* HAY, IAN

BELL, ADRIAN HANBURY (1901-)

NCBEL, IV, 522-523.

BELL, ARTHUR CLIVE HEWARD (1881-1964)

PRIMARY

Donald A. Laing, "A Checklist of the Published Writings of Clive

Bell" in William G. Bywater, Jr. *Clive Bell's Eye.* Detroit: Wayne State University Press, 1975. Pp. [250].

Pp. 213-242, "Checklist." Primary, first British and first American publications, including unsigned writings. Form arrangement. Books: place, publisher, date, occasional note on contents. Periods: volume, date, pages, title of volume in which reprinted.

While aiming at completeness, Laing suggests (p. 213) some of the limitations and possible omissions of this checklist.

GENERAL

Millett; Daiches; Temple & Tucker; NCBEL, IV, 1003-1004.

BELL, HENRY THOMAS MACKENZIE (1856-1930)

NCBEL, III, 612.

BELL, JULIAN HEWARD (1908-1937)

NCBEL, IV, 231-232.

BELL, MARTIN (1918-)

Vinson-Poets.

BELLERBY, FRANCES (-)

Vinson-Poets.

BELLOC, JOSEPH HILAIRE PIERRE (1870-1953)

PRIMARY

Norah Nicholls. "The First Editions of Hilaire Belloc." *Bookman* (London) 81 (1931): 62, 126-127.

Primary books. Chronological arrangement. Publisher, year, format, binding, illustrator. Bibliographical notes.

Patrick Cahill. *The English Editions of Hilaire Belloc.* London: [published by the author], 1953. Pp. 52.

Primary books. Chronological arrangement. Transcribed TP, part collation, binding, date, price, variants, extensive bibliographical notes.

N&Q 198 (1953): 365: "one or two small omissions [these are included in the review] . . .in this otherwise admirable bibliography." P. 452, reply by Cahill.

A list of books and pamphlets (with date and publisher) taken from Cahill is given in Robert Speaight. *The Life of Hilaire Belloc.* London: Hollis and Carter, 1957. Pp. 539-544; and is repeated in Herbert Van Thal, ed. *Belloc. A Biographical Anthology.* London: George Allen and Unwin, Ltd., 1970. Pp. 391-396.

Renée Haynes. *Hilaire Belloc.* London: Longmans, Green, and Co., Ltd. (WTW 35), 1958. Pp. 35.

Pp. 31-35, primary books. Chronological arrangement. Date, genre. P. 35, selected secondary books.

SECONDARY

Above, Haynes, p. 35.

GENERAL

Millett; Longaker & Bolles; Batho & Dobrée; Temple & Tucker; NCBEL, IV, 1004-1010.

BENEDICTUS, DAVID (1938-)

Vinson-Novelists.

BENNETT, ALAN (1934-)

Vinson-Dramatists.

BENNETT, ENOCH ARNOLD (1867-1931)

PRIMARY

Norman Emery. *Arnold Bennett 1867-1931. A Bibliography.* Stoke-on-Trent Central Library, 1967.

Not seen.

John D. Gordan. "Arnold Bennett. The Centenary of his Birth. An Exhibition in the Berg Collection." *Bulletin of the New York Public Library* 72 (1968): 72-122.

Chronological arrangement of primary, secondary, and association material, both published and unpublished. Little specifically bibliographical information; extensive historical and biographical annotations. The catalogue is designed to show that the Berg holds "one of the most extensive accumulations of Arnold Bennett materials in the world."

Kenneth Young. *Arnold Bennett.* Harlow: Longman Group Ltd. (WTW 245), 1975. Pp. 54.

Pp. 48-53, select primary bibliography. Chronological arrangement. Date, genre, contents of collections. Pp. 53-54, secondary books: dates, annotations.

Anita Miller. *Arnold Bennett. An Annotated Bibliography, 1887-1932.* New York and London: Garland Publishing, Inc., 1977. Pp. xciv, 787.

Pp. 1-620, chronological list of primary contributions to periodicals: volume, date, pages, brief description of contents. Reviews include author and title of book reviewed. Each item numbered. Pp. 621-637, primary books listed alphabetically by title: place, publisher, date, pages. Pp. 638-787, indices of titles, names, topics, periodicals, etc.

An outstanding contribution to Bennett studies.

SECONDARY

Above, Young, pp. 53-54.

James G. Hepburn. "Arnold Bennett Bibliography." *English Fiction in Transition* 1 (1957): 7-12.

Annotated secondary bibliography. Books: publisher, place, year. Periods: volume, date, pages. Subsequent issues (later *English Literature in Transition*) add to this list, particularly 6 (1963): i, 19-25; 10 (1967): 204-208; 14 (1971): 55-59; and 17 (1974): 20-29. The Annotated Secondary Bibliography Series on English Literature in Transition, Northern Illinois University Press, is to include a volume on Bennett.

Werner W. Riemer. "Arnold Bennett: A Check List of Secondary Literature." *Bulletin of the New York Public Library* 77 (1974): 342-357.

Form arrangement, alphabetically by author in each section. Books: place, publisher, date. Periods: volume, date, pages.

Less informative and less inclusive than the annotated bibliography cited above, but also, perhaps, simpler to use.

GENERAL

Millett; Longaker & Bolles; Bartho & Dobrée; Temple & Tucker; Adelman & Dworkin; Palmer & Dyson; Breed & Sniderman; NCBEL, IV, 429-436; Bufkin.

BENSON, ARTHUR CHRISTOPHER (1862-1925)

Longaker & Bolles; NCBEL, III, 1420.

BENSON, EDWARD FREDERICK (1867-1940)

Batho & Dobrée; Temple & Tucker.

BENSON, ELEANOR THEODORA ROBY (1906-1968)

NCBEL, IV, 524.

BENSON, STELLA (1892-1933)

PRIMARY

John Gawsworth. *Ten Contemporaries. Notes Toward their Definitive Bibliography (Second Series).* London: Joiner & Steele Ltd., 1933. Pp. 240. 1000 copies.

Pp. 43-51, primary books, first editions, 1915-1932. Chronological arrangement. Transcribed TP, full collation, pagination, binding, date, bibliographical notes.

Siegfried Steinbeck. *Der Ausgesetzte Mensch. Zum Leben und Werk von Stella Benson.* Bern: Francke Verlag (Schweizer Anglistische Arbeiten 48), 1959. Pp. 117.

P. 115. Primary books. Dates.

GENERAL

Millett; Daiches, Temple & Tucker; NCBEL, IV, 524-525; Bufkin.

BENTLEY, EDWARD CLERIHEW (1875-1956)

Batho & Dobrée; NCBEL, IV, 525.

BENTLEY, PHYLLIS ELEANOR (1894-)

PRIMARY

Phyllis Bentley. *'O Dreams, O Destinations' An Autobiography.* London: Victor Gollancz Ltd., 1962. Pp. 272.

P. [2], list of 25 primary books. Other bibliographical information in text, *passim*.

GENERAL

Millett; Temple & Tucker; NCBEL, IV, 525-526; Bufkin.

BERESFORD, ANNE (1929-)

(Mrs. Michael Hamburger)

Vinson-Poets.

BERESFORD, JOHN DAVYS (1873-1947)

PRIMARY

Helmut Gerber. "John Davys Beresford: A Bibliography." *Bulletin of Bibliography* 21 (1956): 201-204.

Primary British and American first editions. Genre arrangement. Books: publisher, place, year. Periods: volume, pages, date. Contents of collections listed with information about previous publication.

–"John Davys Beresford." *English Fiction in Transition* 1 (1957): 12-13.

Locates Beresford's MSS; refers to Gerber's bibliography (above) as "most complete and most accurate"; adds three items to it.

GENERAL

Millet; Batho & Dobrée; Temple & Tucker; Bufkin; NCBEL, IV, 526-528.

BERGER, JOHN PETER (1926-)

Vinson-Novelists; Drescher & Kahrmann; Temple & Tucker.

BERKELEY, ANTHONY: *see* COX, ANTHONY BERKELEY

BERKELEY, REGINALD CHEYNE (1890-1935)

NCBEL, IV, 911-912.

BERMANGE, BARRY (1933-)

Vinson-Dramatists.

BERNERS, LORD (1883-1950)

formerly Gerard Hugh Tyrwhitt

NCBEL, IV, 529.

BERRY, FRANCIS (1915-)

Vinson-Poets; NCBEL, IV, 232.

BESANT, ANNIE (1847-1933)

PRIMARY

Theodore Besterman. *A Bibliography of Annie Besant.* London:

Theosophical Society in England, 1924. Pp. 114.

Not seen.

Besterman later published *The Mind of Annie Besant.* London: Theosophical Publishing House, Litd., 1927. Pp. [xii], 122, providing in the bibliography, pp. 115-117, a selected list of primary books, arranged under four topic headings, with place and date for each book; the footnotes, *passim,* provide additional primary titles.

BESIER, RUDOLPH (1878-1942)

Adelman & Dworkin; Salem; Palmer & Dyson; NCBEL, IV, 912-913.

BETJEMAN, SIR JOHN (1906-)

PRIMARY

Margaret L. Stapleton. *Sir John Betjeman: A Bibliography of Writings by and about Him.* With an essay by Ralph J. Mills, Jr. Metuchen, New Jersey: Scarecrow Press, 1974. Pp. vi, 143.

Pp. 31-97, primary. Form and genre arrangement. Books (all editions): place, publisher, date, limitations of issue, contents. Periods: volume, date, pages. Reviews by Betjeman include title and author of book reviewed. Ten different sections including anthologies with poems by Betjeman and recordings of his poems. Pp. 101-129, secondary bibliography. Arranged alphabetically by author under either Books or Magazines; reviews listed under title of book reviewed. Pp. 131-143, indices.

John Press. *John Betjeman.* London: The Longman Group Ltd. (WTW 237), 1974. Pp. 54.

Pp. 51-53, primary books. Date, genre, place.

A simple checklist of the primary book titles.

GENERAL

Daiches; Temple & Tucker; Vinson-Poets; NCBEL, IV, 233-234.

BINYON, ROBERT LAURENCE (1869-1943)

PRIMARY

"Bibliographies of Modern Authors. Robert Laurence Binyon." *London Mercury* 2 (1920):114-115.

Primary books, 1890-1919. Genre arrangement. Publisher, year, brief notes.

GENERAL

Millett; Longaker & Bolles; Batho & Dobrée; Temple & Tucker; Stratford; NCBEL, III, 612-613.

BIRMINGHAM, GEORGE A. (1865-1950)

Pseudonym of James Owen Hannay.

PRIMARY

W. E. Mackey. "The Novels of George A. Birmingham. A List of First Editions." *Trinity College Dublin Annual Bulletin,* Number 14-16 (1955).

Not seen.

GENERAL

Hogan; NCBEL, IV, 529-530.

BIRRELL, AUGUSTINE (1850-1933)

PRIMARY

"Bibliographies of Modern Authors. The Rt. Hon. Augustine Birrell, K. C." *London Mercury* 4 (1921):435-436.

Primary books. Chronological arrangement. Publisher, year, bibliographical notes.

GENERAL

Batho & Dobrée; NCBEL, III, 1421-1422.

BLACKBURN, THOMAS (1916-)

Vinson-Poets.

BLACKWOOD, ALGERNON HENRY (1869-1951)

Millett; NCBEL, IV, 530-531.

BLAIR, ERIC ARTHUR: *see* ORWELL, GEORGE

BLAKE, GEORGE (1893-1961)

Daiches; NCBEL, IV, 531-532.

BLAKE, NICHOLAS: *see* LEWIS, CECIL DAY

BLAND, HUBERT (1855-1914)

See NESBIT, EDITH.

BLOOM, URSULA (-)

(Mrs. Gower Robinson)

PRIMARY

Ursula Bloom. *Life is no Fairy Tale.* London: Hale, 1976. Pp. 175.

Not seen. An autobiography, reviewed by Susan Kennedy in the *Times Literary Supplement, No.* 3891 (8 October 1976), p. 1281, who points out that Miss Bloom is "the most prolific woman writer in the world, with an entry in the *Guiness Book of Records* to prove it."

BLUNDEN, EDMUND CHARLES (1896-1974)

PRIMARY

A. J. Gasworth and Jacob Schwartz. *Bibliography of Edmund Blunden with Preface and Copious Notes by Edmund Blunden.* London: Ulysses Bookshop, 1931.

Not seen. Although cited by several authorities, this work is not listed in the British Museum Catalogue and may not exist.

Alec M. Hardie. *Edmund Blunden.* London: Longmans, Green and Co. (WTW 93), 1958. Pp. 43.

Pp. 39-42, selected primary books. Form and genre arrangement. Place, year. Pp. 42-43, selected secondary bibliography.

T. Saito. "A Blunden Bibliography." *Today's Japan* 5 (1960).

Not seen.

GENERAL

Millett; Longaker & Bolles; Daiches; Temple & Tucker; Vinson-Poets; NCBEL, IV, 234-238; Stratford.

BLUNT, WILFRID SCAWEN (1840-1922)

PRIMARY

Edith Finch (Countess Russell). *Wilfrid Scawen Blunt 1840-1922.* London: Jonathan Cape, 1938. Pp. 415.

Pp. 397-399, primary books. Genre arrangement. Place, publisher, year. Pp. 400-402, general secondary bibliography. Additional criticism in text, *passim.*

Sister Mary Joan Reinehr. *The Writings of Wilfrid Scawen Blunt. An Introduction and a Study.* Milwaukee: Marquette University, 1941. Pp. [x], 223.

Pp. 199-217, primary and secondary bibliography. One alphabetical by author list (entries for Blunt on pp. 199-202). Books: place, year. Periods: volume, date.

Earl of Lytton. *Wilfrid Scawen Blunt.* London: MacDonald, 1961. Pp. 368.

No bibliography. Information in text, *passim.*

SECONDARY

Above, Finch; Reinehr.

GENERAL

Longaker & Bolles; Batho & Dobrée; Temple & Tucker; NCBEL, III, 614-615.

BLYTON, ENID MARY (1897-1968)

(Mrs. Hugh Alexander Pollock; later Mrs. Kenneth Darrell Waters.)

PRIMARY

A Complete List of Books by Enid Blyton. Foreword by Enid Blyton. [Privately published by John Menzies, 1950]

Not seen. Cited by Stoney (below), pp. 149, 232.

Barbara Stoney. *Enid Blyton, A Biography.* London: Hodder and Stoughton, 1974. Pp. 252.

Pp. 221-224, "Books by Enid Blyton, 1922-1968." Chronological arrangement. Date, publisher.

Important limitations are described on p. 221; there is no listing of the periodical contributions, but many details about them are given in the text, *passim.*

BOLAND, BRIDGET (1913-)

Vinson-Dramatists; NCBEL, IV, 913

BOLD, ALAN NORMAN (1943-)

Vinson-Poets.

BOLITHO, WILLIAM (1890-1930)

Pseudonym of William Bolitho Ryall.

Salem.

BOLT, ROBERT OXTON (1924-)

Coleman & Tyler; Adelman & Dworkin; Salem; Parker & Dyson; Breed & Sniderman; Vinson-Dramatists; Temple & Tucker.

BOLTON, GUY (1884-)

Salem.

BOND, EDWARD (1934-)

Vinson-Dramatists; Temple & Tucker.

BONE, SIR DAVID WILLIAM (1874-1959)

PRIMARY

Harry R. Skallerup. "Sir David Bone 1874-1959: A Selected Bibliography." *Bulletin of Bibliography* 23 (1963): 234-236.

Primary and secondary bibliography. Form arrangement. Books: place, publisher, year, reprints, subsequent editions. Periods: volume, pages, date. Secondary bibliography, pp. 235-236. Reviews of books listed under title of book. Includes obituary notices.

GENERAL

NCBEL, IV, 532.

BOOTH, CONSTANCE GORE-: *see* MARKIEVICZ, COUNTESS DE

BOOTH, MARTIN (1944-)

Vinson-Poets.

BOSLEY, KEITH (1937-)

Vinson-Poets.

BOTTOME, PHYLLIS (1884-1963)

PRIMARY

Phyllis Bottome. *The Goal.* London: Faber and Faber, 1962. Pp. 306.

Limited bibliographical information in this autobiography, *passim.*

GENERAL

Temple & Tucker; NCBEL, IV, 532-533.

BOTTOMLEY, GORDON (1874-1948)

PRIMARY

Claude Colleer Abbott, "Introduction" in Gordon Bottomley, *Poems and Plays.* London: Bodley Head, 1953. Pp. 464.

Pp. 9-19, "Introduction." Bibliographical information in text, *passim.*

–and Anthony Bertram, eds. *Poet and Painter, Being the Correspondence between Gordon Bottomley and Paul Nash, 1910-1946.* London: Oxford University Press, 1955. Pp. 272.

Bibliographical information in "Introduction," pp. xi-xix, and text, *passim.*

GENERAL

Millett; Longaker & Bolles; Batho & Dobrée; Temple & Tucker; Breed & Sniderman; NCBEL, IV, 238-240.

BOTTRALL, FRANCIS JAMES RONALD (1906-)

Daiches; Temple & Tucker; Vinson-Poets; NCBEL, IV, 240-241; Stratford.

BOURN, GEORGE: *see* STURT, GEORGE.

BOWEN, ELIZABETH DOROTHEA COLE (1899-1973)

PRIMARY

J'nan Sellery. "Elizabeth Bowen: A Check List." *Bulletin of the New York Public Library* 74 (1970):219-274.

Primary, secondary. Form arrangement, chronological within each section. Books: place, publisher, date, all editions, contents; reviews of books listed under title of book. Periods: date, volume, pages. Reviews by Bowen include title and author of book reviewed. Some cross-referencing to indicate reprinting of separate pieces. Includes translations of primary writings (pp. 263-264) and list of MSS with lengthy descriptions and location (pp. 265-271).

But for the lack of physical descriptions a full-fledged bibliography.

SECONDARY

Above, Sellery, especially pp. 271-274.

GENERAL

Millett; Longaker & Bolles; Daiches; Temple & Tucker; Adelman & Dworkin (Novel); Vinson-Novelists; NCBEL, IV, 534-535; Bufkin.

BOWEN, JOHN GRIFFITH (1924-)

Bufkin; Adelman & Dworkin (Novel); Vinson-Novelists; Vinson-Dramatists; Drescher & Kahrmann.

BOWEN, MARJORIE: *see* LONG, G. M. V. C.

BOWES-LYON, LILIAN HELEN: *see* LYON, LILIAN HELEN BOWES.

BOYLE, WILLIAM (1853-1922)

NCBEL, III, 1939; Breed & Sniderman.

BRADBURY, MALCOLM STANLEY (1932-)

Temple & Tucker; Vinson-Novelists; Drescher & Kahrmann.

BRADLEY, KATHARINE: *see* FIELD, MICHAEL.

BRAGG, MELVYN (1939-)

Vinson-Novelists; Drescher & Kahrmann.

BRAINE, JOHN GERARD (1922-)

PRIMARY

James W. Lee. *John Braine*. New York: Twayne Publishers, Inc. (TEAS 62), 1968. Pp. 127.

Pp. 123-124, bibliography. Primary, secondary selected. Form arrangement. Books, British and American editions: place, publisher, year. Periods: volume, pages, date, genre. Six critical studies, annotated. Notes, pp. 118-122, provide additional secondary criticism.

SECONDARY

Above, Lee.

GENERAL

Temple & Tucker; Adelman & Dworkin (Novel); Vinson-Novelists; Drescher & Kahrmann; Bufkin.

BRAMAH, ERNEST (1869?-1942)

Pseudonym of Ernest Bramah Smith.

PRIMARY

William White. "Ernest Bramah. A First Checklist." *Bulletin of Bibliography* 22 (1958): 127-131.

Primary and secondary. Form arrangement. Books: place, publisher, date, pages, price, reprints, subsequent editions, contents. Periods: volume, pages, date. Pp. 130-131, secondary bibliography. Reviews listed under title of book reviewed. Annotations for secondary criticism.

--"Some Uncollected Authors, XXXVII: Ernest Bramah 1869?-1942." *Book Collector* 13 (1964): 54-63.

Primary books. Chronological arrangement. Transcribed TP, part collation, binding, date, variants, notes. The authoritative bibliography.

--"Two Bramah Variants." *Papers of the Bibliographical Society of America* 62 (1968): 254-256.

Two additions to *Book Collector* bibliography (above).

--"Ernest Bramah's Published Letters: A Survey." *Bulletin of Bibliography* 31 (1974): 5.

Chronological listing of eight works containing letters. Full bibliographical information with annotations.

--"Ernest Bramah in Periodicals, 1890-1972." *Bulletin of Bibliography* 32 (1975): 33-34, 44.

Primary writings published in periodicals. Chronological arrangement. Volume, date, pages, annotations.

GENERAL

Above, White (1958).

BRANDANE, JOHN: *see* MACINTYRE, JOHN.

BRIDGES, ROBERT SEYMOUR (1844-1930)

PRIMARY

George L. McKay. *A Bibliography of Robert Bridges.* London: Oxford University Press; New York: Columbia University Press, 1933. Pp. xii, 215. 550 copies.

Primary first editions. Form arrangement. Books: transcribed TP, part collation, pagination, illustrations, binding, date, number of copies, notes, contents, subsequent editions with important textual changes. Periods: volume, pages, date. Index of first lines; general index. Pp. 12-13, previous bibliographies of Bridges' work.

The standard bibliography. (See below, Kable).

William S. Kable. *The Ewelme Collection of Robert Bridges: A Catalogue.* Columbia: University of South Carolina (Department of English, Bibliographical Series No. 2), 1967. Pp. 35. 350 copies.

Catalogue of the collection formed by Simon Nowell-Smith. Pp. 5-32, primary bibliography. Additions to McKay; notes on variants from McKay's descriptions; annotations, quotations. Pp. 32-35, secondary criticism. Books: place, publisher, date. Periods: volume, pages, date. Annotations.

L. S. Thompson, *Papers of the Bibliographical Society of America* 62 (1968): 288: "a useful supplement to. . . McKay."

SECONDARY

Above, Kable, pp. 32-35.

GENERAL

Millett; Longaker & Bolles; Batho & Dobrée; Temple & Tucker; Stratford; NCBEL, III, 593-597.

BRIDIE, JAMES (1888-1951)

Pseudonym of Osborne Henry Mavor. Other pseudonyms used by Mavor include Archibald P. Kellock and Mary Henderson.

PRIMARY

Winifred Bannister. *James Bridie and his Theatre.* London: Rockliffe Publishing Co., 1955. Pp. xii, 262.

P. ix, list of Bridie's plays, published and unpublished. Other bibliographical information in text, passim.

Helen L. Luyben. *James Bridie Clown and Philosopher.* Philadelphia: University of Pennsylvania Press, 1965. Pp. 180.

Pp. 177-178, primary books, secondary selected. Publisher, place, date, contents. Other secondary references in Notes, pp. 167-171.

SECONDARY

Above, Bannister; Luyben.

GENERAL

Daiches; Temple & Tucker; Coleman & Tyler; Adelman & Dworkin; Salem; Breed & Sniderman; NCBEL, IV, 914-917.

BRIGHOUSE, HAROLD (1882-1958)

PRIMARY

Harold Brighouse. *What I Have Had. Chapters in Autobiography.* London: Harrap & Co., 1953. Pp. 192.

Bibliographical information in text, *passim.*

GENERAL

Millett; Longaker & Bolles; NCBEL, IV, 917-919.

BRITTAIN, VERA MARY (1897-1970)

(Mrs. George E. G. Catlin).

PRIMARY

Vera Brittain. *Testament of Youth. An Autobiographical Study of the Years 1900-1925.* New York: Macmillan Co., 1933. Pp. [663].

--*Testament of Experience. An Autobiographical Story of the Years 1925-1950.* New York: Macmillan Co., 1957. Pp. 480.

Bibliographical information in text, *passim.*

--*On Becoming an Author* [English title: *On Becoming a Writer*]. New York: Macmillan Co., 1948. Pp. [xviii], 218.

Pp. 144-170 give an account of Brittain's writing career.

GENERAL

See below, HOLTBY, WINIFRED.

BROCK, ARTHUR CLUTTON- (1868-1924)

PRIMARY

"Bibliographies of Modern Authors: Arthur Clutton-Brock." *London Mercury* 1 (1920): 366.

Primary books. Chronological arrangement. Publisher, year, brief notes.

There appears to be no list of Clutton-Brock's contributions to periodicals and books.

BROCK, EDWIN (1927-)

Vinson-Poets.

BROOKE, JOCELYN (1908-)

PRIMARY

Anthony Rota. *Jocelyn Brooke. A Checklist of his Writings, together with some appreciations.* London: Bertram Rota Ltd., 1963. Pp. 4.

Not seen.

GENERAL

Temple & Tucker.

BROOKE, RUPERT (1887-1915)

PRIMARY

Richard M. G. Potter. *Rupert Brooke. A Bibliographical Note on his Works published in Book Form 1911-1919.* Hartford, Connecticut: Privately Published, 1923. Pp. 28. 52 copies.

Primary books. Chronological arrangement. Transcribed TP, part collation, pagination, binding, subsequent editions, variants, notes.

Keynes (below), p. 19: "a description of the more obvious books."

Geoffrey Keynes. *A Bibliography of Rupert Brooke.* London: Rupert Hart-Davis (Soho Bibliography No. 4, Third Edition Revised), 1964. Pp. 158.

Primary, secondary selected books. Genre and form arrangement. Transcribed TP, part collation, pagination, binding, date, price, number of copies, variants, reprints, contents, extensive notes. MSS described and located. Indices of poem titles, first lines, general.

The authoritative bibliography.

John Schroder. *Catalogue of Books and Manuscripts by Rupert Brooke, Edward Marsh, and Christopher Hassall.* Cambridge: Rampant Lions Press, 1970. Pp. [135]. 450 copies.

Catalogue of Schroder's unique collection of manuscripts, letters, association items and secondary criticism relating to Brooke, Marsh, and Hassall. Important descriptions and summaries of unpublished material, accounts of holograph variants in published works; extensive bibliographical, textual, and historical notes which supplement Keyne's bibliography of Brooke. Pp. 97-100, bibliography of primary writings by Marsh, including translations by him. Pp. 115-123, bibliography of primary writings by Hassall. Books: publisher, date. Periods: volume, date.

An indispensable book for study of this particular literary group. *Book Collector* 20 (1971): 247: "a book which no one interested in Brooke should miss."

SECONDARY

Above, Keynes, pp. 137-141.

GENERAL

Millett; Longaker & Bolles; Batho & Dobrée; Temple & Tucker; NCBEL, IV, 241-243.

BROOKE, STOPFORD AUGUSTUS (1832-1916)

PRIMARY

Fred L. Standley. "Stopford Augustus Brooke (1832-1916): A Primary Bibliography." *Bulletin of Bibliography* 24 (1964): 79-82.

Pp. 79-81, primary bibliography. Form arrangement. Books: place, date. Periods: volume, pages, date. Pp. 81-82, secondary bibliography. One alphabetical by author or title list.

SECONDARY

Above, Standley, pp. 81-82.

GENERAL

NCBEL, III, 1422-1423.

BROOKE-ROSE, CHRISTINE: *see* ROSE, CHRISTINE BROOKE.

BROOKS, JEREMY (1926-)

Vinson-Novelists.

BROPHY, BRIGID ANTONIA (1929-)

(Mrs. Michael Levey).

Temple & Tucker; Bufkin; Vinson-Novelists; Vinson-Dramatists; Drescher & Kahrmann.

BROPHY, JOHN (1899-1965)

NCBEL, IV, 539-540.

BROWN, GEORGE DOUGLAS (1869-1902)

PRIMARY

James Veitch. *George Douglas Brown.* London: Herbert Jenkins, 1952. Pp. 197.

P. 189, selected primary and secondary bibliography. Chronological arrangement. Dates. Other bibliographical information in text, *passim;* also in Cuthbert Lennox and Andrew Melrose, *George Douglas Brown,* introduced Andrew Lang. London: Hodder and Stoughton, 1903. Pp. xiv, 248.

SECONDARY

Above, Veitch.

GENERAL

Batho & Dobrée; NCBEL, III, 1046.

BROWN, GEORGE MACKAY (1921-)

Vinson-Poets; Vinson-Novelists.

BROWN, IVOR JOHN CARNEGIE (1891-1974)

Temple & Tucker.

BROWNE, MAURICE (1881-1955)

PRIMARY

Montrose J. Moses and Oscar J. Campbell, eds. *Dramas of Modernism and Their Forerunners.* Boston: Little, Brown and Co., 1941. Pp. xvi, 946.

Pp. 925, 941, bibliography. Primary selected, secondary selected. One alphabetical list. Books: place, publisher, date. Periods: volume, pages, date. Studies or reviews of *Wings over Europe* listed thereunder.

Maurice Browne. *Too Late to Lament.* An Autobiography. London: Victor Gollancz, 1955; Bloomington: Indiana University Press, 1956. Pp. 403.

No bibliography, but references to primary and secondary writings in text, *passim;* also in Index.

BROWNE, WYNYARD BARRY (1911-1964)

NCBEL, IV, 919-920.

BROWNJOHN, ALAN CHARLES (1931-)

Vinson-Poets.

BRUCE, GEORGE (1909-)

Vinson-Poets.

BRYHER (ANNIE WINIFRED ELLERMAN) (1894-)

PRIMARY

Shelby Martin. "Winifred Bryher: A Check List." *Bulletin of the New York Public Library* 79 (1976): 459-471.

Primary, secondary selected. Form and genre arrangement. Books: place, publisher, date, genre. Periods: volume, date, pages. Reviews by Bryher include title and author of book reviewed. Pp. 469-471, secondary bibliography, including reviews under title of book reviewed and also locations of MSS collections.

SECONDARY

Above, Martin, pp. 469-471.

GENERAL

Temple & Tucker; Vinson-Novelists; Bufkin.

BUCHAN, JOHN, LORD TWEEDSMUIR (1875-1940)

PRIMARY

Archibald Hanna, Jr. *John Buchan 1875-1940. A Bibliography.* Hamden, Connecticut: Shoe String Press, 1953. Pp. 135.

Primary complete, secondary selected. Form arrangement. Books: publisher, place, date, pages, contents, notes. Periods: volume, pages, date. Pp. 115-119, secondary bibliography.

B. C. Wilmot. *A Checklist of Works by and about John Buchan in the John Buchan Collection, Douglas Library, Queen's University, Kingston, Ontario.* Boston: G. K. Hall, 1961. Pp. 38, 24.

Primary complete, secondary selected. Form and genre arrangement. Publisher, place, date, pages, height, notes on special bindings and MSS notations.

Janet Adam Smith. *John Buchan.* London: Rupert Hart-Davis, 1965. Pp. 524.

Pp. 476-479, bibliography of primary books. Date, contents. Pp. 480-507, "Sources and References": bibliographical information, *passim.*

Hanna, Wilmot, and Smith together give an almost complete list of primary writings, although the bibliographical descriptions are incomplete.

SECONDARY

Above, Hanna, pp. 115-119; Wilmot, pp. 31-36.

J. Randolph Cox. "John Buchan, Lord Tweedsmuir. An Annotated Bibliography of Writings about Him." *English Literature in Transition* 9 (1966): 241-291, 292-325; 10 (1967):209-211; *et. seq.*

Books: place, publisher, year. Periods: volume, pages, date.

GENERAL

Longaker & Bolles; Daiches; Temple & Tucker; NCBEL, IV, 540-544; Bufkin.

BUCHAN, THOMAS BUCHANAN (1931-)

Vinson-Poets.

BUCHANAN, GEORGE HENRY PERROTT (1904-)

Vinson-Poets; Vinson-Novelists.

BULLETT, GERALD WILLIAM (1893-1958)

Millett; NCBEL, IV, 544-545.

BULLOCK, MICHAEL HALE (1918-)

Vinson-Poets.

BULLOUGH, GEOFFREY (1901-)

Daiches.

BUNTING, BASIL (1900-)

PRIMARY

Roger Guedalla. *Basil Bunting: A Bibliography of Works and Criticism.* Norwood, Pennsylvania: Norwood Editions, 1973. Pp. 183.

Pp. 13-98, 117-131, primary bibliography. Form and genre arrangement, including Letters, Recordings, Principal Readings. Books: transcribed title page, binding, date, price, number of copies, contents, extensive bibliographical and textual notes. Periods: volume, date, pages. Pp. 101-113, 135-138, secondary bibliography including reviews of Bunting's books. Index.

GENERAL

NCBEL, IV, 243-244; Vinson-Poets; Temple & Tucker.

BURGESS, ANTHONY (1917-)

Pseudonym of John Burgess Wilson; another pseudonym: Joseph Kell.

PRIMARY

Paul Boytinck. *Anthony Burgess. An Enumerative Bibliography with Selected Annotations.* Norwood, Pennsylvania: Norwood Editions, 1974. Pp. [iv], 43 (printed on rectos only). 200 copies.

Pp. 1-24, primary bibliography. Form arrangement including translations of Burgess's books. Books: place, publisher, date, all editions, translator. Period: volume, date, pages. Burgess's reviews occasionally include title and author of book reviewd. Pp. 25-40, secondary bibliography, includes reviews of primary books under title of book reviewed. Occasional annotations and notes. Pp. i-ii give important bibliographical details.

A helpful if inconsistently organized checklist of primary and secondary material. If it is not available, then Beverly R. David, "Anthony Burgess: A Checklist (1956-1971)," and the supplement by Carlton Holte, *Twen-*

tieth Century Literature 19 (1973): 181-188; 20 (1974): 44-52, will prove useful.

SECONDARY

Above, Boytinck.

GENERAL

Bufkin; Temple & Tucker; Adelman & Dworkin (Novel); Vinson-Novelists; Drescher & Kahrmann.

BURKE, THOMAS (1886-1945)

PRIMARY

John Gawsworth. *Ten Contemporaries. Notes Toward their Definitive Bibliography. (Second Series).* London: Joiner & Steele Ltd., 1933. Pp. 240. 1000 copies.

Pp. 61-82, primary books, first editions, 1910-1932. Chronological arrangement. Transcribed TP, full collation, pagination, binding, date, bibliographical notes.

GENERAL

Millett; NCBEL, IV, 545-546.

BURN, WILLIAM LAURENCE (1904-1966)

Pseudonym used: Richard Sheldon.

PRIMARY

Lionel Madden. "A Checklist of Books, Articles and Reviews by William Laurence Burn." *Durham University Journal* 67 (1974): 4-12.

Chronological arrangement. Books: place, publisher, date, pages. Periods: volume, date, pages. Reviews by Burn include author, title, place, publisher, and date of book reviewed.

BURNETT, FRANCES ELIZA HODGSON (1849-1924)

PRIMARY

Ann Thwaite. *Waiting for the Party. The Life of Frances Hodgson Burnett 1849-1924.* New York: Charles Scribner's Sons, 1974. Pp. xii, 274.

Pp. [250]-[255], primary and secondary books. Chronological arrangement. First British and American editions: place, publisher, date. Chronological list of first British and American performances of plays by Mrs. Burnett with date and theatre.

Although no one has listed Mrs. Burnett's extensive periodical contributions, this biography provides the starting point for such a listing; additional secondary criticism is provided in the notes, pp. 256-265.

BURNETT, IVY COMPTON-: *see* COMPTON-BURNETT, IVY.

BURNS, ALAN (1929-)

Vinson-Novelists.

BURNS, JIM (1936-)

Vinson-Poets.

BUTLER, SAMUEL (1835-1902)

PRIMARY

A. J. Hoppé. *A Bibliography of the Writings of Samuel Butler and of Writings about Him.* London: Bookman's Journal, 1925. Pp. [xvi], 184. 500 copies.

Primary complete, secondary complete. Form arrangement. Books: transcribed TP, complete collation, pagination, binding, date, price, variants, contents, complete notes. Periods: page, date, reprintings, quotations. Pp. 129-160, secondary bibliography. Form arrangement. Annotations. Harkness (below), p. 11: "a solid and comprehensive record of Butler's achievement up to the year 1925. . . especially notable for the fullness and precision of its information under 'Editiones Principes'. . ."

Stanley B. Harkness. *The Career of Samuel Butler (1835-1902): A Bibliography*. London: Bodley Head, 1955. Pp. 154.

Primary complete, secondary complete. Pp. 29-67, primary bibliography. Chronological arrangement. Books: place, publisher, date, variants, reprints, location of MSS, notes. Periods: volume, pages, date, reprintings. Pp. 71-150, secondary bibliography. Form arrangement. Pp. 153-154, translations of primary writings listed under name of language.

Gerber (below), p. 13: Hoppé and Harkness together give an almost complete record of Butler's writings and of the secondary bibliography.

SECONDARY

Above, Hoppé, pp. 129-160; Harkness, pp. 71-150.

Helmut Gerber. "Samuel Butler." *English Fiction* (later *English Literature*) *in Transition* 1 (1957): 13-18; 6 (1963): i, 23-31; continued in subsequent issues.

Annotated additions to Harkness.

Lee E. Holt. *Samuel Butler.* New York: Twayne Publishers, Inc. (TEAS 2), 1964. Pp. 183.

Pp. 171-176, selected secondary bibliography. Alphabetical by author arrangement. Annotated.

A useful, selected bibliography.

GENERAL

Batho & Dobrée; Temple & Tucker; NCBEL, III, 1406-1411.

BUTTS, MARY FRANCIS (1893-1937)

PRIMARY

Douglas Goldring. *South Lodge. Reminiscences of Violet Hunt, Ford Madox Ford, and the English Review Circle.* London: Constable and Co., Ltd., 1943. Pp. [xx], [240].

P. [240], bibliography of primary books. Genre arrangement. Publisher, date.

GENERAL

NCBEL, IV, 546.

BYATT, ANTONIA SUSAN (1936-)

(Mrs. I. C. R. Byatt)

Vinson-Novelists.

BYRNE, BRIAN OSWALD DONN (1889-1928)

PRIMARY

Winthrop Wetherbee, Jr. *Donn Byrne: A Bibliography.* New York: New York Public Library, 1949. Pp. [xii], 89.

Primary and secondary. Form and genre arrangement. Books: transcribed TP, part collation, binding, subsequent editions, contents, bibliographical notes, reviews. Periods: volume, pages, date. Includes translations, dramatizations, cinematizations, anthologies, MSS. Pp. 68-84, secondary bibliography.

The original typescript of this bibliography (available in the New York Public Library) lists even more titles.

SECONDARY

Above, Wetherbee, pp. 1-47 (reviews of the primary books); pp. 68-84, general secondary bibliography.

BYRNE, JOHN KEYES: *see* LEONARD, HUGH.

CAINE, SIR THOMAS HENRY HALL (1853-1931)

Batho & Dobrée; Temple and Tucker; NCBEL, III, 1042.

CALDER-MARSHALL, ARTHUR (1908-)

Daiches; Vinson-Novelists; NCBEL, IV, 546-547.

CALDERON, GEORGE LESLIE (1868-1915)

NCBEL, IV, 920.

CALVIN, HENRY: *see* HANLEY, CLIFFORD.

CAMERON, JOHN NORMAN (1905-1953)

NCBEL, IV, 244.

CAMPBELL, IGNATIUS ROY DUNNACHIE (1902-1957)

PRIMARY

D. S. J. Parsons. "Roy Campbell: A Bibliography." *Four Decades of Poetry 1890-1930* 1 (1976): 151-167.

Primary, secondary. Form and genre arrangement. Books, all editions: place, publisher, date. Periods: volume, date, pages.

Although lacking bibliographical descriptions, this sensibly arranged and seemingly complete list of all of Campbell's writings includes, in addition to other lists, an alphabetically arranged list of the poems with details of their first publication (but not of the volumes in which they were collected) and a list of Campbell's translations.

SECONDARY

Above, Parsons, pp. 161-167.

GENERAL

Millett; Longaker & Bolles; Daiches; Temple & Tucker; NCBEL, IV, 244-246.

CAMPBELL, JOSEPH (1879-1944)

PRIMARY

Patrick Sarsfield O'Hegarty. "Bibliography of Joseph Campbell." *Dublin Magazine* 15 (October-December 1940): 58-61. Also published as a separate pamphlet.

Primary books. Chronological arrangement. Transcribed TP, part collation, pagination, binding, variants, brief notes.

CAMPTON, DAVID (1924-)

Vinson-Dramatists.

CANAWAY, WILLIAM HAMILTON (1925-)

Vinson-Novelists.

CANNAN, DENIS (1919-)

Formerly Dennis Pullein-Thompson.

Breed & Sniderman; Vinson-Dramatists; NCBEL, IV, 920-921.

CANNAN, GILBERT (1884-1955)

SECONDARY

Richard J. Buhr. "Gilbert Cannan: An Annotated Bibliography of Writings about Him." *English Literature in Transition* 20 (1977): 77-107.

Introductory essay (pp. 77-80) mentions primary titles. Secondary bibliography (pp. 81-107) includes reviews. Arranged by author or (for unsigned work) title in one alphabetical list. Books: place, publisher, date, pages. Periods: volume, date, pages. Annotated.

GENERAL

Millett; Batho & Dobrée; Bufkin; Temple & Tucker; NCBEL, IV, 547-548.

CARPENTER, EDWARD (1844-1929)

PRIMARY

[?Edward Carpenter] . *A Bibliography of the Writings of Edward Carpenter.* London: George Allen and Unwin, 1916. Pp. 14. 150 copies.

Primary, secondary selected. Form arrangement. Books: publisher, place, date, reprints. Periods: dates. Excludes periodical contributions reprinted in book form. Includes translations and musical settings of primary writings. P. 14, secondary bibliography.

Reprinted from pp. 323-332 of Edward Carpenter. *My Days and Dreams.* London: George Allen and Unwin; New York: Charles Scribner's Sons, 1916. Pp. 340.

A Bibliography of Edward Carpenter. A Catalogue of books, manuscripts, letters, etc. by and about Edward Carpenter in the Carpenter Collection in the Department of Local History of the Central Library, Sheffield, with some entries from other sources. Sheffield, Sheffield City Libraries, 1949. Pp. [x] , 83.

Primary, secondary. Pp. 1-59, chronological list of primary writings, including books and references to reviews thereof, periodical contributions, and manuscripts. Books: place, publisher, date, pages, subsequent editions and reprints. Periods: date, pages. Pp. 60-63, personal papers by and about Carpenter. Pp. 64-73, secondary bibliography, alphabetical by author. Pp. 74-76, alphabetical list of translators of Carpenter's works, with titles and dates of their translations. Information varies for each entry, and there are frequently descriptive or bibliographical notes for this collection of unique material.

GENERAL

Millett; Batho & Dobrée; Temple & Tucker; NCBEL, III, 1423.

CARROLL, PAUL VINCENT (1900-1968)

PRIMARY

Paul A. Doyle. *Paul Vincent Carroll.* Lewisburg: Bucknell University Press (Irish Writers Series), 1971. Pp. 115.

Pp. 111-115, selected primary and secondary bibliography. Arranged: Plays, Articles by, Articles about. Books: place, publisher, date, contents of collections, changes of titles, miscellaneous notes. Periods: volume, date, pages.

Doyle points out that there is no complete bibliography, that very few of the short stories have been collected, and that this is "the most complete. . . bibliography of [the] dramas. . . presently available" (p. 111).

Diane Roman and Mary Hamilton. "A Checklist. Short Stories [by Paul Vincent Carroll] published in *Ireland's Own,* 1920-30." *Journal of Irish Literature* 1 (Sept. 1972): 83-84.

Chronological arrangement. Volume, pages, date. See introduction by editors, pp. 72-73, for additional information.

SECONDARY

Montrose J. Moses and Oscar J. Campbell, eds. *Dramas of Modernism and Their Forerunners.* Boston: Little, Brown and Co., 1941. Pp. xvi, 946.

Pp. 933-934, 945, bibliography. Primary selected, secondary selected. Alphabetical by author arrangement. Books: place, publisher, date. Periods: volume, pages, date. Reviews of the two primary books listed under titles. Useful secondary checklist.

GENERAL

Temple & Tucker; Adelman & Dworkin; Palmer & Dyson; Salem;

Breed & Sniderman; Hogan; NCBEL, IV, 921-922.

CARSWELL, CATHERINE ROXBURGH (1879-1946)

NCBEL, IV, 548.

CARTER, FREDERICK (-1967)

PRIMARY

John Gawsworth. *Ten Contemporaries. Notes Toward their Definitive Bibliography. (Second Series).* London: Joiner & Steele, Ltd., 1933. Pp. 240. 1000 copies.

Pp. 93-103, primary books, first editions, 1914-1932. Chronological arrangement. Transcribed TP, full collation, pagination, binding, date, bibliographical notes.

CARY, ARTHUR JOYCE LUNEL (1888-1957)

PRIMARY

James B. Meriwether. "The Books of Joyce Cary: A Preliminary Bibliography of English and American Editions." *Texas Studies in Literature and Language* 1 (1959): 300-310.

Primary books. Chronological arrangement. Transcribed TP, part collation, binding, date, reprints, notes.

Barbara Fisher. "Joyce Cary's Published Writings." *Bodleian Library Record* 8 (1970): 213-228.

One chronological list of primary writings with genre identification of each item. Books: place, publisher, date, later editions, bibliographical notes. Periods: volume, date, pages. Includes published interviews.

The most complete listing of titles--to which Peter L. Shillingsburg adds seven items in "Addenda to Fisher: Joyce Cary." *Papers of the Bibliographical Society of America* 69 (1975): 409.

SECONDARY

Robert Bloom. *The Indeterminate World: A Study of the Novels of Joyce Cary.* Philadelphia: University of Pennsylvania Press, 1962. Pp. 212.

Pp. 205-208, selected secondary. Books: place, publisher, date. Periods: volume, pages, date.

Maurice Beebe, James W. Lee, and Sam Henderson. "Criticism of Joyce Cary: A Selected Checklist." *Modern Fiction Studies* 9 (Autumn 1963): 284-288.

Alphabetical by author arrangement. Books: place, publisher, date. Periods: volume, pages, date.

M. M. Mahood. *Joyce Cary's Africa.* London: Methuen and Co., 1964. Pp. 206.

Pp. 197-201, "List of Sources," Important unpublished material in the Osborn collection, Bodleian Library; official government papers relating to Africa; other African studies.

Peter J. Reed. "Joyce Cary. A Selected Checklist of Criticism." *Bulletin of Bibliography* 25 (1968): 133-134, 151.

Alphabetical by author arrangement. Books: place, publisher, year. Periods: volume, pages, date.

GENERAL

Longaker & Bolles; Daiches; Temple & Tucker; Adelman & Dworkin; NCBEL, IV, 548-551; Bufkin.

CASEMENT, ROGER DAVID (1864-1916)

PRIMARY

Patrick Sarsfield O'Hegarty. "Bibliographies of 1916 and the

Irish Revolution. No. XVII. Roger Casement." *Dublin Magazine* 24 (April-June 1949): 31-34. [Also published as a separate pamphlet.]

Primary books and pamphlets. Chronological arrangement. Transcribed TP, part collation, pagination, binding, bibliographical and textual notes.

Roger Casement. *The Crime against Europe. The Writings and Poetry of Roger Casement.* Collected and edited by Herbert O. Mackey. Dublin: C. J. Fallon Ltd., 1958. Pp. [xvi], 227.

Pp. 91-148, miscellaneous journalism; footnotes give periodical and date of original publication; pp. 159-214, poems (no bibliographical information).

CAUDWELL, CHRISTOPHER: *see* SPRIGG, CHRISTOPHER ST. JOHN.

CAUSLEY, CHARLES STANLEY (1917-)

Vinson-Poets; Stratford.

CAUTE, JOHN DAVID (1936-)

Vinson-Novelists; Vinson-Dramatists; Drescher & Kahrmann.

CECIL, LORD EDWARD CHRISTIAN DAVID GASCOYNE (1902-)

Millett; Longaker & Bolles; Daiches; Temple & Tucker.

CHAMBERS, CHARLES HADDON (1860-1921)

Salem.

CHAMBERS, JONATHAN DAVID (1898-1970)

PRIMARY

A. W. Coats. "Bibliography of Works by Professor J. D. Chambers, B. A., Ph. D." *Renaissance and Modern Studies* 16

(1972): 18-24.

Form and genre arrangement. Books: place, publisher, date. Periods: volume, date, pages. Reviews by Chambers include title and author of book reviewed. P. 24, secondary bibliography.

CHAPIN, HAROLD (1886-1915)

NCBEL, IV, 922-923.

CHAPLIN, SIDNEY (1916-)

Vinson-Novelists.

CHARLES, GERDA (-)

Vinson-Novelists; Bufkin.

CHARTERIS, HUGO FRANCIS GUY (1922-1970)

Drescher & Kahrmann.

CHESTERTON, GILBERT KEITH (1874-1936)

PRIMARY

John Sullivan. *G. K. Chesterton. A Bibliography.* London: University of London Press; New York: Barnes and Noble, 1958. Pp. 208.

Primary first editions, secondary selected. Form arrangement. Books: transcribed TP, full collation, binding, date, price, variants, notes, number of copies. Selected contributions to periodicals, mainly of writings subsequently collected in book form: alphabetical list of periods: dates. Chronological list of books and periodicals illustrated by Chesterton. Chronological list of collections and selections from Chesterton. Chronological list of translations of primary writings. Pp. 161-171, secondary bibliography. Chronological arrangement. Index, pp. 197-208.

TLS, No. 2945 (8 August 1958): 452: "admirably thorough, informative, lucid record."

John Sullivan. *Chesterton Continued. A Bibliographical Supplement.* London: University of London Press, 1968. Pp. [xvi], 120.

Pp. 9-84, additions and corrections to Sullivan's *G. K. Chesterton* (above) in its style and order.

Joseph W. Sprug. *An Index to G. K. Chesterton.* Washington: Catholic University Press, 1965. Pp. xx, 427.

Pp. xiii-xvii, alphabetical list of titles by Chesterton herein indexed. Place, publisher, date, pages.

SECONDARY

Above, Sullivan (1958), pp. 161-171.

Lawrence J. Clipper. *G. K. Chesterton.* New York: Twayne Publishers, Inc. (TEAS 166), 1974. Pp. 190.

Pp. 179-186, selected secondary bibliography, annotated.

GENERAL

Millett; Longaker & Bolles; Batho & Dobrée; Temple & Tucker; Adelman & Dworkin; NCBEL, IV, 1021-1028.

CHILDE, WILFRED ROWLAND MARY (1890-1952)

NCBEL, IV, 246.

CHILDERS, ROBERT ERSKINE (1870-1922)

PRIMARY

Patrick Sarsfield O'Hegarty. "Bibliographies of 1916 and the Irish Revolution. No. XVI. Erskine Childers." *Dublin Magazine* 23 (April-June 1948): 40-43.

Primary books. Chronological arrangement. Transcribed TP, part collation, pagination, binding.

GENERAL

NCBEL, IV, 551.

CHITTY, SIR THOMAS WILLES: *see* HINDE, THOMAS.

CHRISTIE, DAME AGATHA MARY CLARISSA (1891-1976)

(Lady Max E. L. Mallowan).

PRIMARY

G. C. Ramsey. *Agatha Christie. Mistress of Mystery.* New York: Dodd and Co., 1967. Pp. [xiv], 124.

Pp. 77-124, bibliographical appendices. Arranged: alphabetical list of all titles with genre; alphabetical list of novels including plot summary, publisher, and date; alphabetical list of short story collections with contents; alphabetical list of books and stories made into plays, including author of the dramatization; list of books and stories made into films; list of titles published only in America or in Britain; selected writings about Dame Agatha excluding reviews.

SECONDARY

Above, Ramsey, pp. 123-124.

GENERAL

Salem; Palmer & Dyson; Vinson-Novelists; Vinson-Dramatists; NCBEL, IV, 552-554.

CHUBB, RALPH NICHOLAS (1892-1960)

PRIMARY

Anthony Reid. "Ralph Chubb, the Unknown. Part II. His Work." *Private Library* (2nd Series) 3 (1970): 193-213.

Primary, secondary. Form arrangement. Transcribed TP without lineation bars, description of illustrations, binding, number of copies, price, extensive bibliographical notes concerning reprints, variants, and unique copies. Periods: volume, pages, date, annotations.

SECONDARY

Above, Reid.

CHURCH, RICHARD THOMAS (1893-1972)

Daiches; Temple & Tucker; Bufkin; Vinson-Novelists; NCBEL, IV, 246-248.

CHURCHILL, SIR WINSTON LEONARD SPENCER (1874-1965)

PRIMARY

Frederick Woods. *A Bibliography of the Works of Sir Winston Churchill, KG, OM, CH.* Second, revised edition. London: Kaye and Ward; Toronto: University of Toronto Press, 1969. Pp. 396, interleaved with unnumbered blank pages.

Primary complete; secondary books. Form arrangement. Books: transcribed TP, full collation, pagination, binding, descriptions of type-face, paper, and endpapers, date, price, variations, reprints, number of copies, extensive textual and bibliographical notes. Periods: volume, pages, date. Appendices include bibliographical history of *The Second World War* and *The British Gazette;* list of *The Political Warfare Leaflets* (translations of Churchill's writings). Index of titles.

The standard primary bibliography.

SECONDARY

Above, Woods, pp. 325-348. Chronological arrangement. Place, publisher, date.

There appears to be no complete secondary bibliography, but by examining all of the bibliographies in all of the books named by Woods one would begin to get an idea of the size of such a list.

GENERAL

Daiches; NCBEL, IV, 1147-1150.

CLARK, LEONARD (1905-)

Vinson-Poets.

CLARKE, ARTHUR CHARLES (1917-)

Vinson-Novelists.

CLARKE, AUSTIN (1896-1974)

PRIMARY

M. J. MacManus. "Bibliographies of Irish Writers. No. 8. Austin Clarke." *Dublin Magazine* 10 (April-June 1935): 41-43.

Primary books. Chronological arrangement. Transcribed TP, part collation, pagination, binding, bibliographical notes.

Liam Miller. "The Books of Austin Clarke. A Checklist" in *A Tribute to Austin Clarke on his Seventieth Birthday,* ed. John Montague and Liam Miller. Dublin: Dolmen Edns, 1966. Pp. 28. 1000 copies.

Primary books. Chronological arrangement. Transcribed TP without lineation bars, genre, part collation, binding. Notice of later editions and reprints with varying information. Occasional textual or bibliographical notes. [Revised and extended version of list first appearing in *The Dubliner,* No. 6, 1963.]

Thomas Dillon Redshaw. "Appreciation. His Works, A Memorial: Austin Clarke (1896-1974)." *Eire-Ireland* 9, No. 2 (Summer, 1974), 107-115.

Pp. 111-113, primary writings. Form and genre arrangement. Books: place, publisher, date. Periods: volume, date, pages. Pp. 113-115, secondary bibliography.

Supplements titles listed by Miller (above).

GENERAL

Temple & Tucker; Coleman & Tyler; Breed & Sniderman; Hogan; Vinson-Poets; NCBEL, IV, 248-249.

CLARKE, THOMAS JAMES (-1916)

PRIMARY

Patrick Sarsfield O'Hegarty. "Bibliographies of 1916 and the Irish Revolution. VII. Thomas James Clarke." *Dublin Magazine* 11 (July-September 1936): 57.

Primary books. Chronological arrangement. Transcribed TP, part collation, pagination, binding, bibliographical notes.

CLAYTON, RICHARD HENRY MICHAEL: *see* HAGGARD, WILLIAM.

CLEMO, JACK (REGINALD JOHN) (1916-)

Vinson-Poets.

COBBING, BOB (1920-)

Vinson-Poets.

COLE, BARRY (1936-)

Vinson-Poets; Vinson-Novelists.

COLE, GEORGE DOUGLAS HOWARD (1889-1959)

Millett; Daiches.

COLERIDGE, MARY ELIZABETH (1861-1907)

PRIMARY

Mary E. Coleridge. *Poems* [ed. Henry Newbolt]. London: Elkin Matthews, 1907. Pp. [xxii], 214.

Pp. v-xii, Preface by Newbolt: bibliographical details about previous book publication of the poems, *passim.*

Mary Coleridge. *The Collected Poems,* ed. Theresa Whistler. London: Rupert Hart-Davis, 1954. Pp. 266.

Pp. 21-81, Introduction by Whistler: bibliographical information, *passim.*

GENERAL

NCBEL, III, 618-619.

COLLIER, JOHN HENRY NOYES (1901-)

PRIMARY

John Gawsworth. *Ten Contemporaries. Notes Toward their Definitive Bibliography (Second Series).* London: Joiner and Steele, Ltd., 1933. Pp. 240. 1000 copies.

Pp. 112-117, primary first editions, 1930-1932. Chronological arrangement. Transcribed TP, full collation, pagination, binding, date, bibliographical notes.

GENERAL

Temple & Tucker; Vinson-Novelists; NCBEL, IV, 554-555.

COLLINS, MICHAEL (1890-1922)

PRIMARY

Patrick Sarsfield O'Hegarty. "Bibliographies of 1916 and the Irish Revolution. XIII. Michael Collins." *Dublin Magazine* 12 (January-March 1937): 66-67.

Primary books. Chronological arrangement. Transcribed TP, part collation, pagination, binding, bibliographical and biographical notes.

SECONDARY

Rex Taylor. *Michael Collins.* London: Hutchinson, 1958. Pp. 352.

Pp. 335-337, secondary bibliography. Form arrangement. Also notes, pp. 324-333.

COLTON, JOHN (1886-1946)

Salem.

COLUM, PADRAIC (1881-1972)

PRIMARY

Alan Denson. "Padraic Colum: An Appreciation with a Checklist of His Publications." *Dublin Magazine* 6 (1967): i, 50-67, ii, 83-85.

Not seen.

A list of primary books with place and date of all editions, drawn from Denson, is given in Zack Bowen. *Padraic Colum A Biographical-Critical Introduction.* Carbondale: Southern Illinois University Press, 1970. Pp. [xiv], 162. Pp. 155-157.

GENERAL

Millett; Longaker & Bolles; Temple & Tucker; NCBEL, III, 1942-1943; Hogan; Breed & Sniderman.

COMFORT, ALEXANDER (1920-)

PRIMARY

Robert D. Callahan. "Alexander Comfort: A Bibliography in Progress," *West Coast Review* 3 (Winter, 1969): 48-67.

Primary, secondary. Form and genre arrangement. Books: place, publisher, date; includes British and American editions. Periods: volume, pages, date. Includes translations by Comfort; editing by Comfort; letters to editors by Comfort; and reviews by Comfort with title and author of book reviewed; also anthologies including his work. Pp. 64-67, secondary bibliography includes reviews of primary writings. Complete to 31 December 1967.

SECONDARY

Above, Callahan, pp. 64-67.

GENERAL

Daiches; Longaker & Bolles; Bufkin; Temple & Tucker; Vinson-Poets; Vinson-Novelists, NCBEL, IV, 249-250.

COMPTON-BURNETT, DAME IVY (1892-1969)

PRIMARY

Frank Baldanza. *Ivy Compton-Burnett.* New York: Twayne Publishers, Inc. (TEAS 11), 1964. Pp. 142.

Pp. 135-138, primary books, secondary selected. Chronological arrangement. Books: place, publisher, date. Periods: volume, pages, date. Annotations for secondary entries.

R. Glynn Grylls. *I. Compton-Burnett.* London: Longman Group Ltd. (WTW 220), 1971. Pp. 30.

P. 29, primary books. Chronological arrangement. Place, date. Pp. 29-30, secondary selected. Periods: volume, date, pages.

SECONDARY

Above, Baldanza and Grylls.

Charles Burkhart. *Ivy Compton-Burnett.* London: Victor Gollancz, 1965. Pp. 142.

Pp. 135-137, secondary selected, including reviews. Periods: volume, page, date.

GENERAL

Daiches; Temple & Tucker; Adelman & Dworkin (Novel); NCBEL, IV, 555-556; Bufkin.

CONN, STEWART (1936-)

Vinson-Poets; Vinson-Dramatists.

CONNOLLY, CYRIL VERNON (1903-1974)

Daiches; Temple & Tucker; Vinson-Novelists.

CONNOLLY, JAMES (-1916)

PRIMARY

Patrick Sarsfield O'Hegarty. "Bibliographies of 1916 and the Irish Revolution. No. V. James Connolly. Hand List, Notes and Queries." *Dublin Magazine* 11 (April-June 1936): 62-64.

Primary books. Chronological arrangement. All titles listed, but described only if O'Hegarty had seen a copy. Place, publisher, year, part collation, binding, extensive notes and queries.

CONNOR, JOHN ANTHONY AUGUSTUS (1930-)

Vinson-Poets.

CONQUEST, GEORGE ROBERT ACWORTH (1917-)

Vinson-Poets; Vinson-Novelists.

CONRAD, JOSEPH (1857-1924)

Formerly Jósef Teodor Konrad Nalcez Korzeniowski.

BIBLIOGRAPHIES OF BIBLIOGRAPHIES

Theodore George Ehrsam. *A Bibliography of Joseph Conrad.*

Metuchen, New Jersey: Scarecrow Press, Inc., 1969. Pp. 448.

Pp. 373-386, bibliographical materials. Arranged alphabetically by author or title. Pp. 9-258, biographical and critical material. Pp. 259-330, primary bibliography. Arranged alphabetically by title. Books: place, publisher, year, pages. Periods: volume, pages, date. Occasional bibliographical notes and reviews under each primary book title. Other divisions: pp. 331-334, primary prefatory material; pp. 335-372, translations of Conrad (alphabetically arranged by English title of work, including translator's name and occasionally reviews); pp. 387-393, iconography; pp. 394-395, motion picture films; pp. 397-448, index.

The most important of all the Conrad bibliographical aids. Thomas M. Whitehead, *Papers of the Bibliographical Society of America* 63 (1969): 350: "perhaps its greatest achievement [is] a full treatment of books and articles about Conrad and [of] reviews of his works. . .a very useful guide to Conrad and 'Conradiana'." A more recent guide is "Conrad" by J. A. V. Chapple, in A. E. Dyson, ed. *The English Novel. Select Bibliographical Guides.* London: Oxford University Press, 1974, pp. 300-313. Survey and evaluation of texts, critical studies, biographies and letters, bibliographies, and background reading. Also lists of titles (with date and place) arranged under these divisions.

PRIMARY

Thomas J. Wise. *A Bibliography of the Writings of Joseph Conrad (1895-1920).* London: Privately Printed, 1920. Pp. 128. 150 copies. Second edn, revised and enlarged. 1921. 170 copies. Reprinted, London: Dawsons, 1964. *A Conrad Library. A Catalogue of Printed Books, Manuscripts and Autograph Letters by Joseph Conrad.* London: Privately Printed, 1928. Pp. [xx], [68]. 205 (?) copies.

Primary books, miscellaneous letters and MSS; secondary books. Transcribed TP, part collation, pagination, occasionally binding; bibliographical notes mainly concerning unique copies in Wise's library; occasionally subsequent editions.

Wise provides the standard bibliography of Editiones Principes in these two volumes (the 1921 and 1928 edns), each one of which "gives material not contained in the other" (W. Partington, *T. J. Wise in the Original Cloth.* London, 1946. p. 325).

Oliver Warner. *Joseph Conrad.* London: Longmans, Green and Co. (WTW 2), 1964. Pp. 40.

Pp. 34-40, bibliography. Primary books. Chronological arrangement. Date, genre. Also includes French and Polish translations with translator, place; a list of secondary books, chronologically arranged; and an alphabetical list of stories with title of volume in which collected.

A convenient checklist of titles.

Above, Ehrsam, pp. 259-334.

The most inclusive listing.

SECONDARY

Kenneth A. Lohf and Eugene P. Sheehy. *Joseph Conrad at Mid-Century: Editions and Studies, 1895-1955.* Minneapolis: University of Minneapolis Press, 1957. Pp. 114. Reprinted 1968.

Pp. 3-42, primary bibliography. Pp. 43-102, secondary bibliography. Arrangement: Memorial Issues of Periodicals; General; Individual Works (including reviews); Letters; Prefaces; Drama; Parody and Miscellaneous. Index.

Ludwik Krzyzanowski, ed. *Joseph Conrad Centennial Essays.* New York: Polish Institute of Arts and Sciences in America, 1960. Pp. 174.

Pp. 166-174, secondary bibliography of items, mainly in Polish, not in Lohf and Sheehy.

Maurice Beebe. "Criticism of Joseph Conrad: A Selected Checklist." *Modern Fiction Studies* 1 (1955); 30-45; 10 (1964): 81-106.

Arranged: General; Studies of Separate Works, listed under title of work studied.

A selected list of studies conveniently arranged according to the primary work studied; particularly useful to the beginning student.

Above, Ehrsam, pp. 9-258; also pp. 259-330, pp. 335-372.

The most inclusive listing. Thorough study of the Conrad criticism begins with this volume, supplemented by the listings in *Conradiana* and in the Teets-Gerber *Annotated Bibliography*.

Conradiana 1 (1968): 87-88 (continuing).

This periodical, devoted to Conrad studies, includes in each issue a continuing bibliography which supplements Ehrsam.

Edmund A. and Henry T. Bojarski. "Three Hundred and Thirty Six Unpublished Papers on Joseph Conrad. A Bibliography of Masters Theses and Doctoral Dissertations, 1917-1963." *Bulletin of Bibliography* 26 (1969): 61-66, 79-83.

An incomplete list, the deficiencies being noted on p. 61.

Bruce E. Teets and Helmut E. Gerber. *Joseph Conrad An Annotated Bibliography of Writings about Him.* DeKalb: Northern Illinois University Press, 1971. Pp. [xii] , 671.

Pp. 3-6, primary books. Genre arrangement. Place, date, contents of collections. Pp. 7-12, essay survey of secondary criticism. Pp. 13-614, secondary bibliography; 1977 entries, 1895-1967. Books: place, publisher, date. Period: volume, date, pages. Full annotations. Indices of authors, of titles of secondary works, of periodicals and newspapers, of foreign languages, and of primary titles.

Additions to this list are provided by George Monteiro. "Addenda to the Bibliographies of Conrad. . . : Reviews in *Public Opinion.*" *Papers of the Bibliographical Society of America* 70 (1976): 276-278; there are also additions in the checklists and specialized bibliographies published in almost every issue of *English Literature in Transition* and *Conradiana.*

GENERAL

Millet; Longaker & Bolles; Batho & Dobrée; Temple & Tucker; Breed & Sniderman; NCBEL, IV, 395-417; Bufkin.

CONRAN, ANTHONY (1931-)

Vinson-Poets.

CONWAY, OLIVE, pseudonym of Harold Brighouse and John Walton: *see* BRIGHOUSE, HAROLD.

COOPER, EDITH: *see* FIELD, MICHAEL.

COOPER, LETTICE ULPHA (1897-)

Vinson-Novelists.

COOPER, WILLIAM (1910-)

Pseudonym of Harry Summerfield Hoff.

Temple & Tucker; Bufkin; Adelman & Dworkin (Novel); Vinson-Novelists; Drescher & Kahrmann.

COPPARD, ALFRED EDGAR (1878-1957)

PRIMARY

Jacob Schwartz. *The Writings of A. E. Coppard. A Bibliography with Foreword and Notes by A. E. Coppard.* London: Ulysses Bookshop, 1931. Pp. [x], 73. 650 copies, signed by Coppard.

Primary complete. Form arrangement. Transcribed TP, full collation, binding, date, contents with details of previous publication, subsequent editions, extensive notes. Includes sections listing anthologies, translations, selected periodical contributions (including reviews by Coppard with title and author of book reviewed).

Gilbert H. Fabes. *The First Editions of A. E. Coppard, A. P. Herbert, and Charles Morgan, with Values and Bibliographical Points.* London: Myers and Co., 1933. Pp. 154.

Transcribed TP, binding, variants, value in sterling. A book for dealers or collectors.

Schwartz and Fabes together give a fairly complete list to 1933.

GENERAL

Millett; Longaker & Bolles; Daiches; Temple & Tucker; NCBEL, IV, 556-557.

CORELLI, MARIE (1855-1924)

PRIMARY

William Stuart Scott. *Marie Corelli, the Story of a Friendship.* London: Hutchinson, 1955. Pp. 280.

Pp. 265-255, bibliography. Primary books, secondary selected. Publisher, date. Additional secondary criticism in text, *passim.*

Further items and information are provided by Richard L. Kowalczyk. "A Bibliography of Marie Corelli." *Bulletin of Bibliography* 30 (1973): 141-142. Primary. Genre arrangement. Books: place, publisher, date. Periods: volume, date, pages. Occasional annotations.

GENERAL

Batho & Dobrée; Temple & Tucker; NCBEL, III, 1043-1044.

CORKERY, DANIEL (1878-1964)

PRIMARY

George Brandon Saul. *Daniel Corkery.* Lewisburg: Bucknell University Press (Irish Writers Series), 1973. Pp. 69.

Pp. 66-69, bibliography.

Not seen.

GENERAL

Millett; Breed & Sniderman; NCBEL, IV, 923-924.

CORNFORD, FRANCES CROFTS (1886-1960)

PRIMARY

Jenny Stratford. *The Arts Council Collection of Modern Literary Manuscripts 1963-1972. A Catalogue. . . with a Preface by Philip Larkin.* London: Turret Books, 1974. Pp. [xxiv], 168.

Pp. 95-109, 148. A description of the Cornford manuscripts and books in in this collection. Books: place, publisher, date, contents. Periods: volume, date, pages. Extensive bibliographical, historical, and textual notes.

Although not put forward as a bibliography, Stratford's complete descriptions of this collection can almost function as one.

GENERAL

Longaker & Bolles; Daiches; NCBEL, IV, 251.

CORNFORD, RUPERT JOHN (1915-1936)

NCBEL, IV, 251.

CORNWELL, DAVID JOHN MOORE: *see* LÉ CARRE, JOHN.

CORVO, BARON: *see* ROLFE, FREDERICK WILLIAM

COTTON, JOHN (1925-)

Vinson-Poets.

COWARD, SIR NOEL PIERCE (1899-1973)

PRIMARY

Raymond Mander and Joe Mitchenson. *Theatrical Companion to Coward.* London: Rockliff, 1957. Pp. 407.

Pp. 391-396, bibliography of primary first publications. Form arrangement. Publisher, date, of British and American editions. Bibliographical information in text, *passim.*

Milton Levin. *Noel Coward.* New York: Twayne Publishers, Inc. (TEAS 73), 1968. Pp. 158.

Pp. 149-151, primary selected. Genre arrangement. Books: place, publisher, year, contents. Periods: volume, pages, date. Pp. 151-153, secondary selected. Alphabetical-by-author arrangement. Annotated.

SECONDARY

Above, Mander and Mitchenson, *passim;* Levin, pp. 151-153.

GENERAL

Millett; Longaker & Bolles; Daiches; Temple & Tucker; Coleman & Tyler; Adelman & Dworkin; Salem; Palmer & Dyson; Breed & Sniderman; Vinson-Dramatists; NCBEL, IV, 924-927.

COX, ANTHONY BERKELEY (1893-1971

Pseudonyms used: Anthony Berkeley; Francis Iles.

NCBEL, IV, 528.

COX, WILLIAM TREVOR: *see* TREVOR, WILLIAM.

CRACKANTHORPE, HUBERT MONTAGUE (1870-1896)

PRIMARY

Henry Danielson. *Bibliographies of Modern Authors.* London: Bookman's Journal, 1921. Pp. [xii] , [212] .

Pp. 21-23, primary books. Chronological arrangement. Transcribed TP, part collation, pagination, binding, variants, miscellaneous bibliographical notes.

SECONDARY

Wendell Harris. "A Bibliography of Writings about Hubert Crackanthorpe." *English Literature in Transition* 6 (1963): 85-91.

Alphabetical by author. Books: place, publisher, year. Periods: volume, pages, date. All entries annotated.

GENERAL

NCBEL, III, 1044.

CRAIG, EDWARD GORDON (1872-1966)

PRIMARY

Ifan Kyrle Fletcher and Arnold Rood. *Edward Gordon Craig. A Bibliography.* London: Society for Theatre Research, 1967. Pp. 117.

Primary. Form arrangement, chronological within each section. Books: part collation, binding, place, publisher or printer, date, number of copies, subsequent editions, bibliographical notes. Periods: volume, pages, date, annotations. Reviews by Craig include title and author of book reviewed. Periodicals edited by Craig treated like primary books. A complete and authoritative bibliography. For information about specific items and additional notes: Donald Oenslager and Arnold Rood. "Edward Gordon Craig. Artist of the Theatre, 1872-1966: Introduction and Catalogue." *Bulletin of the New York Public Library* 71 (1967): 431-467, 524-541.

SECONDARY

Enid Rose. *Gordon Craig and the Theatre.* New York: Frederick A. Stokes Co., n.d. Pp. [x], 250.

Pp. 225-228, catalogues of Craig's exhibitions: place, date. Pp. 229-239, selected secondary books. Chronological arrangement. Place, publisher, date.

CRAIGIE, PEARL MARY TERESA: *see* HOBBES, JOHN OLIVER.

CREGAN, DAVID APPLETON QUARTUS (1931-)

Vinson-Dramatists.

CRESSWELL, WALTER D'ARCY (1896-1960)

PRIMARY

Roderick Finalyson. *D'Arcy Cresswell.* New York: Twayne Publishers, Inc. (TWAS 205), 1972. Pp. 132.

P. 130, selected primary and secondary bibliography. Books: place, publisher, date. Periods: volume, date, pages.

CRIPPS, ARTHUR SHEARLY (1869-1952)

PRIMARY

John Robert Doyle, Jr. *Arthur Shearly Cripps.* Boston: Twayne Publishers, G. K. Hall and Co. (TWAS 365), 1975. Pp. 264.

Pp. 249-253, primary bibliography, selected secondary bibliography. Genre arrangement. Books: place, publisher, date. Periods: date, pages. Each entry annotated.

SECONDARY

Above, Doyle, pp. 252-253.

CROCKETT, SAMUEL RUTHERFORD (1860-1914)

NCBEL, III, 1044-1045.

CRONIN, ARCHIBALD JOSEPH (1896-)

Millett; Daiches; Temple & Tucker; Bufkin; Adelman & Dworkin (Novel); NCBEL, IV, 557.

CROSS, ALAN BEVERLEY (1931-)

Vinson-Dramatists.

CROSSLEY-HOLLAND, KEVIN JOHN WILLIAMS (1941-)

Vinson-Poets.

CROWLEY, ALEISTER (1875-1947)

PRIMARY

Gerald Yorke. "Bibliography of Aleister Crowley" in John Symonds. *The Great Beast. The Life of Aleister Crowley.*

London: Rider and Co., 1951. Pp. 316.

Pp. 301-310, bibliography. Primary complete. Genre arrangement. Books: publisher, place, date, pages, number of copies. Periods: dates, pages. Secondary criticism in text, *passim.*

Edward Noel Fitzgerald. "The Works of Aleister Crowley, Published or Privately Printed. A Bibliographical List" in Charles Richard Cammell. *Aleister Crowley. The Man. The Mage. The Poet.* London: Richards Press, 1951; New York: University Books, 1962. Pp. 230.

Pp. 207-218, bibliography. Primary first editions. Chronological arrangement. Transcribed TP, binding, pages. Secondary criticism in text, *passim.*

Fitzgerald is less comprehensive than Yorke, but adds bibliographical details.

SECONDARY

Above, Yorke; Fitzgerald.

CRUIKSHANK, HELEN BURNESS (1886-)

Vinson-Poets.

CUMMINGS, BRUCE FREDERICK: see BARBELLION, W. N. P.

CURREY, RALPH NIXON (1907-)

Vinson-Poets.

DAHL, ROALD (1916-)

Vinson-Novelists.

DALE, PETER JOHN (1938-)

Vinson-Poets.

DANE, CLEMENCE (188?-1965)

Pseudonym of Winifred Ashton.

Millett; Temple & Tucker; Adelman & Dworkin; Salem; Breed & Sniderman; NCBEL, IV, 927-929; Bufkin.

DARLINGTON, WILLIAM AUBREY CECIL (1890-)

NCBEL, IV, 929.

DASHWOOD, ELIZABETH M.: *see* DELAFIELD, ELIZABETH M.

DAVIDSON, JOHN (1857-1909)

PRIMARY

C. A. and H. W. Stonehill. *Bibliographies of Modern Authors* (Second Series). London: John Castle, 1925. Pp. [xiv], 162. 750 copies.

Pp. 3-38, primary bibliography. Form arrangement (mainly books). Transcribed TP, full collation, pagination, binding, price, number of copies, variants, bibliographical noes.

J. A. Lester, Jr. *John Davidson. A Grub Street Bibliography.* Charlottesville, Virginia: University of Virginia Press (Bibliographical Society of University of Virginia, Secretary's News Sheet No. 40), 1958. Pp. 30.

Not seen.

J. B. Townsend (below), p. 522: "very useful bibliography of Davidson's journalistic work. . . probably as complete as at present can be compiled."

Maurice Lindsay, ed. *John Davidson. A Selection of His Poems.* London: Hutchinson, 1961. Pp. 220.

Pp. 1-46, introduction: gives titles of primary writings and of secondary criticism. Pp. 215-216, primary books. Genre arrangement. Dates, occasionally place.

SECONDARY

Above, Lindsay.

J. B. Townsend. *John Davidson. Poet of Armageddon.* New Haven: Yale University Press, 1961. Pp. 555.

No bibliography; notes include secondary criticism, quotations from MSS, location of Davidson collections.

GENERAL

Batho & Dobrée, Longaker & Bolles; Temple & Tucker; NCBEL, III, 619-621.

DAVIE, DONALD ALFRED (1922-)

PRIMARY

Calvin Bedient. *Eight Contemporary Poets.* New York: Oxford University Press, 1975. Pp. x, 198.

Pp. 181-182, primary books. Place, publisher, date, names of editors and illustrators.

GENERAL

Temple & Tucker; Vinson-Poets.

DAVIES, HUBERT HENRY (1869-1917)

NCBEL, IV, 929-930.

DAVIES, RHYS (1903-)

PRIMARY

John Gawsworth. *Ten Contemporaries. Notes Toward their Definitive Bibliography.* [First Series]. London: Ernest

Benn Ltd., 1932. Pp. 224.

Pp. 44-52, primary books, first editions, 1927-1932. Chronological arrangement. Transcribed TP, full collation, pagination, binding, date, bibliographical notes.

David Rees. *Rhys Davies.* Cardiff: University of Wales Press for the Welsh Arts Council (Writers of Wales), 1975. Pp. 74.

Not seen.

GENERAL

Millett; Temple & Tucker; Vinson-Novelists; NCBEL, IV, 558.

DAVIES, WILLIAM HENRY (1870-1940)

PRIMARY

George F. Wilson. "A Bibliography of W. H. Davies." *Bookman's Journal* 5 (1922): 202, 6 (1922): 29, 59, Continued by Samuel J. Looker, 17 (1929): 122-127.

Primary books. Chronological arrangement. Transcribed TP, part collation, pagination, binding, subsequent editions, bibliographical notes.

Gwendolen Murphy. "Bibliographies of Modern Authors. No. III. W. H. Davies." *London Mercury* 17 (1927-1928): 76-80, 301-304, 684-688.

Primary books. Chronological arrangement. Transcribed TP, full collation, pagination, binding, price, contents, variants, reprints, subsequent editions, bibliographical notes. Pp. 687-688, chronological list of contributions to the *Nation*, 1907-1923: pages, date. Ends "To be continued," but no other entries appeared in the *London Mercury*.

Richard J. Stonesifer. *W. H. Davies. A Critical Biography.* London: Jonathan Cape, 1963; Middletown, Connecticut: Wesleyan University Press, 1965. Pp. 256.

Pp. 233-234, "A Chronology of Davies' Works." Primary books. Place, publisher, year. Pp. 235-250, notes include references to secondary criticism, *passim.*

SECONDARY

Above, Stonesifer, pp. 235-250.

GENERAL

Millett; Longaker & Bolles; Batho & Dobrée; Temple & Tucker; NCBEL, IV, 251-253.

DAVIN, DANIEL MARCUS (1913-)

Vinson-Novelists.

DAWSON, JENNIFER (-)

Vinson-Novelists; Bufkin.

DAY LEWIS, CECIL: *see* LEWIS, CECIL DAY.

DEAN, BASIL (1888-)

NCBEL, IV, 931.

DEEPING, GEORGE WARWICK (1877-1950)

Daiches; NCBEL, IV, 559-560.

DEEVY, TERESA (1900-1963)

NCBEL, IV, 931-932.

DEHN, PAUL EDWARD (1912-1976)

Vinson-Poets.

DEIGHTON, LEN (1929-)

Vinson-Novelists.

DELAFIELD, ELIZABETH MONICA (1890-1943)

Pseudonym of Edmée Elizabeth Monica de la Pasture.

PRIMARY

John Gawsworth. *Ten Contemporaries. Notes Toward their Definitive Bibliography* (Second Series). London: Joiner and Steele Ltd., 1933. Pp. 240. 1000 copies.

Pp. 123-135, primary books, first editions, 1917-1932. Chronological arrangement. Transcribed TP, full collation, pagination, binding, date.

GENERAL

Millett; Daiches; Temple & Tucker; NCBEL, IV, 560-561.

DE LA MARE, WALTER JOHN (1873-1956)

PRIMARY

Gwendolyn Murphy. "Bibliographies of Modern Authors. I. Walter de la Mare." *London Mercury* 15 (1927): 526-531, 635-639; 16 (1927): 70-71.

Primary books. Genre arrangement. Transcribed TP, full collation, pagination, binding, price, variants, reprints, subsequent editions. Pp. 70-71, musical settings with name of composer.

Leonard Clark. "A Handlist of the Writings in Book Form (1902-1953) of Walter de la Mare." *Studies in Bibliography* 6 (1954): 197-217; "Addendum: A Check List of the Writings of Walter de la Mare." *Studies in Bibliography* 8 (1956): 269-270.

Primary books. Chronological arrangement. Place, publisher, date, price, illustrator, reprints, subsequent editions. Index of titles.

--*Walter de la Mare. A Checklist prepared on the Occasion of an Exhibition of his Books and MSS at the National Book League April 20 to May 19, 1956.* Cambridge: University Press, 1956. Pp. 56. Reprinted: Folcroft Library Editions, 1971.

Primary, secondary selected. Form arrangement. Books: place, publisher, date, size in inches, price, occasional notes. Periods: volume, date. Pp. 54-56, secondary bibliography.

Edward Wagenknecht. "A List of Walter de la Mare's Contributions to the London *Times Literary Supplement.*" Boston University *Studies in English* 1 (Winter 1955-1956): 243-255.

Chronological arrangement. Title of review, number of issue, pages, date; author and title of book reviewed. Pp. 211-212, other periodical contributions by de la Mare.

Luce Bonnerot. *L'Œuvre de Walter de la Mare. Une aventure spirituelle.* [Thèse pour le doctorat ès Lettres, Université de Paris]. Paris: Librairie Marcel Didier, 1969. Pp. [532].

Pp. 475-493, primary bibliography, 1902-1969. Books: place, publisher, date. Periods: date, pages. Pp. 501-510, secondary bibliography. Also includes recordings of de la Mare's works and translations of de la Mare's work, pp. 497-500.

SECONDARY

Above, Clark (1956), pp. 54-56; Bonnerot, pp. 501-510.

Doris R. McCrosson. *Walter de la Mare.* New York: Twayne Publishers, Inc. (TEAS 33), 1966. Pp. 167.

Pp. 164-167, secondary bibliography. Alphabetical by author arrangement. Books: place, publisher, year. Periods: date, pages. Annotated.

GENERAL

Millett; Longaker & Bolles; Batho & Dobrée; Daiches; Temple & Tucker; NCBEL, IV, 256-262; Stratford; Bufkin.

DELANEY, SHELAGH (1929-)

Coleman & Tyler; Adelman & Dworkin; Salem; Palmer & Dyson; Vinson-Dramatists.

DE LA PASTURE, EDMEÉ ELIZABETH MONICA: *see* DELAFIELD, ELIZABETH M.

DE LA ROCHE, MAZO (1879-1961)

PRIMARY

Ronald Hambleton. *Mazo de la Roche of Jalna.* New York: Hawthorn Books, Inc., 1966. Pp. [240].

Pp. 223-229, primary bibliography. Form and genre arrangement. Books: date (publishers' names will be found in text, *passim*). Periods: date. Contents of short story collections listed with date and place of previous publication. Plays include cast of first performance. Secondary criticism (mainly reviews) mentioned in text, *passim*.

GENERAL

Millett.

DELDERFIELD, RONALD FREDERICK (1912-1972)

NCBEL, IV, 932.

DE MORGAN, WILLIAM FREND (1839-1917)

Batho & Dobrée; Temple & Tucker; NCBEL, IV, 561-562.

DENNIS, NIGEL FORBES (1912-)

Temple & Tucker; Coleman & Tyler; Bufkin; Adelman & Dworkin (Novel); Vinson-Novelists; Vinson-Dramatists; Drescher & Kahrmann; NCBEL, IV, 562.

DE SELINCOURT, ERNEST (1870-1943)

Millett; Temple & Tucker; NCBEL, IV, 1038.

DE SÉLINCOURT, HUGH (1878-1951)

NCBEL, IV, 562-563.

DICKENS, MONICA ENID (1915-)

(Mrs. R. O. Stratton).

Vinson-Novelists.

DICKINSON, GOLDWORTHY LOWES (1862-1932)

PRIMARY

R. E. Balfour. "Bibliography" in E. M. Forster. *Goldsworthy Lowes Dickinson.* London: Edwin Arnold and Co., 1934, 1938. Pp. 277.

Pp. 244-268, primary bibliography. Chronological arrangement. Books: place, publisher, date, format, pages, publisher of American edition. Periods: date, occasionally pages. Includes translations of Dickinson and obituary notices.

GENERAL

Millett; Batho & Dobrée; NCBEL, IV, 1158-1159.

DICKINSON, PATRIC THOMAS (1914-)

Daiches; NCBEL, IV, 262; Vinson-Poets; Stratford.

DIVER, KATHERINE HELEN MAUD (1867-1945)

NCBEL, IV, 563.

DOBRÉE, BONAMY (1891-1974)

PRIMARY

Margaret Britton. "A Selected List of the Published Writings of Bonamy Dobrée" in John Butt, ed., *Of Books and Humankind. Essays and Poems Presented to Bonamy Dobrée.* London: Routledge and Kegan Paul, 1964. Pp. 232.

Pp. 217-226, primary bibliography, 1919-1962. Chronological arrangement. Books: place, publisher, date, reprints, contents. Periods: volume, pages, date. Includes unsigned writings.

GENERAL

Millett; Daiches; Temple & Tucker.

DOBRÉE, VALENTINE (1894-)

Daiches.

DOBSON, HENRY AUSTIN (1840-1921)

PRIMARY

Francis Edwin Murray. *A Bibliography of Austin Dobson.* Derby: Frank Murray, 1900. Pp. 347. 635 copies.

Primary, form arrangement, genre subdivisions. Information varies for each entry. Extensive indices.

Alban Dobson. *A Bibliography of the First Editions of Published and Privately Printed Books and Pamphlets by Austin Dobson.* London: First Edition Club, 1925. Pp. 88.

Primary books. Chronological arrangement. Transcribed TP, full collation, binding, date, reprints, notes.

--*Austin Dobson. Some Notes . . . with Chapters by Sir Edmund Gosse and George Saintsbury.* London: Oxford University Press, 1928.

Adds a few items not in Dobson (1925).

Alban T. A. Dobson. *University of London Library, Catalogue of the Collection of the Works of Austin Dobson (1840-1921).* London: Chiswick Press, 1960. Pp. 62.

Primary, secondary. Form arrangement. Minimum of bibliographical details, but a list of the titles by and about Dobson in this virtually complete collection.

Together these four books provide a complete account of Dobson's writings.

SECONDARY

Above, Dobson (1960).

GENERAL

Longaker & Bolles; Batho & Dobrée; NCBEL, III, 1427-1428.

DOUGHTY, CHARLES MONTAGU (1843-1926)

PRIMARY

"Bibliographies of Modern Authors. Charles Montagu Doughty." *London Mercury* 4 (1921): 87.

Primary books, 1866-1921. Genre arrangement. Publisher, year.

Anne Treneer. *Charles Montagu Doughty. A Study of his Prose and Verse.* London: Jonathan Cape, 1935. Pp. 350.

Pp. 333-339, bibliography. Primary books, secondary selected. Genre arrangement. Publisher, place, date. Reviews of Doughty listed under title of book reviewed.

SECONDARY

Above, Treneer.

GENERAL

Millett; Longaker & Bolles; Temple & Tucker; NCBEL, III, 622-623.

DOUGLAS, LORD ALFRED (1870-1945)

PRIMARY

Rupert Croft-Cooke. *Bosie. Lord Alfred Douglas, His Friends and Enemies.* London: W. H. Allen; New York: Bobbs-Merrill Co., 1963. Pp. 414.

No bibliography, but bibliographical references in text, *passim;* also see pp. 385-386 for list of primary and secondary books used by Croft-Cooke.

SECONDARY

Above, Croft-Cooke, *passim.*

GENERAL

NCBEL, III, 623-624.

DOUGLAS, GEORGE NORMAN (1868-1952)

PRIMARY

Edward D. McDonald. *A Bibliography of the Writings of Norman Douglas with Notes by Norman Douglas.* Philadelphia: Centaur Book Shop, 1927. Pp. 165. 400 copies.

Primary, secondary selected. Form arrangement. Books: transcribed TP, full collation, pagination, binding, date, variants, reprints, notes. Periods: volume, date, titles of books in which later collected. Includes unsigned writings. Reviews by Douglas include title of book reviewed. Pp. 149-165, secondary bibliography.

Cecil Woolf. *A Bibliography of Norman Douglas.* London: Rupert Hart-Davis (Soho Bibliography No. 6), 1954; Fair Lawn, New Jersey: Essential Books, 1957. Pp. 201.

Primary. Form arrangement. Books: transcribed TP, full collation, pagination, binding, date, contents, price, variants, reprints, full notes. Periods: volume, pages, dates. Indices.

Continues, supplements, but does not supplant, McDonald.

Ian Greenlees. *Norman Douglas.* London: Longmans, Green and Co. (WTW 82), 1957. Pp. 38.

Pp. 35-37, bibliography. Primary books. Chronological arrangement. Date, genre, textual notes. P. 38, secondary bibliography.

One of the most complete bibliographies in the WTW series.

SECONDARY

Above, McDonald, pp. 149-165; Greenlees, p. 38.

Ralph D. Lindeman. *Norman Douglas.* New York: Twayne Publishers, Inc. (TEAS 19), 1965. Pp. 208.

Pp. 199-200, bibliography. Annotated.

GENERAL

Millett; Longaker & Bolles; Daiches; Temple & Tucker; NCBEL, IV, 563-565; Bufkin.

DOUGLAS, KEITH CASTELLAIN (1920-1944)

PRIMARY

Desmond Graham. *Keith Douglas 1920-1944. A Biography.* London: Oxford University Press, 1974. Pp. [xvi], 295.

Pp. 259-262, select primary and secondary bibliography. Arranged: Books: Uncollected Poems in Periodicals, Uncollected Prose, Unpublished material. Books: place, publisher, date. Periods: date, pages. Locations of MSS material. P. 260, secondary bibliography.

Graham cites his 1969 Leeds thesis as containing "a full bibliography" of primary and secondary material. Further information about the British Library MSS collection will be found in Jenny Stratford. *The Arts Council Collection of Modern Literary Manuscripts 1963-1972. A Catalogue . . . with a Preface by Philip Larkin.* London: Turret Books, 1974. Pp. [xxiv] , 168. For Douglas, see pp. 44-61, 118-130.

SECONDARY

Above, Graham, p. 260.

GENERAL

NCBEL, IV, 262-263; Temple & Tucker.

DOUGLAS, OLIVE CUSTANCE (1879-1944)

(Lady Alfred Douglas)

SECONDARY

Nancy J. Hawkey. "Olive Custance Douglas: An Annotated Bibliography of Writings about Her." *English Literature in Transition* 15 (1972): 52-56.

Selected secondary bibliography, arranged alphabetically by author. Books: place, publisher, date, relevant pages. Periods: volume, date, pages. Annotated. Includes reviews of books by Lady Douglas but no listing of the primary books--a clear case of putting the critic before the poet.

DOUGLAS HOME, WILLIAM: *see* HOME, WILLIAM DOUGLAS.

DOWSON, ERNEST CHRISTOPHER (1867-1900)

PRIMARY

Guy Harrison. "Bibliography" in Victor Plarr. *Ernest Dowson 1888-1897. Reminiscences, Unpublished Letters, and Marginalia.* London: Elkin Matthews, 1914. Pp. 147.

Pp. 131-142, primary first editions, secondary selected bibliography. Genre arrangement. Books: publisher, place, date, part collation, notes. Periods: volume, date, pages.

C. A. and H. W. Stonehill. *Bibliographies of Modern Authors* (Second Series). London: John Castle, 1925. Pp. [xiv], 162. 750 copies.

Pp. 41-63, primary bibliography. Form arrangement. Transcribed TP, full collation, pagination, binding, price, number of copies, variants, bibliographical notes.

SECONDARY

Above, Harrison.

Thomas Burnett Swann. *Ernest Dowson.* New York: Twayne Publishers, Inc. (TEAS 15), 1964. Pp. 122.

Pp. 113-114, primary books, including translations by Dowson. Pp. 114-117, secondary books. Alphabetical by author arrangement. Place, publisher, year, annotations.

Jonathan Ramsey. "Ernest Dowson: An Annotated Bibliography of Writings about Him." *English Literature in Transition* 14 (1971): 17-42.

Alphabetical by author arrangement. Books: place, publisher, date. Periods: volume, pages, date. Full annotations. The best source of information about Dowson. Subsequent issues of this periodical include supplements, particularly 18 (1975): 54-58.

GENERAL

Longaker & Bolles; Batho & Dobrée; NCBEL, III, 624-625.

DOYLE, SIR ARTHUR CONAN (1859-1930)

PRIMARY

Harold Locke. *A Bibliographical Catalogue of the Writings of Sir Arthur Conan Doyle, M. D., Ll. D., 1879-1928.* Tunbridge Wells: D. Webster, 1928. Pp. 84.

Primary. Form and genre arrangement. Transcribed TP, part collation, binding, date, notes on some reprints, other notes. Contributions to periodicals listed under title of the periodical: dates. Index.

A fairly complete bibliography, although difficult to use.

Pierre Nordon. *Conan Doyle. A Biography,* translated Frances Partridge. New York: Rinehart and Winston, 1967. Pp. 370.

Pp. 347-350, bibliography. Nordon refers one to Locke (above) for the primary bibliography, providing additions and corrections to it. Pp. 351-360, selected secondary bibliography. Topic arrangement. Place, publisher, date, pages.

SECONDARY

Above, Nordon, pp. 351-360.

Ronald Burt de Waal. *The World Bibliography of Sherlock Holmes and Dr. Watson. A Classified and Annotated List of Materials Relating to their Lives and Adventures.* Boston: New York Graphic Society, 1974. Pp. [xvi] , 526.

Pp. 1-97, primary bibliography of the Sherlock Holmes tales, including all editions, translations, and manuscripts. Pp. 99-458, secondary bibliography including all references of any sort to Holmes. Pp. 461-526, appendices and indices.

The 6221 entries in this enormous work provide all the information anyone could ever require about Conan Doyle's creation and is the starting point for all studies of the Sacred Writings.

GENERAL

Longaker & Bolles; Batho & Dobrée; Temple & Tucker; NCBEL, III, 1046-1049.

DRABBLE, MARGARET (1939-)

(Mrs. C. W. Swift).

PRIMARY

Valerie Grosvenor Myer. *Margaret Drabble: Puritanism and Permissiveness.* New York: Barnes and Noble (Critical Studies Series), 1974. Pp. 200.

P. 197, list of primary novels with dates; other primary writings are cited in the text. Of limited use to scholars, since the general editor writes of the books in this series that they are "free from cumbersome scholarly apparatus" (p. 7).

GENERAL

Bufkin; Vinson-Novelists; Drescher & Kahrmann; Temple & Tucker.

DRINAN, ADAM: *see* MACLEOD, JOSEPH

DRINKWATER, JOHN (1882-1937)

PRIMARY

Henry Danielson. *Bibliographies of Modern Authors.* London: Bookman's Journal, 1921. Pp. [xii] , [212] .

Pp. 41-60, books and pamphlets. Chronological arrangement. Transcribed TP, part collation, pagination, binding, variants, miscellaneous bibliographical notes.

[Timothy d'Arch Smith]. *John Drinkwater, 1882-1937. Catalogue of an Exhibition.* London: Times Bookshop, 1962. Pp. 51. 100 copies.

Primary books, also MSS, association items and iconography. Transcribed TP without lineation bars, full collation, binding, date, variants, reprints, notes.

Michael Pearce. *John Drinkwater. A Comprehensive Bibliography of His Works.* New York and London: Garland Publishing, Inc., 1977. Pp. [xiv], 157.

Primary, secondary selected. Form arrangement. Transcribed TP, full collation, pagination, date, binding, reprints, contents, bibliographical notes. Periods: dates, pages. Each item numbered, with reviews of Drinkwater listed under title of the work reviewed. Pp. 104-157, indices of titles (arranged by genre) locating all publications of the work in question.

SECONDARY

Above, Pearce, *passim.*

GENERAL

Millett; Longaker & Bolles; Daiches; Temple & Tucker; Salem; NCBEL, IV, 263-266.

DUCLAUX, MARY (1856-1944)

Née Agnes Mary Frances Robinson; (1) Mrs. James Darmesteter; (2) Mrs. Émile Duclaux.

PRIMARY

Ruth Van Zuyle Holmes. "Mary Duclaux. 1856-1944." *English Literature in Transition* 10 (1967): i, 27-46.

Pp. 32-39, primary bibliography. Form arrangement. Books: place, publisher, year. Periods: volume, pages, date, genre. Pp. 39-46, secondary bibliography. Chronological arrangement. Fully annotated. Lists anthologies including Duclaux, also translations by Duclaux; excludes her reviews for the *TLS*. Continued in later issues.

SECONDARY

Above, Holmes, pp. 39-46.

GENERAL

NCBEL, III, 646, 647.

DUFFY, MAUREEN (1933-)

Vinson-Novelists; Vinson-Dramatists; Drescher & Kahrmann.

DUGGAN, ALFRED LEO (1903-1964)

Bufkin; Temple & Tucker; Drescher & Kahrmann.

DUKES, ASHLEY (1885-1959)

PRIMARY

Ashley Dukes. *The Scene is Changed.* London: Macmillan and Co., 1942. Pp. 252.

Bibliographical information in the text, *passim,* of this autobiography.

GENERAL

Millett; NCBEL, IV, 934-935.

DU MAURIER, DAME DAPHNE (1907-)

(Lady Browning).

Bufkin; Temple & Tucker; Vinson-Novelists; NCBEL, IV, 565-566.

DU MAURIER, GEORGE LOUIS PALMELLA BUSSON (1834-1896)

PRIMARY

Trilbyana. The Rise and Progress of a Popular Novel. New York: Critic Company, 1895. Pp. 41.

Material drawn largely from the *Critic* puffing *Trilby;* important information concerning American reception of the novel.

John J. Winterich, "George du Maurier and *Trilby*" in *Books and the Man.* New York: Greenberg, 1929. Pp. [xvi] , 374.

Pp. 102-122, discursive essay with bibliographical information, *passim.*

L. N. Feipel. "The American Issues of *Trilby.*" *Colophon* 2, iv (1937): 537-549.

An essay on the variants in the American issues; detailed bibliographical information.

Derek Pepys Whiteley. *George du Maurier.* London: Art and Technics, 1948. Pp. 112.

Pp. 6-7, list of books illustrated by du Maurier.

GENERAL

Batho & Dobrée; NCBEL, III, 1049.

DUNCAN, RONALD FREDERICK HENRY (1914-)

Temple & Tucker; Breed & Sniderman; Vinson-Poets; Vinson-Dramatists; NCBEL, IV, 935-936.

DUNKERLEY, WILLIAM ARTHUR (1852-1941)

Pseudonym used: John Oxenham.

NCBEL, IV, 696-697.

DUNN, DOUGLAS EAGLESHAM (1942-)

Vinson-Poets.

DUNSANY, EDWARD JOHN MORETON DRAX PLUNKETT, LORD DUNSANY (1878-1957)

PRIMARY

Henry Danielson. *Bibliographies of Modern Authors.* London: Bookman's Journal, 1921. Pp. [xii], [212].

Pp. 67-75, primary books, 1905-1920. Chronological arrangement. Transcribed TP, part collation, pagination, binding, variants, miscellaneous bibliographical notes.

F. G. Stoddard. "The Lord Dunsany Collection." *Library Chronicle of the University of Texas* 9, iii (1967): 27-32.

A discursive essay with particular attention given to the MSS at Texas.

Mark Amory. *Biography of Lord Dunsany.* London: Collins, 1972. P. 288.

Pp. 283-284, primary books, 1905-1954, chronologically arranged. Place, publisher, date, genre.

There appears to be no complete listing of all of Lord Dunsany's extensive output.

GENERAL

Millett; Temple & Tucker; Adelman & Dworkin; Salem; NCBEL, III, 1945-1948; Breed & Sniderman.

DURRELL, LAWRENCE GEORGE (1912-)

PRIMARY

Robert A. Potter and Brooke Whiting. *Lawrence Durrell: A Checklist.* Los Angeles: UCLA Library, 1961. Pp. 50.

Primary. Chronological arrangement. Books (both British and American editions): place, publisher, date, brief notes. Periods: volume, pages, date. Pp. 47-50, title index.

An extremely full list, issued on the occasion of the presentation of the Powell collection to UCLA, and incorporating two earlier bibliographies: A. G. Thomas and L. C. Powell, "Some Uncollected Authors. XXIII. Lawrence Durrell." *Book Collector* 9 (1960): 56-63; and A. Knerr. "Regarding a Checklist of Lawrence Durrell." *Papers of the Bibliographical Society of America* 55 (1961): 142-152.

Alan Thomas. "Bibliography" in G. S. Fraser. *Lawrence Durrell: A Study.* London: Faber and Faber, 1968. Pp. 256. [Second edition, 1973: not seen.]

Pp. 200-250, bibliography. Primary, secondary. Form and genre arrangement. Books: publisher, place, date, format, brief bibliographical notes, remarks by Durrell. Periods: place, volume, date, notes. Includes gramophone records, musical settings, unpublished radio and television appearances by Durrell. Pp. 216-225, secondary bibliography. Chronological arrangement.

Potter-Whiting and Thomas together provide an extensive primary list, to which James A. Brigham in "Note 384. Lawrence Durrell and the *International Post,*" *Book Collector* 24 (1975): 294-295, and "Addenda to the Bibliography of Lawrence Durrell," *Notes and Queries* 23 (July, 1976): 308-310, gives additions.

G. S. Fraser. *Lawrence Durrell.* London: Longman Group Ltd. (WTW 216), 1970, Pp. 47.

Pp. 45-47, primary and secondary books. Chronological arrangement. Date, genre, place.

A convenient checklist of the primary books.

SECONDARY

Above, Thomas, pp. 216-225.

Bernard Stone. "Bibliography" in Alfred Perlès. *My Friend Lawrence Durrell.* London: Scorpion Press, 1961. Pp. 62.

Pp. 47-60, primary bibliography. Pp. 61-62, secondary bibliography, including reviews. Volume, pages.

John A. Weigel. *Lawrence Durrell.* New York: Twayne Publishers, Inc. (TEAS 29), 1965. Pp. 174.

Pp. 165-170, bibliography. Books: place, publisher, date, Period: volume, pages, date. Annotated.

Maurice Beebe. "Criticism of Lawrence Durrell. A Selected Checklist." *Modern Fiction Studies* 13 (1967): 417-421.

Alphabetical by author arrangement. Books: place, publisher, year. Periods: volume, pages, date.

GENERAL

Daiches; Temple & Tucker; Breed & Sniderman; Adelman & Dworkin (Novel); Vinson-Poets; Vinson-Novelists; Vinson-Dramatists; Drescher & Kahrmann; NCBEL, IV, 266-271; Bufkin.

DYER, CHARLES RAYMOND (1928-)

Salem; Vinson-Dramatists.

DYMENT, CLIFFORD HENRY (1914-1971)

Daiches; NCBEL, IV, 271-272.

EAST, MICHAEL, pseudonym of Morris West: *see* WEST, MORRIS.

EDDISON, ERIC RUCKER (1882-1945)

PRIMARY

George Rostrevor Hamilton. "Eric Rucker Eddison." *Book Handbook: An Illustrated Quarterly* [Bracknell] 1, i (1947): 53-57.

Pp. 53-54, biographical details. Pp. 55-57, primary books. Chronological arrangement. Transcribed TP (recto and verso), pagination, part collation, binding, price, miscellaneous bibliographical notes with references to subsequent editions.

EDELMAN, MAURICE (1911-)

Vinson-Novelists; Drescher & Kahrmann.

EGERTON, GEORGE (1859-1945)

Pseudonym of Mary Chavelita Clairmonte, afterwards Mrs. Bright.

PRIMARY

John Gawsworth. *Ten Contemporaries. Notes Toward their Definitive Bibliography* [First Series]. London: Ernest Benn Ltd., 1932. Pp. 224.

Pp. 61-65, primary books, first editions, 1893-1905. Chronological arrangement. Transcribed TP, full collation, pagination, binding, date, bibliographical notes. Includes translations by Egerton.

Terence deVere White, ed. *A Leaf from the Yellow Book. The Correspondence of George Egerton.* London: Richards Press, 1958. Pp. 184.

No bibliography: the text gives information about published and unpublished writings, including periodical contributions and secondary criticism. Index, pp. 181-184.

EGLINTON, JOHN (1868-1961)

Pseudonym of William Kirkpatrick Magee.

Temple & Tucker.

ELIOT, THOMAS STEARNS (1888-1965)

PRIMARY

Hans Willi Bentz. *T. S. Eliot in Ubersetzungen.* Frankfurt am Main: Hans W. Bentz Verlag, 1963. Pp. 58. 500 copies.

List of 222 translations of Eliot after 1945. Titles, names of translators, publishers, places, dates, prices. Various indices.

T. S. Eliot. *The Waste Land A Facsimile and Transcript of the Original Drafts including the Annotations of Ezra Pound*, ed. Valerie Eliot. New York: Harcourt Brace Jovanovich, Inc., 1971. Pp. [xxxii], 149. See the "Introduction," pp. ix-xxx, for details concerning original publication of *The Waste Land.*

Donald [Clifford] Gallup. *T. S. Eliot A Bibliography.* London: Faber and Faber, Ltd., 1969. [Second, revised edition of the London, Faber and Faber, Ltd., 1952 and the New York, Harcourt, Brace, and Co., 1953, edition]. Pp. 414.

Primary. Form arrangement. Books: transcribed TP, part collation, binding, date, price, number of copies, variants, subsequent editions, extensive notes. Periods: volume, pages, date. Reviews by Eliot include title and author of book reviewed. Translations of Eliot listed separately under name of language into which translated. Index. "Introductory Note," pp. 11-14, provides concise statement of Gallup's bibliographical principles.

The authoritative bibliography.

Alexander Sackton. *The T. S. Eliot Collection of the University of Texas at Austin.* (Tower Bibliographical Series No. 9). Austin: Humanities Research Center, University of Texas, 1975. Pp. [410]. 1500 copies.

A description of the Eliot collection arranged and numbered in accord with Gallup (above): descriptions of items provided if there is information additional to that given by Gallup. Unique materials (MSS and letters) identified with letters unused by Gallup. Includes an alphabetical list of Eliot's correspondents as represented in the Texas collection.

An absolutely required addition to Gallup, although the suggested dates of some letters may be open to question.

Elizabeth R. Eames and Alan M. Cohn. "Some Early Reviews by T. S. Eliot (Addenda to Gallup)." *Papers of the Bibliographical Society of America* 70 (1976): 420-424.

Discussion, history, and description of ten pieces by Eliot not listed in Gallup.

SECONDARY

Richard M. Ludwig. "T. S. Eliot" in *Sixteen Modern American Authors. A Survey of Research and Criticism,* ed. Jackson R. Bryher. Durham, North Carolina: Duke University Press, 1974. Pp. xx, 673.

Pp. 181-222. Survey and evaluation in essay form of the Eliot bibliographies, editions, MSS and letters, biographies, and criticism, the last section subdivided into five chronological areas; supplement arranged as above includes material up to 1972. A helpful listing of primary and secondary bibliographies is given on pp. 181-182, 216.

Mildred Martin. *A Half-Century of Eliot Criticism. An Annotated Bibliography of Books and Articles in English, 1916-1965.* Lewisburg: Bucknell University Press, 1972. Pp. 361.

Pp. 19-262, Books and Articles. chronological arrangement. Books: place, publisher, year. Periods: volume, date, pages. Annotated. Pp. 263-303, ephemeral references including reviews and interviews. Indices of authors, of periodicals, and of subjects. Geoffrey Groom, *Library* 28 (1973): 173: "[The] annotations. . .are succinct and to the point."

Both Ludwig and Martin are indispensable to the student, as is the *T. S. Eliot Review* (formerly *T. S. Eliot Newsletter*). Particularly useful is Audrey T. Rodgers' survey and listing of secondary material, "Eliot in the 70's: A Mosaic of Criticism" (2, i [Spring, 1975] : 10-15). The *Review* also includes a "Bibliographical Update"—a listing with précis of criticism in journals—and other bibliographical information.

Charles A. Carpenter. "T. S. Eliot as Dramatist: Critical Studies in English, 1933-1975." *Bulletin of Bibliography* 33 (1976): 1-12.

Secondary. Arrangement by General Studies or under title of play. Books: place, publisher, date. Periods: volume, date, pages. Annotations and cross-references. A supplement to Martin.

GENERAL

Millett; Longaker & Bolles; Temple & Tucker, Coleman & Tyler; Breed & Sniderman; Adelman & Dworkin; Salem; Palmer & Dyson; NCBEL, IV, 157-201.

ELIZABETH (1866-1941)

Pseudonym of Mary Annette Beauchamp; later Grãfin von Arnim; later Countess Russell. Another pseudonym: Alice Cholmondeley.

PRIMARY

Leslie de Charms. *Elizabeth of the German Garden.* London: Heinemann, 1958. Pp. 429.

No bibliography, but there are references in the text to the primary writings, as well as quotations from letters and diaries by Elizabeth.

ELLERMAN, ANNIE WINIFRED: *see* BRYHER.

ELLIS, HENRY HAVELOCK (1859-1939)

PRIMARY

Houston Peterson. *Havelock Ellis. Philosopher of Love.* Boston and New York: Houghton Mifflin Co.; London: Allen and Unwin Ltd., 1928. Pp. 432.

Pp. 394-417, bibliography of primary writings, August 1880 to January 1928. Chronological arrangement. Books: place, publisher, date, reprints. Periods: volume, pages, date. Translations listed under name of language. P. 394: "Although [Ellis] has himself gone over the list three times, it cannot be considered absolutely complete."

Burne (below), p. 100: "excellent bibliography up to 1928."

A. Calder Marshall. *Havelock Ellis. A Biography.* London: Rupert Hart-Davis, 1959. Pp. 292.

Pp. 283-286, bibliography of post-1928 titles; selected secondary bibliography.

Glenn S. Burne. "Havelock Ellis: An Annotated Selected Bibliography of Primary and Secondary Works." *English Literature in Transition* 9 (1966): 55-107.

Pp. 55-74, primary bibliography, excluding "work of a strictly and clearly medical nature." Form arrangement. Books: date, place, publisher, pages, reprints. Periods: volume, pages, date. Pp. 74-107, secondary bibliography. Alphabetical by author arrangement. Annotated.

SECONDARY

Above, Marshall, pp. 285-286, 11-16; Burne, pp. 74-107 (subsequent issues of *English Literature in Transition* continue this bibliography).

GENERAL

Millet; Batho & Dobrée; Temple & Tucker; NCBEL, III, 1429-1431.

EMPSON, WILLIAM (1906-)

PRIMARY

Moira Megaw, "An Empson Bibliography" in *William Empson. The Man and His Work*, ed. Roma Gill. London and Boston: Routledge and Kegan Paul, 1974. Pp. x, 244.

Pp. [213] -244, primary bibliography. Chronological arrangement, subdivided by genre and form. Books: publisher and date of British and American editions. Periods: volume, date, pages. Reviews by Empson include title and author of book reviewed. Limitations of the bibliography are described on p. [213] . If this work is not available, one should turn to Michael L. Johnson. "William Empson: A Chronological Bibliography." *Bulletin of Bibliography* 29 (1972): 134-139, in which practically the same information is given.

GENERAL

Millett; Longaker & Bolles; Daiches; Temple & Tucker; Vinson-Poets; NCBEL, IV, 272-274.

ENRIGHT, DENNIS JOSEPH (1920-)

PRIMARY

William Walsh. *D. J. Enright. Poet of Humanism.* London: Cambridge University Press, 1974. Pp. [viii] , 107.

P. 107, bibliography of primary books, chronologically arranged. Place, publisher, date.

GENERAL

Temple & Tucker; Vinson-Poets; Vinson-Novelists; Stratford.

ESMOND, HENRY VERNON (1869-1922)

Pseudonym of Henry Vernon Jack.

NCBEL, III, 1192.

ERVINE, ST. JOHN GREER (1883-1971)

Millett; Longaker & Bolles; Batho & Dobrée; Temple & Tucker; Adelman & Dworkin; Salem; NCBEL, III, 1945; Hogan; Breed & Sniderman.

EVANS, DAVID CARADOC (1879-1945)

PRIMARY

Oliver Sandys. *Caradoc Evans.* London: Hurst and Blackett, Ltd., 1946. Pp. 167.

Bibliographical information in text, *passim,* of this biography by Mrs. Evans.

Brynmor Jones. *Caradoc Evans 1879-1945.* Welsh Arts Council (Bibliographies of Anglo-Welsh Literature, 2), 1968.

Not seen.

GENERAL

Millett; Daiches; Temple & Tucker; NCBEL, IV, 566.

EVANS, MARGIAD: *see* WILLIAMS, PEGGY EILEEN ARABELLA.

EVELING, HARRY STANLEY (1925-)

Vinson-Dramatists.

EVERETT, PETER (1931-)

Vinson-Novelists; Bufkin.

EWART, GAVIN BUCHANAN (1916-)

Vinson-Poets.

FABIAN SOCIETY (1884-)

PRIMARY

Anne Fremantle. *This Little Band of Prophets. The British Fabians.* London: George Allen and Unwin; New York: New American Library (Mentor Book MT266), 1960. Pp. 320.

Pp. 268-285, "Fabian Publications 1884-1958." Chronological arrangement under three divisions: Tracts, Research Pamphlets, Books and Other Publications. Date, number in series, title and author. General secondary bibliography, pp. 308-314.

SECONDARY

Above, Fremantle, pp. 308-314.

FAGAN, JAMES BERNARD (1873-1933)

NCBEL, IV, 936-937.

FAIRFAX, JOHN (1930-)

Vinson-Poets.

FAIRFIELD, CICILY ISABEL: *see* WEST, REBECCA.

FALCK, COLIN (1934-)

Vinson-Poets.

FALKNER, JOHN MEADE (1858-1932)

PRIMARY

Graham Pollard. "Some Uncollected Authors. XXV. John Meade Falkner. 1858-1932." *Book Collector* 9 (1960): 318-325.

Primary books. Chronological arrangement. Transcribed TP, part collation, binding, date, variants, reprints, notes.

GENERAL

NCBEL, III, 1051.

FALLON, PADRAIC (1905-1974)

Vinson-Poets; Hogan.

FARJEON, ELEANOR (1881-1965)

PRIMARY

Eileen H. Colwell. *Eleanor Farjeon.* London: Bodley Head (Bodley Head Monograph), 1961. Pp. 94.

Pp. 89-94, bibliography. Primary books. Chronological under these headings: Books by Eleanor Farjeon; Books by Eleanor Farjeon and Harry Farjeon; Books by Eleanor Farjeon and Herbert Farjeon; American Editions. Publisher, date, illustrator.

Denise Avril Zeeman. *Eleanor Farjeon: A Bibliography.* Johannesburg: University of the Witwatersrand, 1970. Pp. vi, 37 (mimeographed sheets).

Pp. 1-18, 21, 27-28, primary bibliography. Genre arrangement under divisions Children's Works and Adult Works. Books (all editions and translations): place, publisher, date, illustrator, translator, contents, list of selected reviews. Periods: volume, date, pages. Secondary bibliography, *passim* and pp. 18-27.

FARJEON, HERBERT (1887-1945)

NCBEL, IV, 937-938; also above, FARJEON, ELEANOR.

FARRELL, JAMES GORDON (1935-)

Vinson-Novelists.

FAUSSET, HUGH I'ANSON (1895-1965)

Millett; Temple & Tucker.

FEARN, JOHN RUSSELL (1908-1960)

PRIMARY

Philip Harbottle. *The Multi-Man. A Biographic and Bibliographic Study.* Market Harborough: Wellandside (Photographics) Ltd., 1968. Pp. [ii] , 69.

Pp. 37-69, primary bibliography. Form and genre arrangement. Books: publisher, pages, price, format, date; brief summary of plot of novels. Periods: date, genre of contribution, illustrator, quotation of 'blurb.' For each item, pseudonym under which published: a total of 34 pseudonyms listed.

FEINSTEIN, ELAINE (1930-)

Vinson-Poets.

FFOULKES, MAUDE MARY (1871-1949)

(Mrs. Chester Craven).

PRIMARY

Violet Powell. *A Substantial Ghost: The Literary Adventures of Maude ffoulkes.* London: Heinemann, 1967. Pp. xii, [210].

No bibliography, but references in passing to Mrs. ffoulkes' books. Additional information in Marguerite Steen, *Looking Glass. An Autobiography.* London: Longmans, 1966, pp. 81-84.

FIELD, MICHAEL

Pseudonym of:

BRADLEY, KATHERINE HARRIS (1846-1914)
and
COOPER, EDITH EMMA (1862-1913)

PRIMARY

Mary Sturgeon. *Michael Field.* London: George Harrap and Co., 1922. Pp. 246.

Pp. 245-246, bibliography. Primary books. Chronological arrangement. Publisher, date, reprints. Information about periodical contributions and secondary criticism in text, *passim.*

T. and D. C. Sturge Moore, eds. *Works and Days. From the Journal of Michael Field.* London: John Murray, 1933. Pp. 338.

No bibliography. Information in text, *passim,* and in "Editors' Preface," pp. xv-xxii.

GENERAL

Temple & Tucker; NCBEL, III, 626-627.

FIELDING, GABRIEL (1916-)

Pseudonym of Alan Gabriel Barnsley.

PRIMARY

Alfred Borrello. *Gabriel Fielding.* New York: Twayne Publishers, Inc. (TEAS 162), 1974. Pp. [167].

Pp. 155-157, primary bibliography. Form and genre arrangement. Books (British and American first editions, and paperback editions): place, publisher, date. Periods: volume, date, pages. Pp. 157-159, selected secondary bibliography including major reviews of Fielding's novels. Annotated.

SECONDARY

Above, Borrello.

GENERAL

Temple & Tucker; Bufkin; Adelman & Dworkin (Novel): Vinson-Novelists; Drescher & Kahrmann.

FIGGIS, DARRELL (1882-1925)

PRIMARY

Patrick Sarsfield O'Hegarty. "Bibliographies of 1916 and the Irish Revolution. No. XV. Darrell Figgis." *Dublin Magazine* 12 (July-September 1937): 47-54.

Primary books. Chronological arrangement. Transcribed TP, part collation, pagination, binding, extensive biographical and bibliographical notes.

FINLAY, IAN HAMILTON (1925-)

Vinson-Poets.

FIRBANK, ARTHUR ANNESLEY RONALD (1886-1926)

PRIMARY

Miriam J. Benkovitz. *A Bibliography of Ronald Firbank.* London: Rupert Hart-Davis (Soho Bibliography No. 16), 1963. Pp. 103.

Primary. Form arrangement. Transcribed TP, full collation, pagination, binding, date, price, variants, reprints, extensive notes, contents. Index.

The authoritative bibliography. Praised by Lord Horder, *Book Collector* 12 (1963): 380: "a work which takes Firbank studies in general so much further forward" (also additions and corrections).

SECONDARY

Robert Murray Davis. "Ronald Firbank. A Selected Bibliography of Criticism." *Bulletin of Bibliography* 26 (1969): 108-111.

Alphabetical by author arrangement. Books: place, publisher, date. Periods: volume, date, pages. Reviews are identified, and cross-references are given for related entries.

GENERAL

Temple & Tucker; NCBEL, IV, 567-569; Bufkin.

FISHER, ROY (1930-)

Vinson-Poets.

FITZGIBBON, ROBERT LOUIS CONSTANTINE LEE-DILLON (1919-)

Drescher & Kahrmann.

FITZMAURICE, GEORGE (1877-1963)

PRIMARY

The Plays of George Fitzmaurice. Dublin: Dolmen Press Ltd.

I. *Dramatic Fantasies,* ed. Austin Clarke. 1967. Pp. [xvi] , 159; II. *Folk Plays,* ed. Howard K. Slaughter. 1969. Pp. xx, 153; III. *Realistic Plays,* ed. Howard K. Slaughter. 1970. Pp. xviii, 166.

The title page for each play gives the title of the volume or periodical, place, and date of first publication, while the last pages of each volume provide details of the first production of each play: place, theatre, date, cast of characters, producer. The three Introductions provide references to the secondary bibliography.

Joanne L. Henderson. "Checklist of Four Kerry Writers: George Fitzmaurice . . ." *Journal of Irish Literature* 1 (May 1972): 191-104.

Primary, secondary. Form arrangement. Books: place, publisher, date, pages, contents. Periods: volume, date, pages.

GENERAL

NCBEL, III, 1941-1942; Breed & Sniderman; Hogan.

FLECKER, JAMES ELROY (1884-1915)

PRIMARY

Henry Danielson. *Bibliographies of Modern Authors.* London: Bookman's Journal, 1921. Pp. [xii] , [212] .

Pp. 81-89, primary books, 1906-1921. Chronological arrangement. Transcribed TP, part collation, pagination, binding, variants, miscellaneous bibliographical notes.

Most of this information is reprinted in Douglas Goldring. *James Elroy Flecker. An Appreciation with some Biographical Notes.* London: Chapman and Hall, 1922. Pp. 200. Pp. 191-195, bibliography. Adds the number of copies in each edition.

Thomas Stanley Mercer. *James Elroy Flecker. From School to Samarkand.* Thames Ditton, Surrey: Merle Press, 1952. Pp. 56. 160 copies.

Pp. 47-56, primary bibliography. Genre and form arrangement. Books: transcribed TP, part collation, binding, notes. Periods: volume, pages, dates.

Mercer provides the most complete list of primary writings.

SECONDARY

John Sherwood. *No Golden Journey. A Biography of James Elroy Flecker.* London: Heinemann, 1973. Pp. xviii, 232.

Pp. 229-231, selected secondary bibliography, including reviews of Flecker's books. Other studies and obituary notices are cited in the text.

GENERAL

Millett; Longaker & Bolles; Batho & Dobrée; Temple & Tucker; NCBEL, IV, 274-276.

FLEMING, IAN LANCASTER (1908-1964)

PRIMARY

Kingsley Amis. *The James Bond Dossier.* London: Jonathan Cape, 1965. Pp. 159.

Pp. 156-159, chronological list of novels by Fleming with details of plot.

John Pearson. *The Life of Ian Fleming.* New York: McGraw-Hill, 1966. Pp. [xii], 338.

Bibliographical information in text, *passim.*

David Randall. *The Ian Fleming Collection of 19th-20th Century Source Material concerning Western Civilization together with the Originals of the James Bond-007 Tales.* Bloomington, Indiana: Lilly Library, 1971. Pp. 53.

Not seen. *TLS,* 23 July 1971, p. 868: part III of this catalogue of an exhibition at the Lilly Library gives bibliographical details of primary manuscripts.

SECONDARY

Iwan Hedman. "Ian Fleming." *Armchair Detective* 5 (1972):216-219, 222.

Secondary bibliography, pp. 218-219, 222. Dates only.

GENERAL

Drescher & Kahrmann.

FLETCHER, IAN (1920-)

Vinson-Poets.

FLETCHER, JOSEPH SMITH (1863-1935)

PRIMARY

"A Bibliography of the Works of J. S. Fletcher." *The Borzoi 1925*. New York: Alfred A. Knopf, 1925. Pp. [xiv], 351.

Pp. 73-75, primary books. Genre arrangement. Titles only.

FLINT, FRANK STEWART (1885-1960)

Millett; Longaker & Bolles; Temple & Tucker; NCBEL, IV, 276.

FORD, FORD MADOX [HUEFFER] (1873-1939)

PRIMARY

David Dow Harvey. *Ford Madox Ford, 1873-1939. A Bibliography of Works and Criticism.* Princeton: Princeton University Press, 1962. Pp. xxiv, 633.

Primary, secondary. Form arrangement. Books: transcribed TP, part collation, binding, date, price, variants, reprints, full notes, MSS, previous publication of contents, contents. Periods: volume, pages, date. Sections on Manuscripts; Letters; Miscellanea; Contributions to Periodicals: précis, annotations, quotations. Complete, extensive annotations and quotations for all secondary criticism and many of the primary writings.

H. E. Gerber, *English Literature in Transition* 6 (1963): 57: "the basic bibliographical record. . .accurate, thorough, and as nearly complete as any volume of this kind is ever likely to be or need be even for the most discriminating scholar."

SECONDARY

Above, Harvey, pp. 275-610, for criticism before 1962. After 1962, consult issues of *English Literature in Transition* for annotated lists of secondary bibliography.

Charles G. Hoffmann. *Ford Madox Ford.* New York: Twayne Publishers, Inc. (TEAS 55), 1967. Pp. 156.

Pp. 145-147, primary books. Pp. 147-150, secondary bibliography. Alphabetical by author arrangement. Books: place, publisher, year. Periods: volume, pages, date. Annotated.

GENERAL

Millett; Longaker & Bolles; Temple & Tucker; NCBEL, IV, 569-575; Bufkin.

FORESTER, CECIL SCOTT (1899-1966)

Temple & Tucker; Bufkin; NCBEL, IV, 576-577.

FORSTER, EDWARD MORGAN (1879-1970)

PRIMARY

Louis K. Greiff. "Edward Morgan Forster. A Bibliography." *Bulletin of Bibliography* 24 (1964): 108-112.

Primary books. Genre arrangement. Place, publisher, date, pages, reprints, subsequent editions, translations. Includes stage adaptations of Forster's writings.

B[rownlee] J[ean] Kirkpatrick. *A Bibliography of E. M. Forster.* London: Rupert Hart-Davis (Soho Bibliography No. 19, Revised Edition), 1968. Pp. 205.

Primary. Form arrangement. Books: transcribed TP, part collation, pagination, binding, date, price, number of copies, variants, reprints, subsequent editions, contents, extensive notes. Periods: volume, pages, date. Includes unsigned primary writings; reviews by Forster include title and author of book reviewed. Separate list of translations of Forster. Index.

R. J. Roberts, *Book Collector* 15 (1966): 75-79: "one of the most careful and useful of recent additions to the study of contemporary English literature" (review of the first edition).

John B. Shipley. "Additions to the E. M. Forster Bibliography." *Papers of the Bibliographical Society of America* 60 (1966): 224-225.

Adds six items to Kirkpatrick (first edition); other information. A guide to both primary and secondary material is provided by Malcom Bradbury, "Forster," in A. E. Dyson, ed. *The English Novel. Select Bibliographical Guides.* London: Oxford University Press, 1974, pp. 314-333. Survey and evaluation of texts, critical studies, biographies and letters, bibliographies, and background reading. Also lists of titles (with date and place) arranged under these divisions.

SECONDARY

W. Heffer and Sons Ltd., Booksellers, Cambridge. *Heffer Catalogue Seven, E. M. Forster.* With introduction by A. N. L. Munby, Cambridge, 1971. Pp. 96.

Books owned by Forster offered for sale. *Book Collector* 21 (1972): 125: "a mine of Forsterological research material."

Alfred Borrello. *E. M. Forster. An Annotated Bibliography of Secondary Materials.* Metuchen, N. J.: The Scarecrow Press, Inc., 1973. Pp. [xiv], 188.

Secondary. Chronological arrangement from 1907 to 1970. Books: place, publisher, date, pages. Periods: volume, date, pages, occasionally place. All items annotated. Pp. 157-188, indices of authors; of titles; of periodicals; of reviews of Forster listed under title of the book reviewed; of reviews of books about Forster; and of bibliographies, doctoral dissertations, obituaries, and dramatizations.

An extremely useful book by the author of *An E. M. Forster Dictionary* (1971), which also provides miscellaneous primary and secondary bibliographical information.

Frederick P. W. McDowell. *E. M. Forster: An Annotated Bibliography of Writings about Him.* DeKalb, Illinois: Northern Illinois University Press, 1976.

Not seen. This work incorporates the numerous listings of annotated, secondary criticism compiled by McDowell and others in different issues of *English Literature in Transition*, to which reference should be made for later listings of criticism of Forster.

GENERAL

Millett; Longaker & Bolles; Batho & Dobrée; Daiches, Temple & Tucker; NCBEL, IV, 437-444; Bufkin.

FORSYTH, JAMES LAW (1913-)

Vinson-Dramatists.

FOWLER, HON. ELLEN THORNEYCROFT (1860-1929)

(Mrs. A. L. Felkin).

NCBEL, IV, 577.

FOWLES, JOHN (1926-)

PRIMARY

Prescott Evarts, Jr. "John Fowles: A Checklist." *Critique* 13, No. 3 (1972): 105-107.

Primary, secondary selected. Books (English-language editions): place, publisher, date. Periods: volume, pages, date. Includes major reviews of primary works.

Karen Magee Myers. "John Fowles: An Annotated Bibliography, 1963-1976." *Bulletin of Bibliography* 32 (1976): 162-169.

Primary, pp. 162-164. Form and genre arrangement. Books (all editions and translations): place, publisher, date, translator. Periods: volume, date, pages. Secondary bibliography, pp. 164-169. Reviews listed under title of work reviewed. Only the entries for articles and books are annotated.

SECONDARY

Above, Evarts, pp. 106-107; Myers, pp. 164-169.

GENERAL

Vinson-Novelists; Drescher & Kahrmann; Temple & Tucker.

FRANKAU, GILBERT (1884-1952)

NCBEL, IV, 577-578.

FRASER, SIR ARTHUR RONALD (1888-)

NCBEL, IV, 579.

FRASER, CLAUD LOVAT (1890-1921)

PRIMARY

Christopher S. Millard. *The Printed Work of Claud Lovat Fraser.* London: Henry Danielson, 1921. Pp. x, 106. 275 copies.

Primary. Genre arrangement. Detailed description of Fraser's art work.

SECONDARY

Haldane Macfall. *The Book of Claud Lovat Fraser.* London: J. M. Dent and Sons, 1923. Pp. 183.

No bibliography; information in text, *passim.*

FRASER, GEORGE SUTHERLAND (1915-)

Daiches; Temple & Tucker; Vinson-Poets; NCBEL, IV, 276-277.

FRAYN, MICHAEL (1933-)

Vinson-Novelists; Vinson-Dramatists; Drescher & Kahrmann; Temple & Tucker; Bufkin.

FRAZER, SIR JAMES GEORGE (1854-1941)

PRIMARY

Theodore Bestermann. *A Bibliography of Sir James George Frazer, O. M.*

London: Macmillan, 1934. Pp. xxi, 100. Reprinted, London: Dawsons of Pall Mall, 1968.

Primary complete, 1884-1933. Chronological arrangement. Books: transcribed TP without lineation bars, size, pages, brief notes on later reprints. Periods: volume, pages, date; notes on volumes in which later collected; reviews by Frazer include title and author of book reviewed. Pp. [85] -93, primary titles listed by form and genre. Index.

The standard bibliography.

GENERAL

Batho & Dobrée; NCBEL, III, 1482-1484.

FREELING, NICOLAS (1927-)

Vinson-Novelists.

FREEMAN, GILLIAN (1929-)

Vinson-Novelists; Drescher & Kahrmann.

FREEMAN, JOHN (1880-1929)

PRIMARY

"Bibliographies of Modern Authors: John Freeman." *London Mercury* 1 (1920): 497.

Primary books. Genre arrangement. Publisher, date.

Gertrude Freeman and Sir John Squire, eds. *John Freeman's Letters.* London: Macmillan and Co., 1936. Pp. 395.

No bibliography; information in text, *passim.*

SECONDARY

Janet M. Irvin. "John Freeman: An Annotated Bibliography of Writings about Him." *English Literature in Transition* 19 (1976): 35-47.

Selected secondary bibliography, arranged alphabetically by author. Books: place, publisher, date, relevant pages. Periods: volume, date, pages. Annotated.

GENERAL

Millet, Longaker & Bolles; Bartho & Dobrée; Daiches; Temple & Tucker.

FREEMAN, RICHARD AUSTIN (1862-1943)

PRIMARY

"Checklist Bibliographies of Modern Authors. Richard Austin Freeman." *Book Trade Journal,* No. 64 (31 July, 1936), pp. 20-21.

Primary books. Chronological arrangement. Publisher, date, binding.

FRIEL, BRIAN (1929-)

PRIMARY

Desmond E. S. Maxwell. *Brian Friel.* Lewisburg: Bucknell University Press (Irish Writers Series), 1973. Pp. 112.

Pp. 111-112, selected primary and secondary bibliography. Books: place, publisher, date, with selected reviews listed under title of work reviewed. Period: volume, date, pages.

GENERAL

Salem; Breed & Sniderman; Hogan; Vinson-Dramatists; Temple & Tucker.

FRY, CHRISTOPHER (1907-)

PRIMARY

Bernice Larson Schear and Eugene C. Prater. "A Bibliography on Christopher Fry." *Tulane Drama Review* 4 (March 1960). 88-98.

Primary and secondary. Arranged: pp. 88-89, primary writings in one list, alphabetical by title of book or name of periodical; translations by Fry listed under name of original author. Pp. 89-98, secondary bibliography: books alphabetical by author, periods alphabetical by title, reviews of Fry listed under title of work reviewed. Books: place, publisher, date, pages. Periods: volume, pages, date.

Stanley Wiersma. *Christopher Fry. A Critical Essay.* Grand Rapids, Michigan: William B. Eerdmans Publishing Co. (Contemporary Writers in Christian Perspective Series), 1970. Pp. 48.

Pp. 46-48, selected primary and secondary bibliography. Books: publisher, date. Periods: volume, date, pages.

SECONDARY

Above, Schear-Prater, pp. 89-98; Wiersma, pp. 47-48.

GENERAL

Daiches; Temple & Tucker; Coleman & Tyler; Adelman & Dworkin; Salem; Palmer & Dyson; Breed & Sniderman; Vinson-Poets; Vinson-Dramatists; NCBEL, IV, 938-941.

FRY, ROGER ELIOT (1866-1934)

PRIMARY

Solomon Fishman. *The Interpretation of Art.* Berkeley and Los Angeles: University of California Press, 1963. Pp. 196.

Pp. 101-105, chronology of Fry's life; includes primary books.

Quentin Bell. *Roger Fry. An Inaugural Lecture.* Leeds University Press, 1964. Pp. [22]; and Arts Council of Great Britain. *Vision and Design. The Life, Work and Influence of Roger Fry* [Catalogue of an exhibition]. London: Shenval Press, 1966. Pp. [48].

No bibliographies in these two pamphlets; information in text and notes, *passim.*

While the primary books are listed in these books, there is no list of all of Fry's writings.

GENERAL

Millett; Daiches; Temple & Tucker; NCBEL, IV, 1042-1044.

FULLER, JOHN LEOPOLD (1937-)

Vinson-Poets.

FULLER, ROY BROADBENT (1912-)

Longaker & Bolles; Daiches; Bufkin; Temple & Tucker; Vinson-Poets; Stratford; Vinson-Novelists; Drescher & Kahrmann; NCBEL, IV, 278.

FULTON, ROBIN (1937-)

Vinson-Poets.

GALE, NORMAN ROWLAND (1862-1942)

PRIMARY

Alfred Hayes, Richard LeGallienne, Norman Gale. Rugby: Rugby Press, 189?, Pp. 11.

Pp. 6-11, primary books. Chronological arrangement. Date, part collation, publisher, binding, number of copies.

GENERAL

Millett; NCBEL, III, 627.

GALSWORTHY, JOHN (1867-1933)

PRIMARY

H. V. Marrot. *A Bibliography of the Works of John Galsworthy.* London: Elkin Matthews and Marrot; New York: Charles Scribner's Sons, 1928. Pp. xiv, 252. 210 copies.

Primary, secondary selected. Form arrangement. Books (subdivided by genre): transcribed TP, part collation, pagination, binding, date, contents, number of copies, variants, reprints, notes; includes both British and American editions, although descriptions of the latter are less complete than of the former. Periods: dates. Includes translations of Galsworthy, iconography, index. Pp. 195-208, secondary bibliography.

Ralph Mottram. *John Galsworthy.* London: Longmans, Green and Co. (WTW 38), 1953. Pp. 40.

Pp. 37-40, primary books. Date, genre.

Genji Takahashi. *Studies in the Works of John Galsworthy.* Tokyo: Shinozaki Shorin, 1954. Pp. [xiv], [393].

Pp. 306-319, primary, secondary bibliography of books published in Japan. Primary: annotated editions and translations. Editor or translator, publisher, date. Secondary: publisher, date.

English Fiction in Transition 1 (1958): 27: "Valuable bibliography of translations into Japanese of Galsworthy."

SECONDARY

Above, Marrot, pp. 195-208.

Alice T. McGirr. "Reading List of John Galsworthy." *Bulletin of Bibiolography* 7 (1913): 113.

Reviews listed under title of book reviewed. Periods: volume, pages, date, quotations.

Helmut Gerber, *et al.* "John Galsworthy." *English Fiction* (later *English Literature) in Transition* 1 (1957): 23-24; 2 (1958): 7-29; 7 (1964): 93-110. (Continued in subsequent issues).

Annotated. Books: place, publisher, year. Periods: volume, pages, date.

One should also note that the Annotated Secondary Bibliography Series on English Literature in Transition, Helmut E. Gerber, general editor, Northern Illinois University Press, is to include a volume on Galsworthy.

E. H. Mikhail. *John Galsworthy the Dramatist: A Bibliography of Criticism.* Troy, New York: Whitston Publishing Company, Inc., 1971. Pp. [x], 91.

Form and genre arrangement, with material arranged alphabetically by author in each division. Books: place, publisher, date. Periods: volume, date, pages. Includes reviews of theatrical productions and unpublished dissertations.

GENERAL

Millett; Longaker & Bolles; Batho & Dobrée; Daiches; Temple & Tucker; Coleman & Tyler; Adelman & Dworkin; Salem; Palmer & Dyson; Breed & Sniderman; NCBEL, IV, 579-586; Bufkin.

GARIOCH, ROBERT (1909-)

Pseudonym of Robert Garioch Sutherland.

Daiches; Vinson-Poets; NCBEL, IV, 278.

GARLICK, RAYMOND ERNEST (1926-)

Vinson-Poets.

GARNETT FAMILY

CONSTANCE (1862-1946)

DAVID (1892-)

EDWARD WILLIAM (1868-1937)

RICHARD (1835-1906)

PRIMARY

Carolyn G. Heilbrun. *The Garnett Family.* London: George Allen and Unwin, 1961. Pp. 214.

Pp. 202-210, separate bibliographies for each of the four Garnetts. Primary books. Form and genre arrangement. Place, publisher, year.

GENERAL

Millett (Edward, David); Batho & Dobrée; NCBEL, III, 1431 (Richard); Daiches; Vinson-Novelists; NCBEL, IV, 586; Bufkin (David).

GASCOYNE, DAVID EMERY (1916-)

PRIMARY

Ann Atkinson. "David Gascoyne: A Check-List." *Twentieth Century Literature* 6 (1961): 180-192.

Primary, secondary selected. Form arrangement. Books: place, publisher, date, pages. Periods: volume, pages, date. Occasional annotations. List of anthologies including Gascoyne.

Jenny Stratford. *The Arts Council Collection of Modern Literary Manuscripts 1963-1972. A Catalogue. . .with a Preface by*

Philip Larkin. London: Turret Books, 1974. Pp. [xxiv], 168.

Pp. 79-87: a description of the Gascoyne books and manuscripts in this collection and location of other manuscripts. Books: place, publisher, date, contents. Periods: volume, date, pages. Extensive bibliographical, historical, and textual notes.

A very useful supplement to Atkinson.

GENERAL

Longaker & Bolles; Daiches; Temple & Tucker; Vinson-Poets; NCBEL, IV, 279.

GAWSWORTH, JOHN (1912-1970)

Pseudonym of Terence Ian Fytoon Armstrong.

Longaker & Bolles; NCBEL, IV, 279-281.

GEORGE, WALTER LIONEL (1882-1926)

GENERAL

Stanley J. Kunitz and Howard Haycraft. *Twentieth Century Authors.* New York: H. W. Wilson Co., 1942. Pp. [viii], 1577.

Pp. 524-525, titles by and about George.

Longaker & Bolles; NCBEL, IV, 586-587.

GERAHTY, DIGBY GEORGE: *see* STANDISH, ROBERT.

GERHARDIE, WILLIAM ALEXANDER (1895-1977)

Millett; Daiches; Bufkin; Temple & Tucker; Vinson-Novelists; NCBEL, IV, 587-588.

GIBBON, LEWIS GRASSIC: *see* MITCHELL, JAMES LESLIE.

GIBBON, WILLIAM MONK (1896-)

Vinson-Poets.

GIBBONS, STELLA DOROTHEA (1902-)

(Mrs. Allan Bourne Webb).

Daiches; Bufkin; Temple & Tucker; Vinson-Novelists; NCBEL, IV, 589.

GIBBS, SIR PHILIP HAMILTON (1877-1962)

PRIMARY

Philip Gibbs. *The Pageant of the Years. An Autobiography.* London: Heinemann, 1946. Pp. 530. *Crowded Company.* London and New York: Allan Wingate, 1949. Pp. 286.

Bibliographical information in texts, *passim,* of these two autobiographies.

GENERAL

Millett; Temple & Tucker.

GIBSON, WILFRID WILSON (1878-1962)

PRIMARY

John Gawsworth. *Ten Contemporaries. Notes Toward their Definitive Bibliography.* [First Series]. London: Ernest Benn Ltd., 1932. Pp. 224.

Pp. 74-94, primary books, first editions, 1902-1932. Chronological arrangement. Transcribed TP, full collation, pagination, binding, date, bibliographical and textual notes.

GENERAL

Millett; Longaker & Bolles; Batho & Dobrée; Daiches; Temple &

Tucker; NCBEL, IV, 281-282.

GIELGUD, VAL HENRY (1900-)

NCBEL, IV, 941-942.

GILL, ARTHUR ERIC ROWTON (1882-1940)

PRIMARY

Evan R. Gill. *Bibliography of Eric Gill.* London: Cassell and Co., 1953. Pp. 224. 1000 copies. Reprinted: Folkstone and London: Dawsons of Pall Mall, 1974.

Primary, secondary. Form arrangement. Books: transcribed TP, full collation, pagination, binding, date, price, variants, reprints, contents, reviews of the book. Periods: volume, pages, date. Pp. 152-193, secondary bibliography. Index.

J. G. Physick. *The Engraved Work of Eric Gill.* London: HMSO (Victoria and Albert Museum Publication), 1963. Pp. 266.

Chronological list of the engravings with full information.

Evan R. Gill. *The Inscriptional Work of Eric Gill. An Inventory.* London: Cassell and Co., 1964. Pp. 140 plus plates.

Complete description of 762 inscriptions: informative prefaces, various indices. Additional details and corrections are provided by David Peace. *Addendum and Corrigenda to The Inscriptional Work of Eric Gill.* San Francisco: Brick Row Book Shop, 1972. Pp. [37].

SECONDARY

Above, Gill (1953).

Wolfgang Kehr. "Eric Gill als Schriftkünstler." *Archiv für Geschichte des Buchwesens* 4 (1962): 454-621.

Pp. 614-621, secondary bibliography.

GILLIATT, PENELOPE (-)

Vinson-Novelists.

GINSBURY, NORMAN (1902-)

NCBEL, IV, 942-943.

GISSING, GEORGE ROBERT (1857-1903)

PRIMARY

Pierre Coustillas. "Gissing's Short Stories: A Bibliography." *English Literature in Transition* 7 (1964): 59-72.

Arranged: collections; translations into Japanese; individual stories. Books: place, publisher, date, pages. Periods: volume, pages, date. Extensive bibliographical and textual notes.

John Spiers and Pierre Coustillas. *The Rediscovery of George Gissing. A Reader's Guide* [Guide to National Book League Exhibition, London, June-July, 1971]. London: National Book League, 1971. Pp. [viii], 163.

An important bibliographical and biographical supplement to Collie (below).

Michael Collie. *George Gissing. A Bibliography.* Toronto and Buffalo: University of Toronto Press, 1975. Pp. xiv, 129.

Primary books. Arranged in two chronological lists: Books published in Gissing's lifetime; Books published after Gissing's death which had not appeared in any form during his lifetime. Transcribed TP, full collation, pagination, binding, contents. Details for all editions. Full bibliographical and historical notes concerning the publication of each title. Index and appendices, including chronological listing of Gissing's books. Collie describes the scope of his work on pp. xi-xiv and 19-22.

This meticulously detailed bibliography should assist both the literary student and the bibliophile; but they should keep in mind Pierre Coustillas' evaluation *[English Literature in Transition* 20 (1977): 46-47] of the book: "a pretentious, inaccurate production against which all potential users should be warned." Only Gissing's serial publications remain unlisted.

SECONDARY

Pierre Coustillas and Colin Partridge, editors. *Gissing. The Critical Heritage.* London and Boston: Routledge and Kegan Paul, 1972. Pp. [xviii] , 564.

An anthology of representative reviews of Gissing's books, arranged under title of book reviewed.

A useful supplement to Wolff (below).

Joseph Wolff. *George Gissing. An Annotated Bibliography of Writings about Him.* DeKalb, Illinois: Northern Illinois University Press, 1974. Pp. x, 293.

Pp. 10-265, selected secondary bibliography, 1880-1970. Chronologically arranged. Books: place, publisher, date. Periods: volume, date, pages. Précis of each entry. Pp. 267-293, indices. See pp. v-vi for titles of earlier secondary bibliographies which supply additional entries.

The starting point for study of criticism of Gissing.

GENERAL

Longaker & Bolles: Batho & Dobrée; Temple & Tucker; NCBEL, III, 1000-1004.

GITTINGS, ROBERT WILLIAM VICTOR (1911-)

Vinson-Poets; NCBEL, IV, 282-283.

GLANVILLE, BRIAN LESTER (1931-)

Vinson-Novelists; Drescher & Kahrmann; Bufkin.

GLEN, DUNCAN (1933-)

Vinson-Poets.

GLYN, ELINOR SUTHERLAND (1864-1943)

(Mrs. Clayton Glyn).

PRIMARY

Anthony Glyn [Sir Anthony Geoffrey Leo Simon, né Davson]. *Elinor Glyn. A Biography* London: Hutchinson and Co., 1968 (Revised Edition). Pp. 356.

P. [345], bibliography of primary books. Chronological arrangement. Publisher, date. Other important bibliographical information in text, *passim.* Index.

There is no list of the extensive periodical contributions, nor a complete account of the very detailed history of the primary books.

GENERAL

NCBEL, IV, 589-590.

GODDEN, MARGARET RUMER (1907-)

(Mrs. James L. Haynes-Dixon)

PRIMARY

Hassell A. Simpson. *Rumer Godden.* New York: Twayne Publishers, Inc. (TEAS 151), 1973. Pp. 160.

Pp. 149-155, bibliography. Primary selected, secondary selected. Form and genre arrangement. Books, selected British and American editions: place, publisher, year. Periods: volume, pages, date. Notes, pp. 136-148, provide additional primary titles and secondary criticism. See pp. 7-8, 149, for acknowledged limitations of the bibliography.

SECONDARY

Above, Simpson.

GENERAL

Longaker & Bolles; Bufkin; Temple & Tucker; Adelman & Dworkin (Novel); Vinson-Novelists; NCBEL, IV, 590-591.

GOGARTY, OLIVER ST. JOHN (1878-1957)

PRIMARY

Michael Hewson. "Gogarty's Authorship of *Blight*." *Irish Book* 1 (Spring 1959): 19-20.

Not seen.

Ulick O'Connor. *Oliver St. John Gogarty. A Poet and His Times.* London: Jonathan Cape, 1964. Pp. 317.

Pp. 305-310, general bibliography. Author, title. Other bibliographical information in text, *passim.* Index.

GENERAL

Longaker & Bolles; Temple & Tucker; NCBEL, IV, 283-284.

GOLDING, LOUIS (1895-1958)

PRIMARY

Louis Golding. *The World I Knew.* London: Hutchinson and Co., [1940] . Pp. 328.

Bibliographical information in text, *passim,* of this autobiography.

J. B. Simons. *Louis Golding. A Memoir.* London: Mitre Press, 1958. Pp. 139.

Bibliographical information in text, *passim.*

GENERAL

Millett; Daiches; Temple & Tucker; NCBEL, IV, 591-592; Bufkin.

GOLDING, WILLIAM GERALD (1911-)

PRIMARY

Jack I. Biles. "A William Golding Checklist." *Twentieth Century Literature* 17 (1971): 107-121.

Pp. 108-112, primary. Pp. 112-121, secondary selected. Form arrangement. Books: place, publisher, date of British and American first editions; reviews listed under primary title. Periods: date, pages.

Virginia Tiger. *William Golding. The Dark Fields of Discovery.* London: Calder and Boyars, 1974. Pp. 244.

Pp. 230-234, primary. Form arrangement. Books (first British and American editions): place, publisher, date. Periods: date, pages, title of volume in which collected. Pp. 234-240, secondary selected (last entry, 1972).

Stephen Medcalf. *William Golding.* Harlow: Longman Group Ltd. (WTW 243), 1975. Pp. [47].

Pp. 41-42, select primary: date, genre. Pp. 42-43, select secondary: date, place, annotations.

SECONDARY

Above, Biles, pp. 112-121; Tiger, pp. 234-240; Medcalf, pp. 42-43.

Jerry Don Vann. "William Golding: A Checklist of Criticism." *Serif* 8, ii (1971): 21-26.

Secondary bibliography. Arranged: biography and general studies, reviews and studies of individual novels, listed under title of work discussed. Books: place, publisher, date. Periods: date, volume, pages. Latest entry: 1969.

Golding's more popular novels have been the subjects of numerous case books and study guides designed for high school students and undergraduates; these works contain secondary bibliographies selected for and generally limited to the needs of the audience to whom the book is addressed.

GENERAL

Temple & Tucker; Breed & Sniderman; Adelman & Dworkin (Novel); Vinson-Novelists; Drescher & Kahrmann; Bufkin.

GOLDRING, DOUGLAS (1887-1960)

PRIMARY

Douglas Goldring. *Odd Man Out. The Autobiography of a "Propaganda Novelist."* London: Chapman and Hall, 1935.

Bibliographical information in text, *passim.*

GENERAL

Temple & Tucker.

GOPALEEN, MYLES NA: *see* O'NOLAN, BRIAN.

GORDON, GILES ALEXANDER ESME (1940-)

Vinson-Poets.

GORE-BOOTH, CONSTANCE: *see* MARKIEVICZ, COUNTESS DE.

GOSSE, SIR EDMUND WILLIAM (1849-1928)

PRIMARY

Norman Gullick, "Bibliography" in Evan Charteris. *The Life and*

Letters of Sir Edmund Gosse. London: Heinemann; New York: Harper, 1931. Pp. 525.

Pp. 511-518, bibliography of primary books, restricted to Gosse's "more important writings." Chronological arrangement. Place, publisher, date, bibliographical notes.

Elias Bredsdorff, ed. *Sir Edmund Gosse's Correspondence with Scandinavian Writers.* Copenhagen: Gyldendal (Scandinavian University Books), 1960. Pp. 354.

Pp. 316-342, primary bibliography. Arranged: Gosse's writings on Scandinavian subjects; contributions to the *Encyclopaedia Britannica* on Scandinavian subjects; contributions to Scandinavian periodicals and newspapers. Pp. 343-346, secondary bibliography. Chronological arrangement. Books: place, date. Periods: number, pages, date. Reviews by Gosse include author and title of book reviewed.

There is no complete primary bibliography.

SECONDARY

Above, Bredsdorff, pp. 343-346.

James D. Woolf. "Sir Edmund Gosse. An Annotated Bibliography of Writings about Him." *English Literature in Transition* 11 (1968): 126-172. Continued in later issues, especially 14 (1971): 71-73; 16 (1973): 148-152; 17 (1974): 37-43; 18 (1975): 59-62.

Alphabetical by author arrangement. Books: place, publisher, year. Periods: volume, pages, date. Annotations.

GENERAL

Millett; Longaker & Bolles; Batho & Dobrée; Temple & Tucker; NCBEL, III, 1432-1435.

GOULD, GERALD (1885-1936)

Millett; Temple & Tucker; NCBEL, IV, 284-285.

GOW, RONALD (1897-)

Vinson-Dramatists; NCBEL, IV, 943-944.

GRAHAM, ROBERT BONTINE CUNNINGHAME (1852-1936)

PRIMARY

Leslie Chaundy. *A Bibliography of the First Editions of Robert Bontine Cunninghame Graham.* London: Dulau and Co., 1924. Pp. 16. 500 copies.

Primary books. Chronological arrangement. Transcribed TP, part collation, binding, date, notes.

Herbert Faulkner West. *The Herbert Faulkner West Collection of Robert Bontine Cunninghame Graham* [in the Dartmouth College Library). Dartmouth: Privately Published, 1938. Pp. 20. 85 copies.

Primary, secondary selected. Form arrangement. Books: place, publisher, date, reprints, variants. Periods: volume, pages, dates. Includes MSS, letters. Pp. 18-19, secondary bibliography.

The catalogue of a "*virtually* complete" (p. 5) collection.

C. T. Watts. "Robert Bontine Cunninghame Graham (1852-1936). A List of his Contributions to Periodicals." *Bibliotheck* (Glasgow) 4, v (1965): 186-199.

Chronological arrangement under literary form. Volume, date, pages. Includes list of periodicals examined by Watts. Book reviews by Graham include author, title, and date of book reviewed.

SECONDARY

Above, West, pp. 18-19.

Helmut Gerber. "Robert Bontine Cunninghame Graham." *English Fiction* (later *English Literature*) *in Transition* 1 (1957): 19. Continued in later issues.

Annotated.

GENERAL

Millett; Longaker & Bolles; Batho & Dobrée; Temple & Tucker; NCBEL, IV, 1318-1319.

GRAHAM, WILLIAM SYDNEY (1918-)

PRIMARY

Calvin Bedient. *Eight Contemporary Poets.* New York: Oxford University Press, 1975. Pp. x, 198.

P. 182, primary books. Place, publisher, date, names of illustrators.

GENERAL

Daiches; Temple & Tucker; Vinson-Poets; NCBEL, IV, 285.

GRAHAM, WINSTON MAWDESLEY (-)

Vinson-Novelists.

GRAHAME, KENNETH (1859-1932)

PRIMARY

Roger Lancelyn Green. "Kenneth Grahame." *TLS,* 9 June 1945, p. 276.

Primary first editions. Chronological arrangement. Books: transcribed TP, pages, number of copies for the limited editions. Periods: date.

Green states that of Grahame's periodical contributions it is "unlikely that much remains unrecorded."

Eleanor Graham. *Kenneth Grahame.* London: Bodley Head (Bodley Head Monograph), 1963. Pp. 72.

Pp. 70-71, bibliography of primary books. Publisher, date, illustrator. Additional information about reprints and subsequent editions of the primary titles listed by Green (above).

SECONDARY

Peter Morris Green. *Kenneth Grahame 1859-1932. A Study of his Life, Work and Times.* London: John Murray; New York: World, 1959. Pp. 400.

Pp. 377-385, primary bibliography derived from Green (above). Pp. 381-385, general secondary bibliography. Additional secondary criticism in text and notes, *passim.*

GENERAL

Batho & Dobrée; Temple & Tucker; NCBEL, IV, 593.

GRANVILLE-BARKER, HARLEY (1877-1946)

PRIMARY

Frederick May and Margery M. Morgan. "A List of Writings" in Charles B. Purdom. *Harley Granville-Barker. Man of the Theatre, Dramatist and Scholar.* London: Rockliff, 1955. Pp. 322.

Pp. 293-309, bibliography. Primary. Form and genre arrangement. Books: part collation, binding, variants, reprints, notes. Periods: volume, pages, date. Includes MSS and an account of works written in collaboration.

SECONDARY

Mary Louise Davis. "Reading List on Harley Granville-Barker." *Bulletin of Bibliography* 7 (1913): 130-132.

Primary, secondary. Topical arrangement. Books: place, publisher, date, reprints, contents (British and American editions. Periods: volume, pages, date, quotations, annotations.

Margery M. Morgan. *A Drama of Political Man. A Study in the Plays of Harley Granville-Barker.* London: Sidgwick and Jackson, 1961. Pp. 337.

No bibliography. References to secondary criticism in text and in notes, *passim.*

GENERAL

Millett, Longaker & Bolles; Batho & Dobrée; Temple & Tucker; Coleman & Tyler; Adelman & Dworkin; Breed & Sniderman; NCBEL, IV, 944-946.

GRAVES, ALFRED PERCEVAL (1846-1932)

PRIMARY

Alfred Perceval Graves. *To Return to All That. An Autobiography.* London: Jonathan Cape, 1930. Pp. 350.

Pp. 347-350, bibliography of primary books. Genre arrangement. Publisher, occasionally date.

GENERAL

NCBEL, III, 1907-1908.

GRAVES, CHARLES PATRICK RANKE (1899-1971)

PRIMARY

Jane Gordon. *Married to Charles.* London: Heinemann, 1950. Pp. 283.

Bibliographical information in text, *passim,* of this informal biography by Mrs. Graves.

GRAVES, ROBERT RANKE (1895-)

PRIMARY

Fred H. Higginson. *A Bibliography of the Works of Robert Graves.* London: Nicholas Vane Ltd., 1966. Pp. 328.

Primary, secondary selected. Form arrangement. Books: transcribed TP, part collation, pagination, binding, date, price, number of copies, variants, reprints, subsequent editions, contents, notes. Periods: volume, pages, date, genre; reviews by Graves include title and author of book reviewed.

Pp. 283-297, secondary bibliography; selected reviews of primary books listed under book titles. Pp. 300-328, Index.

The authoritative primary bibliography. Corrections and additions to it are provided by A. S. G. Edwards and J. Pinsent, and by John Woodrow Presley, in the *Papers of the Bibliographical Society of America* 68 (1974): 67-68; 69 (1975): 568-569. Primary publications after 1964 are listed by A. S. G. Edwards and Diane Tolomeo. "Robert Graves: A Check-List of his Publications, 1965-1974." *Malahat Review*, No. 35 (July, 1975), pp. 168-179. The compilers employ the divisions in Higginson, but they do not continue the enumeration of items.

Howard Gerwing. "The Robert Graves Manuscript Collection at the University of Victoria." *Malahat Review*, No. 35 (July, 1975), pp. 180-185.

General description of this important collection of primary and secondary material.

John W. Presley. *The Robert Graves Manuscripts and Letters at Southern Illinois University: an Inventory.* Troy, N.Y.: Whitston Publishing Company, 1976. Pp. [viii] , 262.

Primary material, including letters received by Graves. Genre arrangement, with manuscripts arranged alphabetically by title within each section; letters to Graves, pp. 165-236, arranged under name of writer. Complete description of each manuscript and letter. Pp. 253-261, Index of names and titles.

In his Introduction (pp. ii-vi) Presley describes the history of the collection, points out that it "almost covers Graves' entire career," and states that it "is a primary source for the study of Graves as a novelist, critic, translator, essayist, or mythographer."

SECONDARY

Above, Higginson, pp. 283-297.

Jean-Paul Forster. *Robert Graves et la dualité du réel.* Berne: Herbert Lang et Cie (Publications Universitaires Européenes, Série XIV [Langue et littérature anglo-saxonnes, 24]), 1975. Pp. 372.

P. 352, titles by Graves translated into French (publisher, place, date); pp. 353-357, secondary bibliography (supplements Higginson, and continues through 1972).

GENERAL

Millett; Daiches; Temple & Tucker; Vinson-Poets; Vinson-Novelists; NCBEL, IV, 201-207; Bufkin.

GRAY, JOHN HENRY (1866-1934)

PRIMARY

Alan Anderson, "Bibliography" in Father Brocard Sewell, ed. *Two Friends, John Gray and André Raffalovich. Essays Biographical and Critical.* Aylesford: St. Albert's Press, 1963. Pp. 193.

Pp. 178-187, primary bibliography. Form arrangement. Books: transcribed TP, size in inches, binding, occasional notes. Books with contributions: dates. List of periodicals to which Gray contributed; no specific entries.

G. A. Cevasco. "John Gray (1866-1934): A Primary Bibliography and an Annotated Bibliography of Writings about Him." *English Literature in Transition* 19 (1976): 49-63.

Pp. 49-54, primary bibliography. Chronological arrangement. Books: place, publisher, date. Periods: volume, date, pages. Brief description of contents or genre for each entry. Pp. 54-63, selected secondary bibliography, annotated.

Cevasco provides a complete list of writings, while Anderson offers the bibliographical details for each book.

SECONDARY

Above, Sewell, *passim;* and Cevasco, pp. 54-63.

GENERAL

NCBEL, III, 628.

GRAY, SIMON (1936-)

Vinson-Novelists; Vinson-Dramatists; Drescher & Kahrmann.

GREEN, FREDERICK LAWRENCE (1902-1953)

NCBEL, IV, 593-594.

GREEN, HENRY (1905-1973)

Pseudonym of Henry Vincent Yorke.

PRIMARY

John Russell. *Henry Green: Nine Novels and an Unpacked Bag.* New Brunswick: Rutgers University Press, 1960. Pp. 251.

Pp. 245-246. "Books, Stories, and Articles by Henry Green." Chronological arrangement. Books: place, publisher, date. Periods: volume, pages, date. Includes reviews by Green. No secondary bibliography, although there are references to secondary criticism in notes, pp. 237-243.

SECONDARY

Above, Russell, pp. 237-243.

Edward Stokes. *The Novels of Henry Green.* London: Hogarth Press, 1959. Pp. 248.

Notes, pp. 237-243, provide references to secondary bibliography.

Robert S. Ryf. *Henry Green.* New York: Columbia University Press (Columbia Essays on Modern Writers 29), 1967. Pp. 48.

Pp. 47-48, secondary bibliography. Alphabetical by author arrangement. Books: place, publisher, date. Periods: date.

GENERAL

Longaker & Bolles; Daiches; Temple & Tucker; Adelman & Dworkin (Novel); Vinson-Novelists; NCBEL, IV, 594-595; Bufkin.

GREEN, PETER MORRIS (1924-)

Vinson-Novelists; Bufkin.

GREENE, GRAHAM (1904-)

PRIMARY

Neil Brennan. "Bibliography" in Robert O. Evans, ed. *Graham Greene. Some Critical Considerations.* Lexington: University of Kentucky Press, 1963. Pp. 286.

Pp. 245-276, bibliography. Primary books, secondary selected. Chronological arrangement. Books: place, publisher, date, reviews and relevant secondary criticism. No details of periodical contributions, but titles and dates of periodicals for which Greene has written. Pp. 263-274, secondary bibliography. Genre arrangement.

De Vitis (below), p. 161: "A nearly complete bibliography."

Gene D. Phillips, S. J. *Graham Greene: The Films of his Fiction.* New York and London: Teachers College Press, Columbia University, 1974. Pp. [xxviii], [204].

Pp. 188-189, primary books, chronologically arranged: original date of publication; date, place, and publisher of current edition. Pp. 189-190, shorter primary pieces, mainly on the cinema. Pp. 190-191, general secondary bibliography. Pp. 192-193, Film Scripts written by Greene; pp. 193-194, Film Adaptations of Greene's Fiction by other Screenwriters: title, director, producer, company, writer or co-writers, actors, length of film.

There appears to be no complete list of Greene's post-1963 writings.

R. A. Wobbe. "Graham Greene's Literary and Theater Reviews and Articles in *The Spectator,* 1932-1941." *Bulletin of Bibliography* 34 (1977): 21-28.

Chronological arrangement. Reviews include title and author of book reviewed, and title of volume by Greene in which collected. Theater reviews give play title and author. See introduction for references to other unlisted primary writings.

SECONDARY

Above, Brennan, pp. 263-274; Phillips, pp. 190-191.

William Birmingham. "Graham Greene Criticism, A Bibliographical Study." *Thought* 27 (Spring, 1952): 72-100.

Pp. 72-98, essay on studies of Greene. Pp. 98-100, alphabetical by author list of secondary criticism (mainly in periodicals), highly selective.

Maurice Beebe. "Criticism of Graham Greene. A Selected Checklist with an Index to Studies of Separate Works." *Modern Fiction Studies* 3 (1957): 281-288.

Alphabetical by author list of general criticism; specific studies listed under alphabetically arranged titles of the primary books.

Donald P. Costello. "Graham Greene and the Catholic Press." *Renascence* 12 (Autumn 1959): 3-28.

Pp. 3-26, essay; pp. 26-28, bibliography of "items . . . representative of the interest the Catholic Press . . . has shown in Greene . . . "

A. A. DeVitis. *Graham Greene.* New York: Twayne Publishers, Inc. (TEAS 3), 1964. Pp. 175.

Pp. 161-165, primary bibliography. Form and genre arrangement. Books: place, publisher, year. Periods: volume, pages, date. Pp. 165-171, secondary bibliography. Alphabetical by author arrangement. Annotated.

J. Don Vann. *Graham Greene. A Checklist of Criticism.* Kent, Ohio: Kent State University Press (Serif Series No. 14), 1970. Pp. [viii] , 69.

Form and genre arrangement. Book reviews listed under title of book reviewed, primary books being chronologically arranged. Pp. 2-3, list of primary and secondary bibliographies. Books: place, publisher, date (reviews of books about Greene listed under title of the book reviewed). Periods: volume, date, pages.

Vann attempts to list omissions from previous bibliographies and to bring "Greene scholarship from [Brennan, above] up to date" (p. v). Together these secondary bibliographies give a fairly complete listing of the available information.

GENERAL

Longaker & Bolles; Daiches; Temple & Tucker; Coleman & Tyler; Adelman & Dworkin; Salem; Palmer & Dyson; Breed & Sniderman; Adelman & Dworkin (Novel); Vinson-Dramatists; Vinson-Novelists; NCBEL, IV, 503-512; Bufkin.

GREENWOOD, WALTER (1903-1974)

Palmer & Dyson; Vinson-Dramatists; NCBEL, IV, 947.

GREGORY, LADY ISABELLA AUGUSTA PERSSE (1859-1932)

PRIMARY

Eileen E. Coxhead. *Lady Gregory. A Literary Portrait.* London: Macmillan and Co., 1961. Pp. 241. (Second edition, revised and enlarged, 1966. Not seen).

Pp. 231-232, "Lady Gregory's Principal Publications." Primary books. Chronological arrangement. Publisher, year.

--*John Millington Synge and Lady Gregory.* London: Longmans, Green and Co. (WTW 149), 1962. Pp. 35.

Pp. 34-35, bibliography of primary books. Chronological arrangement. Place, year, contents of collections.

SECONDARY

Edward Halim Mikhail. "The Theater of Lady Gregory." *Bulletin of Bibliography* 27 (1970): 10, 9.

Alphabetical by author arrangement. Books: place, publisher, date. Periods: volume, pages, date. More emphasis on the Irish theater in general than on Lady Gregory's plays.

Edward A. Kopper, Jr. *Lady Isabella Persse Gregory*. Boston: Twayne Publishers, G. K. Hall and Co. (TEAS 194), 1976. Pp. 160.

Pp. 151-152, selected primary bibliography. Pp. 152-156, selected secondary bibliography. Books: place, publisher, date. Periods: volume, date, pages. All entries annotated.

GENERAL

Millett; Batho & Dobrée; Longaker & Bolles; Temple & Tucker; Coleman & Tyler; Adelman & Dworkin; Salem; NCBEL, III, 1939-1941; Hogan; Breed & Sniderman.

GRENFELL, JULIAN HENRY FRANCIS (1892-1915)

Longaker & Bolles; NCBEL, IV, 285.

GRIERSON, SIR HERBERT JOHN CLIFFORD (1866-1960)

Batho & Dobrée; Daiches; Temple & Tucker.

GRIEVE, CHRISTOPHER MURRAY: *see* MACDIARMID, HUGH.

GRIFFIN, GWYN (1922-)

Bufkin.

GRIFFITH, ARTHUR (1872-1922)

PRIMARY

Patrick Sarsfield O'Hegarty. "Bibliographies of 1916 and the Irish Revolution. XII. Arthur Griffith." *Dublin Magazine* 12 (January-March 1937): 61-66.

Primary books. Chronological arrangement. Transcribed TP, part collation, pagination, binding, bibliographical and biographical notes.

GRIFFITHS, BRYN (-)

Vinson-Poets.

GRIGSON, GEOFFREY EDWARD HARVEY (1905-)

Longaker & Bolles; Daiches; Temple & Tucker; Vinson-Poets; Stratford; NCBEL, IV, 1052-1053.

GRUBB, FREDERICK CRICHTON-STUART (1930-)

Vinson-Poets.

GUEDALLA, PHILIP (1889-1944)

Millett; Longaker & Bolles; Daiches; Temple & Tucker; NCBEL, IV, 1167-1168.

GUEST, HENRY (HARRY) BAYLY (1932-)

Vinson-Poets.

GUNN, NEIL MILLER (1891-1973)

PRIMARY

W. R. Aitken, "Neil M. Gunn: A Bibliography" in *Neil M. Gunn: The Man and the Writer,* ed. Alexander Scott and Douglas Gifford. New York: Barnes and Noble, 1973. Pp. [viii], 400.

Pp. [389]-397, "Bibliography." Primary books including translations of these titles, Selected secondary (thirteen titles). Place, publisher, date. Occasional bibliographical notes. This checklist was first published in *Bibliotheck* (Glasgow) 3, iii (1961): 89-95.

SECONDARY

Above, Aitken.

GENERAL

Daiches; NCBEL, IV, 595; Vinson-Novelists; Bufkin.

GUNN, THOMSON (THOM) WILLIAM (1929-)

Temple & Tucker; Vinson-Poets.

GUTHRIE, THOMAS ANSTEY: *see* ANSTEY, F.

GUTHRIE, SIR WILLIAM TYRONE (1900-1971)

PRIMARY

David E. Jones and Alfred Rossi. "The Writings of Sir Tyrone Guthrie: A Selective Bibliography." *Drama Survey* 3 (1963): 104.

Thirteen items. Books: place, publisher, date. Periods: volume, date, pages.

GENERAL

NCBEL, IV, 947-948.

GWYNN, STEPHEN LUCIUS (1864-1950)

Temple & Tucker.

HACKETT, WALTER (1876-1944)

NCBEL, IV, 948-949.

HADDON, CHRISTOPHER: *see* PALMER, JOHN LESLIE.

HAGGARD, SIR HENRY RIDER (1856-1925)

PRIMARY

George L. McKay. *A Bibliography of the Writings of Sir Rider*

Haggard. London: Bookman's Journal, 1930. Pp. 110. 475 copies.

Primary. Form arrangement. Books: transcribed TP, part collation, pagination, binding, date, contents, number of copies, full notes. Periods: volume, pages, date. Publications other than books listed together in one list.

--and J. E. Scott. *Additions and Corrections to the Haggard Bibliography.* London: Mitre Press, 1939. Pp. 28. 100 copies.

Considerable expansion of McKay (1930); especially pp. 3-9, list of American editions, 1886-1891; pp. 10-24, corrections and additional information concerning first editions; pp. 25-28, additional writings other than books.

J. E. Scott. *A Bibliography of the Works of Sir Henry Rider Haggard 1856-1925.* Bishop's Stortford, Herts: Elkin Matthews Ltd., 1947. Pp. 258. 500 copies.

Primary, secondary selected. Form and genre arrangement. Books: transcribed TP, part collation, pagination, binding, date, number of copies, contents, variants, MSS, reprints, full bibliographical notes. Periods: date. Divisions include letters to the *Times* and other newspapers; reports of speeches; reviews by Haggard (including title and author of book reviewed); dramatizations and film productions of Haggard's novels; parodies of Haggard. Pp. 236-246, secondary bibliography. Dates, annotations. Index.

The authoritative bibliography.

SECONDARY

Above, Scott, pp. 236-246.

Morton Cohen. "Henry Rider Haggard." *English Fiction* (later *English Literature) in Transition* 1, iii (1958): 36-38. Continued in later issues.

Annotated.

--*Rider Haggard. His Life and Works.* London: Hutchinson and

Co., 1960. Pp. 327.

Pp. 310-322, secondary bibliography. Arranged: reviews of primary books listed under title of book; other writings about Haggard; general literary and historical background.

GENERAL

Batho & Dobrée; Temple & Tucker; NCBEL, III, 1055-1056.

HAGGARD, WILLIAM (1907-)

Pseudonym of Richard Henry Michael Clayton.

Vinson-Novelists.

HALE, JOHN (1926-)

Vinson-Dramatists.

HALL, JOHN CLIVE (1920-)

Vinson-Poets.

HALL, MARGUERITE RADCLYFFE (1886-1943)

PRIMARY

Sheila Bolton. "A Radclyffe Hall Collection." *Private Library* 2 (1958-1959): 50-52.

An essay in which the primary books in their various editions are mentioned along with date, publisher, place, and genre. Extensive bibliographical notes.

GENERAL

Bufkin; Temple & Tucker; NCBEL, IV, 596.

HALL, WILLIS (1929-)

Breed & Sniderman; Vinson-Dramatists.

HALLIWELL, DAVID WILLIAM (1936-)

Vinson-Dramatists.

HAMBURGER, MICHAEL PETER LEOPOLD (1924-)

Vinson-Poets.

HAMILTON, ANTHONY WALTER PATRICK (1904-1962)

Salem; NCBEL, IV, 949-950.

HAMILTON, SIR GEORGE ROSTREVOR (1888-1967)

Temple & Tucker; NCBEL, IV, 286.

HAMILTON, ROBERT IAN (1938-)

Vinson-Poets.

HANKIN, ST. JOHN EMILE CLAVERING (1869-1909)

PRIMARY

St. John Hankin. *The Dramatic Works,* ed. John Drinkwater. New York: Mitchell Kennerley, 1912. 3 vols. 1000 copies.

Bibliographical information in "Introduction," I, 3-28, by Drinkwater. Casts and dates of original performances, III, 225-231. Collection includes essays and reviews by Hankin with place and date of original publication.

Gertrud Engel. *St. John Hankin als Dramatiker.* Giessen: Buchdruckerei Nitschkowski, 1931. Pp. 100.

P. 6, list of newspaper reviews of Hankin's plays: date only. P. 4, primary books (seven titles): place, publisher, date.

GENERAL

NCBEL, IV, 950-951; Breed & Sniderman.

HANLEY, CLIFFORD (1922-)

Pseudonym used: Henry Calvin.

Vinson-Novelists.

HANLEY, GERALD ANTHONY (1916-)

Vinson-Novelists; Drescher & Kahrmann; Bufkin.

HANLEY, JAMES (1901-)

Millett; Daiches; Bufkin; Temple & Tucker; Vinson-Novelists; Vinson-Dramatists; NCBEL, IV, 596-597.

HANNAY, JAMES OWEN: *see* BIRMINGHAM, G. A.

HARDY, THOMAS (1840-1928)

PRIMARY

Henry Danielson. *The First Editions of the Writings of Thomas Hardy and their Values.* London: George Allen and Unwin, 1916. Pp. 40. A. P. Webb. *A Bibliography of the Works of Thomas Hardy.* London: Frank Hollings, 1916. Pp. [xiv], [128].

Two typical bibliographies of the first-edition-craze period: still informative, but inferior to Purdy (below).

Richard Little Purdy. *Thomas Hardy, A Bibliographical Study.* London: Oxford University Press, 1954. Pp. [x], [388]. New Impression, 1968.

Primary. Form arrangement. Books (pp. 3-276): transcribed TP, part collation, pagination, binding, variants, reprints, later editions; extensive textual and bibliographical notes. Collected Editions (pp. 279-288): brief descriptions, including contents. Uncollected Contributions to Books, Periodicals, Newspapers (pp. 291-325): dates, pages. Six appendices on special Hardy topics. Index, pp. 355-388.

The authoritative bibliography. F. B. Adams, *Book Collector* 4 (1955): 82-84: "this virtually flawless book."

Additional bibliographical information is provided by James Osler Bailey. *The Poetry of Thomas Hardy. A Handbook and Commentary.* Chapel Hill: University of North Carolina Press, 1970. Pp. xxviii, 712. The primary texts, critical studies, biographies and letters, bibliographies and general background material are surveyed and evaluated by F. B. Pinion, "Hardy," in A. E. Dyson, ed. *The English Novel. Select Bibliographical Guides.* London: Oxford University Press, 1974, pp. 264-279.

SECONDARY

Above, Webb, pp. 103-117.

Helmut E. Gerber and W. Eugene Davis, eds. *Thomas Hardy An Annotated Bibliography of Writings about Him.* DeKalb: Northern Illinois University Press, 1973. Pp. x, 841.

Pp. 3-7, primary books. Form and genre arrangement. Place, date, contents of collections. Pp. 9-18, essay survey of secondary criticism. Pp. 19-755, secondary bibliography, 3153 entries, 1871 to 1969, fully annotated. Books: place, publisher, date. Period: volume, date, pages. Indices of authors, of titles of secondary works, of periodicals and newspapers, of foreign languages, and of primary titles.

Additional information is provided by Margaret Hutchins. "A Selected List of References on Thomas Hardy's Works." *Bulletin of Bibliography* 12 (1924): 51-55; by George Monteiro. "Addenda to the Bibliographies of. . .Hardy. . . : Reviews in *Public Opinion*." *Papers of the Bibliographical Society of America* 70 (1976): 276-278; and by Weber (below).

Carl J. Weber. *The First Hundred Years of Thomas Hardy 1840-1940. A Centenary Bibliography of Hardiana.* Waterville, Maine: Colby College Library, 1942. Pp. 276. Reprinted: New York: Russell and Russell, Inc., 1965.

One list including studies, reviews, translations, etc., arranged alphabetically by author or title of periodical. Books: place, publisher, date. Periods: volume, pages, date. Occasional brief annotations.

One of the most comprehensive secondary bibliographies ever compiled for a modern author.

GENERAL

Millett; Batho & Dobrée; Longaker & Bolles; Temple & Tucker; NCBEL, III, 980-992.

HARRIS, FRANK (1856-1931)

PRIMARY

Robert Brainard Pearsall. *Frank Harris.* New York: Twayne Publishers, Inc. (TEAS 103), 1970. Pp. 196.

Pp. 183-186, primary books. Chronological arrangement. British and American first editions; place, publisher, date, contents of collections, languages into which translated, occasional notes. P. 186, list of periodicals with which Harris was associated, with relevant dates. Pp. 187-189, secondary bibliography, annotated. Additional secondary items are given in the Notes, pp. 177-181.

For additional secondary items and information concerning MSS sources, see Vincent Brome. *Frank Harris.* London: Cassells and Co., 1959; reprinted, London: World Distributors, 1965, pp. 5-7, 242-248.

SECONDARY

Above, Pearsall and Brome.

GENERAL

Temple & Tucker; NCBEL, IV, 1054-1055.

HARRISON, TONY (1937-)

Vinson-Poets.

HART, SIR BASIL HENRY LIDDELL: *see* LIDDELL-HART, SIR BASIL HENRY.

HARTLEY, LESLIE POLES (1895-1972)

PRIMARY

Peter Bien. "A L. P. Hartley Bibliography." *Adam International Review* 29, Numbers 294-296 (1961): 63-70.

Primary. Form arrangement. Books: date, publisher, place, reprints or subsequent editions, translations, contents with details of original publication. Periods: volume, date, pages; information concerning later publication in book form.

More informative and extensive than the bibliography in Bien's book (below).

--*L. P. Hartley.* London: Chatto and Windus; University Park: Pennsylvania State University Press, 1963. Pp. 288.

Pp. 267-269, bibliography. Primary. Genre arrangement. Dates. P. 268, list of book reviews by Hartley (N. B.: "The reviews are too numerous to list in detail. A fuller listing is available from University Microfilms, Ann Arbor, Michigan, publication No. 62-1912.") Pp. 268-269, selected secondary bibliography.

Paul Bloomfield. *L. P. Hartley.* London: Longman Group Ltd. (WTW 217, Revised Edition), 1970. Pp. 36.

Pp. 35-36, primary books, selected secondary criticism. Chronological arrangement. Date, genre.

SECONDARY

Above, Bien (1963), pp. 268-269; Bloomfield, pp. 35-36.

GENERAL

Daiches; Temple & Tucker; Adelman & Dworkin (Novel); Vinson-Novelists; NCBEL, IV, 597-598; Bufkin.

HARWOOD, HAROLD MARSH (1874-1959)

Salem; NCBEL, IV, 951-952.

HARWOOD, LEE (1939-)

Vinson-Poets.

HASSALL, CHRISTOPHER VERNON (1912-1963)

PRIMARY

Christopher Hassall. *Ambrosia and Small Beer. The Record of a Correspondence between Edward Marsh and Christopher Hassall.* London: Longmans, 1964. Pp. 374.

Although there is no bibliography, these letters (mainly from Marsh) throw light on the literary work of both men. Especially informative about Marsh's editorial work.

See above: BROOK, RUPERT. John Schroder. *A Catalogue . . .*

GENERAL

Temple & Tucker; Breed & Sniderman; NCBEL, IV, 952-953.

HASTINGS, MICHAEL GERALD TAILOR (1938-)

Vinson-Dramatists.

HAWKES, JACQUETTA HOPKINS (1910-)

(Mrs. J. B. Priestley).

Palmer & Dyson.

HAWKINS, SIR ANTHONY HOPE: *see* HOPE, ANTHONY.

HAY, IAN (1876-1952)

Pseudonym of John Hay Beith.

Breed & Sniderman; NCBEL, IV, 598-600.

HAYES, ALFRED (1857-1936)

PRIMARY

Alfred Hayes, Richard LeGallienne, Norman Gale. Rugby: Rugby Press, 189?. Pp. 11.

P. 1, primary books. Chronological arrangement. Date, part collation, publisher, binding, number of copies.

GENERAL

NCBEL, III, 629.

HEADLAM, WALTER GEORGE (1866-1908)

PRIMARY

Lawrence Haward, "Bibliography" in Cecil Headlam. *Walter Headlam. His Letters and Poems, With a Memoir.* London: Duckworth and Co., 1910. Pp. [x], [171].

Pp. 111-[171], bibliography. Chronological arrangement. Books: place, publisher, date, part collation, pagination, reviews of the book. Periods: volume, date, pages. Reviews include author and title of book reviewed. Extensive bibliographical and textual notes. Includes list of obituary notices.

A full listing of primary writings, with a helpful list of secondary writings.

HEANEY, SEAMUS (1930-)

PRIMARY

Robert Buttel. *Seamus Heaney.* Lewisburg: Bucknell University Press (Irish Writers Series), 1975. Pp. 88.

Not seen.

GENERAL

Temple & Tucker

HEATH-STUBBS, JOHN FRANCIS ALEXANDER (1918-)

Daiches; Temple & Tucker; Vinson-Poets; NCBEL, IV, 287.

HEISS, JOHN STANGER (1871-1936)

Pseudonym used: Oscar Asche.

NCBEL, IV, 908.

HENDERSON, MARY: *see* BRIDIE, JAMES.

HENDRY, JAMES FINDLAY (1912-)

Daiches; NCBEL, IV, 287-288.

HENLEY, WILLIAM ERNEST (1849-1903)

PRIMARY

Kennedy Williamson. *William Ernest Henley. A Memoir.* Harold Shaylor, 1930. Pp. 296.

Pp. 287-290, bibliography. Primary, secondary selected. Arranged: Magazine and Newspaper Articles on Henley; Books containing material on Henley; Works edited by Henley; Writings by Henley not included in the *Collected Works* (1921). Dates. Additional primary writings mentioned in text, *passim.*

Michael Sadleir. "Some Uncollected Authors, X. William Ernest Henley." *Book Collector* 5 (1956): 162-168.

Primary books. Chronological arrangement. Publisher, date, format, pages, binding, subsequent editions.

SECONDARY

Above, Williamson.

Jerome Hamilton Buckley. *William Ernest Henley. A Study in the 'Counter-Decadence' of the 'Nineties.* Princeton: Princeton University Press, 1945. Pp. xii, 234.

Pp. 217-224, all inclusive secondary bibliography.

Joseph M. Flora. *William Ernest Henley.* New York: Twayne Publishers, Inc. (TEAS 107), 1970. Pp. 171.

Pp. 157-159, primary bibliography. Form and genre arrangement. Pp. 159-162, secondary bibliography. Alphabetical by author arrangement. Annotated. Additional information in notes, *passim,* pp. 149-156.

GENERAL

Longaker & Bolles; Batho & Dobrée; NCBEL, III, 629-631.

HENRI, ADRIAN MAURICE (1932-)

Vinson-Poets.

HEPPENSTALL, JOHN RAYNER (1911-)

Temple & Tucker; Vinson-Poets; Vinson-Novelists; Drescher & Kahrmann; Bufkin.

HERBERT, SIR ALAN PATRICK (1890-1971)

PRIMARY

Gilbert Fabes. *The First Editions of A. E. Coppard, A. P. Herbert, and Charles Morgan, with Values and Bibliographical Points.* London: Myers and Co., 1933. Pp. 154.

Pp. 55-125, bibliography of primary books. Chronological arrangement. Transcribed TP, binding, variants, current price.

GENERAL

Millett; Daiches; Temple & Tucker; Vinson-Novelists; NCBEL, IV, 288-290

HESELTINE, PHILIP (1894-1930)

PRIMARY

Cecil Gray. *Peter Warlock: A Memoir of Philip Heseltine.* London: Jonathan Cape, 1934. Pp. 319.

Pp. 307-313, "Complete List of Published Works." Pp. 307-313, original music. P. 313, literary works: publisher, date.

HEWITT, JOHN HAROLD (1907-)

Vinson-Poets.

HEWITT, REGINALD MAINWARING (1887-1948)

PRIMARY

Vivian de Sola Pinto, ed. *Reginald Mainwaring Hewitt (1887-1948) A Selection from his literary remains . . . with a memoir.* Oxford: Blackwell (for the subscribers), 1955. Pp. 149.

No bibliography, but many references in passing to Hewitt's contributions to periodicals and to other writings.

HEWLETT, MAURICE HENRY (1861-1923)

PRIMARY

Percy H. Muir. "A Bibliography of the First Editions of Books by Maurice Henry Hewlett (1861-1923)" in *Bibliographies of Modern Authors,* 3rd Series. London: Bookman's Journal, 1927. Pp. 9-36, plus 4 pp. "Addenda and Corrigenda" (1931).

Primary books. Chronological arrangement. Transcribed TP, full collation, pagination, binding, variants, notes. The "Addenda and Corrigenda" adds important information.

A "collector's bibliography."

Bruce Sutherland. *Maurice Hewlett: Historical Romancer* [A Dissertation . . .]. Philadelphia: University of Pennsylvania, 1938. Pp. [x], 199.

Pp. 189-192, primary bibliography. Arranged: Books and Pamphlets; Translations of Hewlett's novels; Book reviews, prefaces, and speeches by Hewlett. Chronological in each section. Place, publisher, date, occasional notes. Author and title of books reviewed or introduced by Hewlett. Pp. 193-199, secondary bibliography, arranged alphabetically by author. Includes reviews of Hewlett.

SECONDARY

Above, Sutherland, pp. 193-199.

Marie T. Tate. "Maurice Hewlett." *English Literature in Transition* 6 (1963): 33-36.

Annotated. Continued in subsequent issues of ELT.

GENERAL

Millett; Longaker & Bolles; Batho & Dobrée; Temple & Tucker; NCBEL, IV, 600-602; Bufkin.

HICHENS, ROBERT SMYTHE (1864-1950)

PRIMARY

Robert Hichens. *Yesterday. The Autobiography of Robert Hichens.* London: Cassell and Co., Ltd., 1947. Pp. 464.

No bibliography, but much information concerning Hichen's literary career. Index.

GENERAL

Temple & Tucker; NCBEL, IV, 602-603.

HIGGINS, BRIAN (1930-1965)

Stratford.

HIGGINS, FREDERICK ROBERT (1896-1941)

PRIMARY

M. J. MacManus. "Bibliography of F. R. Higgins." *Dublin Magazine* 21 (July-September 1946): 43-45.

Primary books. Chronological arrangement. Transcribed TP, part collation, pagination, binding, price, occasional notes.

GENERAL

NCBEL, IV, 290.

HILL, GEOFFREY (1932-)

Vinson-Poets; Temple & Tucker.

HILTON, JAMES (1900-1954)

PRIMARY

"Checklist Bibliographies of Modern Authors. James Hilton." *Book Trade Journal*, No. 62 (17 July 1936), p. 20.

Primary books. Chronological arrangement. Publisher, date, binding and binding variants.

P. G. Scott. "Note 366. The First Printing of *Goodbye Mr. Chips.*" *Book Collector* 22 (1973): 534-535.

Detailed description of the printing history of this novel.

GENERAL

Temple & Tucker; WWW 51-60; NCBEL, IV, 604.

HINDE, THOMAS (1926-)

Pseudonym of Sir Thomas Willes Chitty.

Adelman & Dworkin (Novel); Vinson-Novelists; Drescher & Kahrmann; Temple & Tucker; Bufkin.

HOBBES, JOHN OLIVER (1867-1906)

Pseudonym of Pearl Mary Theresa Craigie.

Batho & Dobrée; NCBEL, III, 1058.

HOBSBAUM, PHILIP DENNIS (1932-)

Vinson-Poets.

HODGE, HORACE EMERTON (MERTON) (1904-1958)

NCBEL, IV, 953.

HODGSON, RALPH (1871-1962)

PRIMARY

Colin Fenton, ed. Ralph Hodgson, *Collected Poems.* London: Macmillan and Co., Ltd., 1961. Pp. 185.

Pp. 179-181, poems by Hodgson arranged alphabetically by title. For each, name of periodical in which first published and date.

Wesley D. Sweetser. *Ralph Hodgson: A Bibliography.* Oswego, N. Y. Privately Printed for the Author, 1974. Not for sale.

Not seen. Reviewed by Nicholas A. Salerno, *English Literature in Transition* 19 (1976): 65-66, who describes the contents and points out some defects.

GENERAL

Millett; Longaker & Bolles; Batho & Dobrée; Temple & Tucker; Stratford; NCBEL, IV, 291.

HOFF, HARRY SUMMERFIELD: *see* COOPER, WILLIAM.

HOGARTH PRESS: *see* WOOLF, VIRGINIA.

HOLBROOK, DAVID KENNETH (1923-)

Vinson-Poets; Vinson-Novelists.

HOLDEN, MOLLY (1927-)

Vinson-Poets.

HOLLOWAY, JOHN (1920-)

Temple & Tucker; Vinson-Poets.

HOLME, CONSTANCE (-1955)

(Mrs. F. B. Punchard).

PRIMARY

Bertram Rota. "Some Uncollected Authors, XI: Constance Holme." *Book Collector* 5 (1956): 250-255.

Primary books. Chronological arrangement. Publisher, date, binding, bibliographical notes. Includes books with contributions by Holme.

GENERAL

Daiches; NCBEL, IV, 604; Bufkin.

HOLTBY, WINIFRED (1898-1935)

PRIMARY

Geoffrey Handley-Taylor. *Winifred Holtby. A Concise and Selected Bibliography together with Some Letters.* London: A.

Brown and Sons, Ltd., 1955. Pp. 76. 1000 copies.

Primary, secondary select. Form arrangement. Part collation, publisher, place, date, contents; notes on subsequent editions, reprints, and translations. Periodical contributions arranged alphabetically by subject matter: dates. Includes list of MSS with locations. Index.

References to primary writings not listed here are made in the following:

Vera Brittain. *Testament of Friendship. The Story of Winifred Holtby.* London: Macmillan and Co., Ltd., 1940. Pp. 442.

--and Geoffrey Handley-Taylor, eds. *Selected Letters of Winifred Holtby and Vera Brittain* (1920-1935). London: A. Brown and Sons, Ltd., 1960. Pp. 384. 500 copies.

SECONDARY

Above, Handley-Taylor (1955), pp. 41-52.

GENERAL

Temple & Tucker; NCBEL, IV, 605; Bufkin.

HOME, HON. WILLIAM DOUGLAS- (1912-)

PRIMARY

William Douglas Home. *Half-Term Report, An Autobiography.* London: Longmans, Green and Co., 1954. Pp. 209.

A certain amount of bibliographical assistance can be deduced from this volume.

--*The Plays of William Douglas Home.* London: Heinemann, 1958. Pp. 434.

Bibliographical references in the introduction, pp. 7-11.

GENERAL

Palmer & Dyson; Breed & Sniderman; Vinson-Dramatists; NCBEL; IV, 933-934.

HOPE, ANTHONY (1863-1933)

Pseudonym of Sir Anthony Hope Hawkins.

PRIMARY

Sir Charles Mallet. *Anthony Hope and his books, Being the Authorised Life of Sir Anthony Hope Hawkins.* London: Hutchinson and Co., 1935. Pp. 290.

Bibliographical information in text, *passim.*

GENERAL

Batho & Dobrée; Temple & Tucker; NCBEL, III, 1058-1059.

HOPKINS, GERARD MANLEY, S. J. (1844-1889)

PRIMARY

Tom Dunne. *Gerard Manley Hopkins. A Comprehensive Bibliography.* Oxford: Clarendon Press, 1976. Pp. xxvi, 394.

Pp. [3]-98, primary complete. Arranged: Poetry; Prose; Anthologies; Translations; Dubia. Primary books: transcribed TP, full collation, pagination, size in centimeters, paper, binding, extensive textual, bibliographical, and historical notes, with details of reprints and later editions. Other books: place, publisher, date. Periods: volume, date, pages, notes. Reviews are listed under the title of the work being reviewed. Pp. [101]-325, secondary bibliography. Arranged: Bibliographies; Biography; Books and Pamphlets; Periodical Articles and Reviews; Theses and Dissertations; Criticism of individual poems [listed under title of the poem studied]; Miscellaneous. All entries annotated and cross-referenced. Pp. 329-356, Writings about Hopkins in languages other than English. Pp. [359]-362, Location of Manuscripts. Index. Material in each section is arranged chronologically, and all items are identified by letter and number.

This model of bibliographical completeness and honesty is worthy of its subject, and all students of Hopkins will find that it assists them in their studies, even though the termination date for entries is 1969-1970.

SECONDARY

Above, Dunne, pp. [3] -98, *passim;* pp. 101-356.

Edward H. Cohen. *Works and Criticism of Gerard Manley Hopkins: A Comprehensive Bibliography.* Washington, D. C.: Catholic University of America Press, 1969. Pp. [xvi] , 217.

Pp. 1-5, primary; pp. 15-163, secondary. Chronological within each section; alphabetical by author within the year in the secondary bibliography. Books: place, publisher, date, pages; reviews within year of publication listed after book title, otherwise book title is repeated for following year(s) and reviews are listed there. Periods: volume, date, pages. Index of Critics.

Ruth Seelhammer. *Hopkins Collected at Gonzaga.* Chicago: Loyola University Press, 1970. Pp. xiv, 272.

Catalogue of the collection in the Crosby Library, Gonzaga University, Spokane, Washington. Arranged: Primary writings; Association items; Secondary writings. Alphabetical by author within second and third section, by title within first. Books: place, publisher, date; brief description of any unique autograph inscriptions. Periods: volume, date, pages. The collection includes every edition and impression of the primary writings. Index of names and relevant topics.

GENERAL

Longaker & Bolles; NCBEL, III, 581-593; Temple & Tucker.

HOPKINS, JOHN RICHARD (1931-)

Vinson-Dramatists.

HOPKINSON, HENRY THOMAS (1905-)

Daiches.

HOPKINSON, TOM (1905-)

Vinson-Novelists.

HOROVITZ, MICHAEL (1935-)

Vinson-Poets.

HOUÉDARD, DOM PIERRE-SYLVESTER (1924-)

Vinson-Poets.

HOUGHTON, CLAUDE (1889-1961)

Pseudonym of Claude Houghton Oldfield.

PRIMARY

Sir Hugh S. Walpole and Clemence Dane. *Claude Houghton. Appreciations . . . with a bibliography.* London: William Heinemann, 1935. Pp. 15.

Not seen.

Ben Abramson. "Claude Houghton Bibliography." *Reading and Collecting* 2 (December, 1937): 6.

Primary books. Chronological arrangement. Place, date.

HOUGHTON, WILLIAM STANLEY (1881-1913)

Longaker & Bolles; Batho & Dobrée; Salem; Breed & Sniderman; NCBEL, IV, 954.

HOULT, NORAH (1901-)

Millett; NCBEL, IV, 605-606.

HOUSEHOLD, GEOFFREY EDWARD WEST (1900-)

Vinson-Novelists; NCBEL, IV, 606.

HOUSMAN, ALFRED EDWARD (1859-1936)

PRIMARY

A. S. F. Gow. *A. E. Housman. A Sketch together with a List of his Writings and Indexes to his Classical Papers.* Cambridge: University Press; New York: Macmillan Company, 1936. Pp. [xiv], [137].

Pp. 65-78, Writings on Greek and Latin. Alphabetical list of subjects (reviews included). For books: place, publisher, date. For periodicals: volume and page numbers, date. Reviews by Housman include author and title of book reviewed. Indices, pp. 83-[137], divided Passages in Greek and Latin Authors (alphabetical list of authors with references to specific pages in Housman's writings) and subjects. Pp. 79-80, English Writings (information as above). Pp. 58-59, icongraphy; pp. 60-61, lectures by Housman with dates.

The definitive list of Housman's classical work.

John Carter and John Sparrow. "A. E. Housman. An Annotated Checklist," *The Library*, N. S. 21 (September, 1940): 160-191.

Primary first editions, secondary selected. Chronological arrangement. Information varies, but generally for books: place, publisher, date, size, number of leaves, binding, number of copies, various annotations. For periodicals: date and page number. Includes brief account of The Poetical Manuscripts. This work is reproduced in *A. E. Housman An Annotated Hand-List.* London: Rupert Hart-Davis (Soho Bibliography Number 2), 1952. Pp. 54. Reviewed by W. White, *Library* 7 (December, 1952): 285: "It has been corrected and slightly revised, the appendix on the poetical manuscripts being considerably enlarged . . . only two new entries are listed... authoritatively written small gem of a bibliographical hand-list."

William White, et al. "A. E. Housman, An Annotated Check-List. Additions and Corrections," *The Library* 23 (June, 1942): 31-44; (September-December, 1942): 133.

Information as in Carter and Sparrow (1940), above.

William White, "A. E. Housman, An Annotated Check-List. Additions and Corrections: III, " *The Library* 7 (September, 1952): 201-210.

Information as in Carter and Sparrow (1940), above. Particularly informative concerning reprints and numbers of copies in editions. Note especially White's introduction, p. 201, for brief survey of Housman bibliography.

G. B. A. Fletcher. "A. E. Housman Bibliography," *The Library* 8 (March, 1953): 51.

Addition to White (1952), above.

William White. "A. E. Housman Anthologized," *Bulletin of Bibliography* 21 (1954): 43-48, 68-72.

Chronological list of anthologies containing Housman. For each title: publisher, place, date, title of Housman contribution.

William White. "An Unrecorded Housman MS Item," *Papers of the Bibliographical Society of America* 49 (1955): 78-79.

Letters and a poem in the Fitzwilliam Museum, Cambridge.

William White. "Published Letters of A. E. Housman," *Bulletin of Bibliography* 22 (1957): 80-82.

Alphabetical listing by authors of printed sources. For books: publisher, place, date. For periodicals: volume and page numbers, date. Extensive annotations and quotations.

William White. "A Checklist of A. E. Housman's Writings in Latin," *Papers of the Bibliographical Society of America* 54 (1960): 188-190.

A list of the twelve known items with finding information.

William White. "Housman in French and Music," *Papers of the Bibliographical Society of America* 56 (1962): 257-259.

A short study of translations of Housman.

Tom Burns Haber. "Three Unreported Letters of A. E. Housman." *Papers of the Bibliographical Society of America* 57 (1963): 230-233.

There are no short-cuts in finding Housman's writings: in order to locate all of the primary material one should consult all of the above entries, noting as well the references within these items to other bibliographies of Housman.

SECONDARY

Above, Carter and Sparrow (1940, 1952); White (1942, 1952); Fletcher (1953).

Theodore G. Ehrsam. *A Bibliography of Alfred Edward Housman.* Boston: F. W. Faxon Company (Useful Reference Series No. 66), 1941. Pp. 44.

Put forward as a primary bibliography, this work was described by White (1942) as "incomplete and inaccurate": its value lies in its listing of secondary material, although there are inaccuracies here. Pp. 11-21, titles by Housman, followed by listing of reviews: volume and page numbers, dates. Pp. 21-43, Material written about Housman: alphabetical by author. Pp. 43-44, Bibliographical Material about Housman.

Robert W. Stallman. "Annotated Bibliography of A. E. Housman: A Critical Study," *PMLA* 60 (1945): 463-502.

Essay with checklists; material arranged by topics, which are listed on p. 464, fn. 1. Books: publisher, place, date, pages. Periods: volume, date, pages.

Benjamin F. Fisher IV. "Writing about A. E. Housman: 1962-1972." *Housman Society Journal* [London] 1 (1974): 7-15.

Not seen.

GENERAL

Millet; Batho & Dobrée; Longaker & Bolles; Temple & Tucker; NCBEL, III, 601-606.

HOUSMAN, LAURENCE (1865-1959)

PRIMARY

Anna Rudolf. *Die Dichtung von Laurence Housman.* Breslau: Priebatschs Buchhandlung (English Series Volume II), 1930. Pp. 93.

Pp. 85-89, bibliography. Primary books, secondary selected. Chronological arrangement. Place, publisher, year (88 items to 1928). Includes reviews of Housman.

GENERAL

Millett; Longaker & Bolles; Batho & Dobrée; Temple & Tucker; Salem; NCBEL, III, 632; Breed & Sniderman.

HOWARD, ELIZABETH JANE (1923-)

(Mrs. Kingsley Amis).

Temple & Tucker; Vinson-Novelists; Drescher & Karhmann.

HOWARD, PETER DUNSMORE (1908-1965)

PRIMARY

Anne Wolrige Gordon. *Peter Howard. Life and Letters.* London: Hodder and Stoughton, 1969. Pp. 318.

Pp. 313-314, "Books and Plays by Peter Howard." Primary books. Chronological arrangement. Publisher, date. Additional primary and secondary references in text, *passim,* including unpublished letters. Index.

HOWARD, ROGER (1938-)

Vinson-Dramatists.

HOYLE, FRED (1915-)

Vinson-Novelists.

HUBBARD, WILFRANC (1857-)

Millett.

HUDSON, STEPHEN (1868-1944)

Pseudonym of Sydney Alfred Schiff.

PRIMARY

John Gawsworth. *Ten Contemporaries. Notes Toward their Definitive Bibliography.* [First Series]. London: Ernest Benn Ltd., 1932. Pp. 224.

Pp. 102-109, primary first editions, 1913-1931. Chronological arrangement. Transcribed TP, full collation, pagination, binding, date, bibliographical notes.

Theophilus E. M. Boll. "Biographical Note" and "Critical Essay" in Stephen Hudson. *Richard, Myrtle and I.* Philadelphia: University of Pennsylvania Press, 1962. Pp. 140.

Pp. 15-89. No bibliography, but text and notes provide primary and secondary references. See also the review by Helmut Gerber of this volume: *English Fiction in Transition* 5, ii (1962): 35-36.

SECONDARY

Above, Boll, pp. 15-89.

GENERAL

Millett; Daiches; Temple & Tucker; NCBEL, IV, 606-607; Bufkin.

HUDSON, WILLIAM HENRY (1841-1922)

PRIMARY

George F. Wilson. *A Bibliography of the Writings of W. H. Hudson.* London: Bookman's Journal, 1922. Pp. 80. Reprinted 1968.

Primary. Two sections: "First editions, pamphlets, leaflets, etc." and "Contributions to periodical literature, prefaces to books, etc., which--unless otherwise stated--have not been reprinted." Chronological arrangement. Books: transcribed TP, part collation, pagination, binding, date, variants, notes; subsequent editions included with full descriptions. Periods: genre, date, pages.

[*The Collected Works of W. H. Hudson, in Twenty-four Volumes.* London and Toronto: J. M. Dent and Sons Ltd.; New York: E. P. Dutton and Co., 1923. 885 copies.

Includes almost all of Hudson's writings.]

Sidonia C. Rosenbaum. "W. H. Hudson: Bibliografía." *Revista Hispanica Moderna* 10 (1944): 222-230.

Primary, secondary select. Form arrangement. Books: place, publisher, date, subsequent editions listed under first edition; translations in separate list. Periods: volume, date, pages. Secondary bibliography: arranged alphabetically by author. In Spanish.

SECONDARY

Above, Rosenbaum.

Helmut Gerber. "W. H. Hudson." *English Fiction in Transition* 1 (1957): 28-29; Marie T. Tate, *English Literature in Transition* 6 (1963): 36-48; 164-165; continued in subsequent issues.

Annotated.

GENERAL

Millett; Batho & Dobrée; Longaker & Bolles; Temple & Tucker; NCBEL, III, 1059-1060.

HUGHES, GLYN (1935-)

Vinson-Poets.

HUGHES, RICHARD ARTHUR WARREN (1900-1976)

PRIMARY

Peter Thomas. *Richard Hughes.* Cardiff: University of Wales Press for the Welsh Arts Council (Writers of Wales), 1973. Pp. [104]. 1000 copies.

Pp. 97-99, primary first British editions and selected periodical contributions. Books: place, publisher, date. Periods: date, pages. Pp. 99-100, selected secondary bibliography. Many additional primary and secondary references are quoted in the text.

SECONDARY

Above, Thomas, pp. 99-100, and text, *passim.*

GENERAL

Millett; Daiches; Temple & Tucker; Breed & Sniderman; Adelman & Dworkin (Novel); Vinson-Novelists; NCBEL, IV, 607; Bufkin.

HUGHES, TED (1930-)

PRIMARY

Calvin Bedient. *Eight Contemporary Poets.* New York: Oxford University Press, 1975. Pp. x, 198.

Pp. 182-183, primary books. Place, publisher, date, names of editors and illustrators.

Keith Sagar. *The Art of Ted Hughes.* Cambridge: Cambridge University Press, 1975. Pp. [viii], 213.

Pp. 175-197, primary and secondary bibliography. Genre arrangement, including translations by and of Hughes, recordings, musical settings of his work, reviews by Hughes (with title and author of book reviewed), and writings for children. Primary books (all first editions): place, publisher, date, reviews, limitations of limited editions. Periods: date. Section D. 1 (pp. 182-191) "constitutes a complete check-list of Hughes' poems for adults;" includes title of volume in which the poem is collected. Secondary bibliography: pp. 175-181 (reviews); pp. 196-197 (studies).

SECONDARY

Above, Sagar.

GENERAL

Temple & Tucker; Vinson-Poets; Stratford.

HULME, THOMAS ERNEST (1883-1917)

PRIMARY

Alun Richard Jones. *Life and Opinions of T. E. Hulme.* London: Victor Gollancz Ltd., 1960. Pp. 233.

Pp. 221-224, "Bibliography of T. E. Hulme's Published Writings." Primary. Chronological arrangement. Books: place, publisher, date. Periods: volume, date, pages. Pp. 225-226, secondary bibliography. Arranged alphabetically by author. Additional secondary criticism in footnotes, *passim.*

T. E. Hulme. *Further Speculations,* ed. Sam Hynes. Minneapolis: University of Minnesota Press, 1955. Pp. 226.

Pp. 221-223, bibliography. Primary. Chronological arrangement. Books: place, publisher, date. Periods: date, volume, pages. P. 224, secondary bibliography.

Wallace Martin. "T. E. Hulme: A Bibliographical Note." *Notes and Queries,* N. S., 9 (1962): 307.

Adds twelve items to Jones and Hynes.

SECONDARY

Above, Jones, pp. 225-226; Hynes, p. 224.

GENERAL

Longaker & Bolles; Temple & Tucker; NCBEL, IV, 1059-1061.

HUMPHREYS, EMYR OWEN (1919-)

Vinson-Novelists; Drescher & Kahrmann; Bufkin.

HUNT, VIOLET (1862-1942)

PRIMARY

Douglas Goldring. *South Lodge. Reminiscences of Violet Hunt, Ford Madox Ford, and the English Review Circle.* London: Constable and Co., Ltd., 1943. Pp. [xx] , [240] .

Pp. 238-[240] , bibliography of primary books. Chronological arrangement. Publisher, date. Suggestions of periodical contributions are found in the text, *passim.*

GENERAL

NCBEL, IV, 607-608.

HUNTER, JIM (1939-)

Vinson-Novelists.

HUNTER, NORMAN CHARLES (1908-1971)

NCBEL, IV, 955.

HUTCHINSON, ARTHUR STUART MENTETH (1879-1971)

NCBEL, IV, 608.

HUTCHINSON, RAY CORYTON (1907-)

Daiches; Temple & Tucker; Vinson-Novelists; NCBEL, IV, 609; Bufkin.

HUTTON, EDWARD (1875-1969)

PRIMARY

Dennis Everard Rhodes. *The Writings of Edward Hutton. A Bibliographical Tribute Compiled and Presented to Edward Hutton on his Eightieth Birthday.* London: Hollis and Carter, 1955. Pp. 64.

Pp. 7-61, primary writings. Chronological arrangement. Books: transcribed TP, part collations, printer's colophon, number of copies, binding, subsequent editions and reprints, translations. Periods: volume, date, pages, brief notes. Reviews by Hutton include title and author of book reviewed. Includes unsigned primary writings. P. 62, books announced but not published. Pp. 63-64, index. A comprehensive listing, although the information is not consistently given.

HUXLEY FAMILY

ALDOUS (Also below). (1894-1963)

ANTHONY (1920-)

ELSPETH JOSCELINE (Mrs. Gervas Huxley). (1907-)

FRANCIS

GERVAS (1894-1971)

HENRIETTA

JULIAN (1887-)

JULIETTE

LAURA

LEONARD (1860-1933)

PRIMARY

Ronald W. Clark. *The Huxleys.* London: Heinemann, 1968. Pp. xvi, 398.

Pp. 367-373, selected primary books. Arranged by author (as above). Place, publisher, date.

HUXLEY, ALDOUS LEONARD (1894-1963)

PRIMARY

Hanson R. Duval. *Aldous Huxley. A Bibliography.* New York: Arrow Editions, 1939. Pp. 205.

Primary. Form arrangement. Books: transcribed TP, full collation, pagination, binding, date, variants, contents, bibliographical notes; all English language editions described, foreign editions listed with publisher. Reprints of books listed separately. Books with contributions by Huxley listed alphabetically by main author. Periods: arranged alphabetically by title of periodical with Huxley's contributions listed chronologically thereunder: date, pages. Includes reviews by Huxley with title of book reviewed. Index.

Complete to September, 1939.

Claire John Eschelbach and Joyce Lee Shober. *Aldous Huxley. A Bibliography 1916-1959.* Berkeley and Los Angeles: University of California Press, 1961. Pp. x, 150.

Primary, secondary. Form and genre arrangement. Books: publisher, place, date, pages. Periods: volume, date, pages, Arrangement within each division is alphabetical by title. All editions and contents of books and pamphlets listed. For poems, essays and short pieces, all places of publication listed. Books reviewed by Huxley listed alphabetically by author, as are books with contributions by Huxley. Secondary bibliography (pp. 91-123) arranged by form. Includes list of earlier bibliographies (p. 91) and criticism of primary works under the title of the work. Additions to this list are provided by Thomas D. Clareson and Carolyn S. Andrews. "Aldous Huxley: A Bibliography 1960-1964." *Extrapolation* 6 (1964): 2-21; by Eschelbach and Joyce Shober Marthaler in "Aldous Huxley: A Bibliography, 1914-1964 *(A Supplementary Listing).*" *Bulletin of Bibliography* 28 (1971): 114-117; and by Dennis Douglas Davis.

"Aldous Huxley: A Bibliography 1965-1973." *Bulletin of Bibliography* 31 (1974): 67-70. These four works compose the best available bibliography.

SECONDARY

Above, Eschelbach and Shober, pp. 91-123; Clareson and Andrews, pp. 11-20; Eschelbach and Marthaler, pp. 116-117; and Davis, pp. 68-70.

GENERAL

Millett; Longaker & Bolles; Daiches; Temple & Tucker; Coleman & Tyler; Salem; Breed & Sniderman; Adelman & Dworkin (Novel); NCBEL, IV, 609-617; Bufkin.

HYDE, DOUGLAS (1860-1949)

PRIMARY

Patrick Sarsfield O'Hegarty. "A Bibliography of Dr. Douglas Hyde." *Dublin Magazine* 14 (January-March, 1939): 57-66; (April-June, 1939): 72-78. Reprinted as pamphlet, Dublin: Privately Published, 1939. Pp. 19. 40 copies.

Primary books, and books edited by Hyde. Chronological arrangement. Transcribed TP, part collation, pagination, binding, notes. Includes "the more important" of Hyde's contributions to books and a two-paragraph description of contributions to periodicals.

Tomas De Bhaldraithe. "Aguisin le clar saothair An Chraoibhin." *Galvia* 4 (1957): 18-24.

Not seen.

GENERAL

Millett; NCBEL, III, 1909-1910; Breed & Sniderman.

INGE, WILLIAM RALPH (1860-1954)

Longaker & Bolles; Batho & Dobrée; NCBEL, III, 1613.

INNES, MICHAEL: *see* STEWART, JOHN INNES MACKINTOSH.

INNES, RALPH HAMMOND (1913-)

Vinson-Novelists.

IRWIN, MARGARET EMMA FAITH (-1967)

NCBEL, IV, 618-619.

ISHERWOOD, CHRISTOPHER WILLIAM BRADSHAW (1904)

PRIMARY

Selmer Westby and Clayton M. Brown. *Christopher Isherwood. A Bibliography 1923-1967.* Los Angeles: California State College, for the J. F. Kennedy Memorial Library, 1968. Pp. [xii], 51.

Pp. 3-29, primary bibliography. Form and genre arrangement. Books: first and subsequent editions: place, publisher, year, pages. Periods: volume, pages, date, reprintings; reviews by Isherwood include title and author of book reviewed. Pp. 33-51, secondary bibliography. Two sections: general criticism (alphabetical by author) and reviews of the primary books (listed under titles of books, alphabetically arranged).

Stathis Orphanos. "Christopher Isherwood: A Checklist 1968-1975." *Twentieth Century Literature* 22 (1976): 354-361.

Pp. 354-358, primary bibliography including first paperback editions, translations, and reissues. Pp. 358-361, secondary bibliography, arranged: Books, Articles, Interviews, Reviews (listed under title of work reviewed).

A continuation of the Westby and Brown *Bibliography* (above), providing the same type of information.

SECONDARY

Above, Westby-Brown, pp. 33-51, Orphanos, pp. 358-361.

Alan Wilde. *Christopher Isherwood.* New York: Twayne Publishers, Inc. (TUSAS 173), 1971. Pp. 171.

Pp. 161-162, checklist of selected primary titles. Pp. 162-164, general secondary bibliography, annotated. P. 165, eighteen reviews of Isherwood's books.

GENERAL

Daiches; Temple & Tucker; Palmer & Dyson; Breed & Sniderman; Adelman & Dworkin (Novel); Vinson-Novelists; Vinson-Dramatists; NCBEL, IV, 619-620; Bufkin.

JACK, HENRY VERNON: *see* ESMOND, HENRY VERNON.

JACKSON, HOLBROOK (1874-1948)

Millett.

JACOBS, WILLIAM WYMARK (1863-1943)

PRIMARY

E. A. Osborne. "Epitome of a Bibliography of W. W. Jacobs." *American Book Collector* 5 (1934): 201-204, 268-272, 286-288, 331-334, 358-362.

A bibliographically informative, chatty, informal essay. No listings provided.

GENERAL

Millett; Longaker & Bolles; Batho & Dobrée; Temple & Tucker; NCBEL, IV, 620-621.

JAMES, MONTAGUE RHODES (1862-1936)

PRIMARY

S. G. Lubbock. *A Memoir of M. R. James.* Cambridge: Cambridge University Press, 1939. Pp. 87.

Pp. 49-87, A. F. Scholfield, "List of his Writings." Primary. Subject arrangement: Bible and Apocrypha; Manuscripts and Books; History and

Antiquities; Friends and Contemporaries; Inscriptions; Miscellaneous. Chronological in each section. Books: publisher, date, place, format. Periods: date, volume, pages.

A. F. Scholfield. "Additions to a List of the Writings of Dr. M. R. James." *Transactions of the Cambridge Bibliographical Society* 2 (1954-1958), 95.

Additions to Scholfield's list in Lubbock (above).

SECONDARY

J. Randolph Cox. "Montague Rhodes James: An Annotated Bibliography of Writings about Him. *English Literature in Transition* 12 (1969): 203-210.

One alphabetical by author list. Books: place, publisher, date. Periods: volume, date, pages. Annotations.

GENERAL

Batho & Dobrée; NCBEL, IV, 621-622.

JAMESON, MARGARET STORM (1897-)

(Mrs. Guy Chapman)

Millett; Daiches; Temple & Tucker; Vinson-Novelists; NCBEL, IV, 622-623; Bufkin.

JELLICOE, PATRICIA ANN (1927-)

(Mrs. Roger Mayne).

Coleman & Tyler; Palmer & Dyson; Breed & Sniderman; Temple & Tucker; Vinson-Dramatists.

JENKINS, JOHN ROBIN (1912-)

Vinson-Novelists.

JENNINGS, ELIZABETH JOAN (1926-)

Temple & Tucker; Vinson-Poets; Stratford.

JENNINGS, GERTRUDE ELEANOR (1877-1958)

NCBEL, IV, 956-957.

JEROME, JEROME KLAPFA (1859-1927)

PRIMARY

Ruth Marie Faurot. *Jerome K. Jerome.* New York: Twayne Publishers, Inc. (TEAS 164), 1974. Pp. 200.

Pp. 189-191, selected primary books ("editions . . . used in this study and not necessarily first editions"). Genre arrangement. Place, publisher, date. Includes plays produced but not published. Pp. 191-194, selected secondary bibliography, annotated.

A useful list of titles, but otherwise a very scrappy production.

GENERAL

Batho & Dobrée; Temple & Tucker; Palmer & Dyson; NCBEL, III, 1062.

JESSE, FRYNIWYD MARSH TENNYSON (1889-1958)

(Mrs. H. M. Harwood).

Millett; Daiches; NCBEL, IV, 623-624.

JOB, THOMAS (1900-1947)

Salem.

JOHNSON, BRYAN STANLEY (1933-)

Vinson-Poets; Vinson-Novelists; Drescher & Kahrmann; Temple & Tucker.

JOHNSON, LIONEL PIGOT (1867-1902)

PRIMARY

Henry Danielson. "A Bibliography of Lionel Johnson." *Bookman's Journal* V (1921): 29, 68, 103-104.

Primary books. Chronological arrangement. Transcribed TP, part collation, pagination, binding, subsequent editions, extensive bibliographical notes.

Provides information about the physical form of the books not given in Fletcher (below).

Iain Fletcher, ed. *The Complete Poems of Lionel Johnson.* London: Unicorn Press, 1953. Pp. 395. 1000 copies.

Pp. 289-294, "Select Bibliography." Primary. Arranged: MSS Sources; Printed Sources; Books with Contributions by Johnson; Periodicals with Contributions by Johnson. Books: editor, publisher, place, date, pages. Periods: date. Additional bibliographical information in Introduction, pp. xi-xliv, and in Textual Notes, pp. 325-395. Secondary bibliography, pp. 292-294.

SECONDARY

Above, Fletcher, pp. 292-294.

GENERAL

Longaker & Bolles; Batho & Dobrée; NCBEL, III, 633-634.

JOHNSON, PAMELA HANSFORD (1912-)

(Rt. Hon. Lady Snow).

PRIMARY

Isabel Quigly. *Pamela Hansford Johnson.* London: Longmans, Green and Co. (WTW 203), 1968. Pp. 48.

Pp. 47-48, bibliography of primary books. Chronological arrangement. Place, date, genre. Includes works written in collaboration with C. P. Snow. P. 48, secondary bibliography (four entries).

GENERAL

Temple & Tucker; Adelman & Dworkin (Novel); Vinson-Novelists; Drescher & Dahrmann; NCBEL, IV, 624-625; Bufkin.

JOHNSTON, WILLIAM DENIS (1901-)

PRIMARY

Kaspar Spinner. *Die Alte Dame Sagt: Nein! Irische Dramatiker. Lennox Robinson, Sean O'Casey. Denis Johnston.* Bern: Francke Verlag (Schweizer Anglistische Arbeiten 52), 1961. Pp. 210.

Pp. 208-209, bibliography. Primary selected. Arranged: Drama, Other Writings. Books: publisher, date. Plays: date of first performance. Pp. 209-210, general secondary bibliography, selected.

SECONDARY

Above, Spinner, pp. 209-210.

GENERAL

Daiches; Temple & Tucker; Salem; Breed & Sniderman; Hogan; Vinson-Dramatists; NCBEL, IV, 957-958.

JONES, DAVID MICHAEL (1895-1974)

PRIMARY

Samuel Rees. *David Jones. An Annotated Bibliography and Guide to Research.* New York and London: Garland Publishing, Inc., 1977. Pp. x, 97.

Pp. 5-16, primary bibliography. Books (all editions): place, publisher, date, textual notes. Periods: volume, date, pages. Pp. 19-92, annotated secondary bibliography with extensive notes. Pp. 93-97, index.

SECONDARY

Above, Rees, pp. 19-92.

GENERAL

Temple & Tucker; NCBEL, IV, 292, Vinson-Poets; Bufkin.

JONES, GLYN (1905-)

Temple & Tucker; Vinson-Poets; Vinson-Novelists.

JONES, GWYN (1907-)

Temple & Tucker; Vinson-Novelists.

JONES, HENRY ARTHUR (1851-1929)

PRIMARY

Frank K. Walter. "Reading List on Henry Arthur Jones." *Bulletin of Bibliography* 6 (1911):273-275.

Primary, secondary selected. Arranged: Plays; Annotated List of Selected Non-Dramatic Works; Annotated List of Criticism of Jones. Alphabetical by title in each section. For each entry: place, publisher, date, price, reprints, subsequent editions; also brief quotation of criticism of each primary title and a list of reviews of that title.

Doris Arthur Jones. *The Life and Letters of Henry Arthur Jones.* London: Victor Gollancz Ltd., 1930. Pp. 448.

Pp. 411-431, bibliography. Primary. Form and genre arrangement. Books: publisher, place, date. Periods: date. For plays: details of first and subsequent performances: theatre, date, actors.

SECONDARY

Above, Walter.

GENERAL

Millett; Batho & Dobrée; Temple & Tucker; Coleman & Tyler;

Adelman & Dworkin; Salem; NCBEL, III, 1164-1166; Breed & Sniderman.

JONES, JACK (1884-1970)

PRIMARY

Keri Edwards. *Jack Jones.* Cardiff: University of Wales Press for the Welsh Arts Council (Writers of Wales), 1974. Pp. 94. 1000 copies.

Pp. 85-87, selected primary. Form and genre arrangement. Books (all editions): place, publisher, date. Period: volume, date. Pp. 88-89, selected secondary.

GENERAL

Breed & Sniderman.

JONES, MERVYN (1922-)

Vinson-Novelists.

JOYCE, JAMES AUGUSTINE ALOYSIUS (1882-1941)

BIBLIOGRAPHIES OF BIBLIOGRAPHIES

Robert H. Deming. *A Bibliography of James Joyce Studies.* Lawrence, Kansas: University of Kansas (Library Series No. 18), 1964. Pp. [viii] , 180.

Pp. 1-4, "Bibliography of Exhibitions, Collections, Checklists and Bibliographies." Books: place, publisher, date. Periods: volume, pages, date. Brief annotations.

The most important listing of bibliographical information for material published before December, 1961. In 1973 a second edition, to be published by G. K. Hall and Company, was announced; but by early 1977 it had not yet appeared.

Alan M. Cohn. "Joyce Bibliographies: A Survey." *American Book Collector* 15 (Summer, 1965): 11-16.

An essay on the history of Joyce bibliography to 1964. Bibliographies cited are listed on p. 16 (with information as for Deming, above); Cohn reproduces and supplements Deming's list. A more recent guide to both primary and secondary material is provided by A. Walton Litz, "Joyce," in A. E. Dyson, ed. *The English Novel. Select Bibliographical Guides.* London: Oxford University Press, 1974, pp. 264-279. Survey and evaluation of texts and concordances, critical studies, biographies and letters, bibliographies, and background reading; also lists of titles (with date and place) arranged under these divisions.

PRIMARY

John J. Slocum and Herbert Cahoon. *A Bibliography of James Joyce.* London: Rupert Hart-Davis (Soho Bibliography No. 5); New Haven: Yale University Press, 1953. Pp. [x], 195.

Primary first editions. Form arrangement. Books: transcribed TP, full collation, pagination, binding, date, price, number of copies, extremely full bibliographical, textual, and publishing notes. Periods: volume, pages, dates, annotations, reprintings. Includes unsigned writings; reviews by Joyce include author and title of book reviewed. Sections on Translations of Joyce's work (alphabetical listing by language, each language subdivided by form); Manuscripts; Musical Settings of Works by Joyce; Miscellany. Index. The definitive primary bibliography. Supplemental information given in Cohn and Kain, *James Joyce Quarterly*, below.

SECONDARY

See above, Deming, and Cohn, for titles of earlier checklists of secondary writings. Deming reprints most of the entries in these earlier works, dividing them by subject matter (General and Biographical; Reviews; Studies of Separate Works; and others). Each entry is annotated, and there is an index. Deming provides the basic secondary bibliography, being supplemented by the *James Joyce Quarterly* listings, below.

Alan M. Cohn and Richard M. Kain. "Supplemental James Joyce Checklist, 1962." *James Joyce Quarterly* 1 (Winter, 1964): 15-22.

Primary, secondary, and translations (excluding items listed in the PMLA annual bibliography). Books: place, publisher, date. Periods: volume, pages, date.

One or more numbers of each succeeding volume of the *James Joyce Quarterly* contains a "Supplemental Checklist" by Cohn, as well as specialized checklists by other compilers: see the *Ten Year Cumulative Index* (1974) by John Van Voorhis and John Metzner and the subsequent annual indices for details.

Maurice Beebe, Phillip F. Herring, Walton Litz. "Criticism of James Joyce: A Selected Checklist." *Modern Fiction Studies* 15 (Spring, 1969): 105-182.

Primary selected, secondary selected. Arranged: Primary Writings; Bibliographies; Biographical Material; General Studies; Studies of Individual Works (listed under primary titles). Books: place, publisher, date. Periods: volume, pages, dtae. Restrictions and principles of selection described on pp. 105-106.

Useful as a secondary bibliography complete in itself (particularly for the beginning student) and also for the additions it provides in its bibliography of bibliographies (pp. 108-109).

Another basic list of secondary criticism for the beginning student is provided by William M. Chace, ed. *Joyce: A Collection of Critical Essays.* Englewood Cliffs, N. J.: Prentice-Hall, Inc. (Spectrum Book), 1974, pp. 180-184.

GENERAL

Millett; Longaker & Bolles; Daiches; Temple & Tucker; Coleman & Tyler; Adelman & Dworkin; Salem; Palmer & Dyson; Breed & Sniderman; NCBEL, IV, 444-472.

KAVANAGH, PATRICK (1905-1967)

PRIMARY

Peter Kavanagh. *Garden of the Golden Apples. A Bibliography of Patrick Kavanagh.* New York: The Peter Kavanagh Hand Press, 1972. Pp. 47.

Primary complete, secondary selected. Form and genre arrangement. Books: place, publisher, date, various bibliographical and historical notes. Periods: dates. Pp. 40-47, secondary bibliography including reviews.

The authoritative bibliography.

John Nemo. "A Bibliography of Writings By and About Patrick Kavanagh." *Irish University Review* 3 (1973): 80-106.

Primary selected, secondary. Genre and form arrangement. Books: place, publisher, date. Periods: date. Pp. 101-106, secondary bibliography including reviews.

SECONDARY

Above, Kavanagh, pp. 40-47; Nemo, pp. 101-106.

GENERAL

Vinson-Poets, Temple & Tucker; NCBEL, IV, 292-293.

KAVANAGH, PATRICK JOSEPH (1931-)

Vinson-Poets.

KAYE-SMITH, SHEILA (1887-1956)

SECONDARY

Paul A. Doyle. "Sheila Kaye-Smith: An Annotated Bibliography of Writings about Her." *English Literature in Transition* 15 (1972): 189-198.

Selected secondary bibliography, arranged alphabetically by author. Books: place, publisher, date, relevant pages. Periods: volume, pages, date. Annotated.

There appears to be no bibliography of the primary writings.

GENERAL

Millett; Longaker & Bolles; Temple & Tucker; NCBEL, IV, 625-626; Bufkin.

KEANE, JOHN B. (1928-)

PRIMARY

Joanne L. Henderson. "Checklists of Four Kerry Writers: . . . John B. Keane (1928-) . . . " *Journal of Irish Literature* 1 (May 1972): 118-119.

Primary, secondary. Books: place, publisher, date; reprintings and reviews of each title. Periods: volume, date, pages.

GENERAL

Breed & Sniderman; Hogan.

KEATING, JOSEPH IGNATIUS PATRICK, S. J. (1865-1939)

PRIMARY

Edmund Felix Sutcliffe. *Bibliography of the English Province of the Society of Jesus.* London, Manresa Press, 1957. Pp. xii, 247.

Pp. 92-98, primary writings. Form and genre arrangement. Books: publisher, date, part collation, subsequent editions, translations, extensive notes. Periods (Contributions listed under title of periodical): volume, date, pages. A total of 435 entries.

KELL, JOSEPH: *see* BURGESS, ANTHONY.

KELLOCK, ARCHIBALD P.: *see* BRIDIE, JAMES.

KENDON, FRANK SAMUEL HERBERT (1893-1959)

NCBEL, IV, 293.

KENNEDY, MARGARET MOORE (1896-1967)

(Lady Davies).

Millett; Daiches; Temple & Tucker; NCBEL, IV, 626-627; Bufkin.

KETTLE, THOMAS (1880-1916)

PRIMARY

Bonnie K. Scott. "A Selected Kettle Bibliography." *Journal of Irish Literature* 3, ii (1974): 89-91.

Primary, secondary. Genre arrangement. Books: place, publisher, date. Secondary bibliography, p. 91.

KEYES, SIDNEY ARTHUR KILWORTH (1922-1943)

PRIMARY

Michael Meyer, ed. *The Collected Poems of Sidney Keyes.* London: Routledge, 1945. Pp. 124; Michael Meyer, ed. *Sidney Keyes. Minos of Crete. Plays and Stories with Selections from his Notebook and Letters and Some Early Unpublished Poems.* London: Routledge, 1948. Pp. 190.

No bibliographies; the introductory material in these two volumes provides miscellaneous bibliographical information.

John Guenther. *Sidney Keyes. A Biographical Inquiry.* London: London Magazine Edns, 1967. Pp. [223].

Bibliographical information in text, *passim.*

SECONDARY

Above, Guenther, *passim.*

GENERAL

Longaker & Bolles; Daiches; NCBEL, IV, 294.

KIELY, BENEDICT (1919-)

PRIMARY

Grace Eckley. *Benedict Kiely.* New York: Twayne Publishers, Inc.

(TEAS 145), 1972. Pp. 184.

Pp. 173-178, primary and secondary selected bibliographies. Genre arrangement. Books: British and American editions, place, publisher, date. Periods: volume, date, pages. Additional secondary criticism provided in notes, pp. 163-172. A few additional primary and secondary titles are given by Daniel J. Casey. *Benedict Kiely.* Lewisburg: Bucknell University Press (Irish Writers Series), 1975, pp. 105-107.

SECONDARY

Above, Eckley and Casey.

KING, FRANCIS HENRY (1923-)

Vinson-Novelists; Drescher & Kahrmann; Bufkin.

KING-HALL, WILLIAM STEPHEN RICHARD, BARON KING-HALL (1893-1966)

NCBEL, IV, 958-959.

KINSELLA, THOMAS (1928-)

PRIMARY

Calvin Bedient. *Eight Contemporary Poets.* New York: Oxford University Press, 1975. Pp. x, 198.

Pp. 183-184, primary books. Place, publisher, date, names of illustrators.

GENERAL

Vinson-Poets; Temple & Tucker.

KIPLING, RUDYARD (1865-1936)

PRIMARY

E. W. Martindell. *A Bibliography of the Works of Rudyard Kipling (1881-1923) A New Edition Much Enlarged Illustrated with 52 Plates.* London: John Lane The Bodley Head Ltd.,

1923. Pp. [xviii], [222]. 700 copies.

Primary, secondary selected. Form arrangement. Books: transcribed TP, partial collation, abbreviated pagination, binding, date, contents occasionally with details of original printing, bibliographical notes. Brief account of collected editions. Uncollected periodical contributions: dates. Manuscripts, proofs, and author's working copies: varying details. Brief account of later editions. Index.

The first bibliography to be compiled: most, but not all, of its information is given in Livingston (below).

Flora V. Livingston. *Bibliography of the Works of Rudyard Kipling.* New York: Edgar H. Wells and Co., 1927. Pp. xviii, 523. *Supplement to Bibliography of the Works of Rudyard Kipling (1927).* Cambridge: Harvard University Press, 1938. Pp. [xvi], 333.

Primary books and pamphlets. Chronological arrangement. Transcribed TP without line bars; partial collation, brief pagination, binding, date, contents with details of original printing, bibliographical notes. *Supplement* arranged: Continuation of bibliography for 1926-1937; Additions and corrections to the 1927 Bibliography; Brief account of pirated pamphlets and issues. Translations of primary writings: original and translated title, place, publisher, date, translator; arranged under name of language. Titles of books printed in Braille. Checklist of secondary criticism. Index to Bibliography and Supplement.

Livingston has long been the standard Kipling bibliography; see also comments on Stewart (below).

Catalogue of the Works of Rudyard Kipling Exhibited at the Grolier Club. New York: Grolier Club, 1930. Pp. [xii], 201. 34 plates. 325 copies.

Primary selected, secondary selected.

A catalogue and not a complete bibliography which offers much incidental information not given in Livingston and Stewart.

James McG. Stewart. *Rudyard Kipling A Bibliographical Catalogue,* ed. A. W. Yeats. Toronto: Dalhousie University Press, and University of Toronto Press, 1959. Pp. [xviii], [674]. 750 copies.

Primary. Arranged: Major works; Other works; Appendices. Chronological within each section. Transcribed TP, partial collation, pagination, full details of bindings with variants; date, subsequent editions, contents with details of original printing. Appendices include: Items in Sales Catalogues; Uncollected Prose and Verse; Works in Anthologies and Readers; Collected Sets; Musical Settings; Unauthorized editions. Index.

Adds many details to Livingston; particularly strong on accounts of editions later than the first British. R. J. Roberts, *Book Collector* 9 (Winter, 1960): 482: "the most comprehensive and detailed . . . invites acceptance as the standard bibliography of Kipling in succession to that of E. W. Martindell and Mrs. Livingston."

George Monteiro. "Rudyard Kipling: Early Printings in American Periodicals." *Papers of the Bibliographical Society of America* 61 (1967): 127-128.

Adds five items to Livingston and Stewart.

SECONDARY

Above, Martindell, pp. 193-203; Grolier Club, pp. 185-192; Livingston, Supplement, pp. 237-261.

Helmut E. Gerber and Edward Lauterbach, eds. "Rudyard Kipling: An Annotated Bibliography of Writings about Him." *English Fiction in Transition* 3, iii, iv, v (1960): 1-235.

Approximately 1630 items, annotated. Note description of limitations, 3: iii: 1-2, and references to other secondary sources. Books: place, publisher, date, pages. Periods: volume, pages, date. Supplements to this list appear in later issues of *English Fiction* (later *English Literature*) *in Transition;* see particularly 8, iii-iv (1965): 136-241.

Probably the most complete single checklist of critical studies, to which additions are made in later issues of the journal.

Reginald Engledon Harbord (successor to Roger L. Green), ed. *The Reader's Guide to Rudyard Kipling's Work.* The Kipling

Society. Privately printed by Gibbs and Sons, Canterbury; issued unbound and unsewn in parts; limited to 100 copies. 1961-1965. Subsequent volumes appeared in 1966 and 1969 [not seen], and others are projected.

An enormous work, over two thousand pages long, written by and for members of the Kipling Society, providing detailed references found nowhere also. Helmut Gerber, *English Literature in Transition* 9 (1966): 49: "simply no other tool [is] as useful for close analyses of Kipling's work. . ."

GENERAL

Millett; Longaker & Bolles; Batho & Dobrée; Temple & Tucker; NCBEL, III, 1019-1032.

KIRKUP, JAMES FALCONER (1923-)

Daiches; Vinson-Poets; NCBEL, IV, 294-295.

KITCHIN, CLIFFORD HENRY BENN (1895-1967)

NCBEL, IV, 627.

KNOBLOCK, EDWARD (1874-1945)

Palmer & Dyson; NCBEL, IV, 959-960.

KNOTT, FREDERICK (1919-)

Salem.

KNOX, EDMUND GEORGE VALPY (1881-1971)

NCBEL, IV, 295.

KOESTLER, ARTHUR (1905-)

PRIMARY

Jenni Calder. *Chronicles of Conscience. A Study of George Orwell and Arthur Koestler.* London: Secker and Warburg. 1968. Pp. 303.

Pp. 291-292, primary books. Genre arrangement. Publisher, date. Pp. 293-294, brief selected secondary bibliography of Koestler and Orwell.

SECONDARY

Above, Calder, pp. 293-294.

Peter Alfred Huber. *Arthur Koestler. Das Literarische Werk.* Zürich: Fretz und Wasmuth Verlag A. G., 1962. Pp. 173.

Pp. 166-168, secondary bibliography.

GENERAL

Temple & Tucker; Adelman & Dworkin (Novel); Vinson-Novelists; NCBEL, IV, 628-629; Bufkin.

KOPS, BERNARD (1926-)

Coleman & Tyler; Breed & Sniderman; Vinson-Poets; Temple & Tucker; Vinson-Novelists; Vinson-Dramatists; Bufkin.

KOTELIANSKY, SAMUEL SOLOMONOVICH (1882-1955)

PRIMARY

George T. Zytaruk. "S. S. Koteliansky's Translations of Russian Works into English." *Bulletin of Bibliography* 25 (1967): 65-66.

Arrangement: alphabetical by author of work translated. Books: place, publisher, date, pages. Periods: date, pages. Includes names of collaborators; other notes. Introduction, p. 65, provides brief list of secondary criticism.

LANG, ANDREW (1844-1912)

PRIMARY

C. M. Falconer. *Catalogue of a Library Chiefly the Writings of Andrew Lang.* Dundee: Privately Published, 1898. Pp. 32. 25 copies.

A list of 495 items in Falconer's collection; the idiosyncratic arrangement defies description. The collection is now a part of the Darlington Collection in the Lilly Library, Indiana University (see below).

Roger Lancelyn Green. *Andrew Lang. A Critical Biography.* Leicester: Edmund Ward, 1946. Pp. 265.

Pp. [241]-259, "A Short-Title Bibliography of the Works of Andrew Lang." Primary selected. Form arrangement with books listed chronologically and periodical contributions under title of period. Books: date. Periods: date. Pp. [223]-231: notes include primary and secondary entries not elsewhere listed. Pp. [236]-240, secondary selected bibliography.

The most comprehensive checklist yet compiled, though not complete.

Roger Lancelyn Green. "Andrew Lang–'The Greatest Bookman of his Age' "; "Descriptions from the Darlington Collection of Andrew Lang." *Indiana University Bookman* 7 (April, 1965): 10-72, 73-101.

An important essay on the Lang bibliography with special reference to the Darlington-Falconer Collection, followed by descriptions as follows: titles of 12 MSS; descriptions of 25 rare or unique primary books and pamphlets. Transcribed TP, part collation, pagination, binding, date, number of copies, price, notes; chronological list of primary titles with dates; List of contributions to Encyclopedias.

Green's various writings together provide a fairly complete primary bibliography.

SECONDARY

Above, Green (1946), pp. [223] -231, [236] -240.

GENERAL

Batho & Dobrée; Temple & Tucker; NCBEL, III, 1440-1444.

LARKIN, PHILIP ARTHUR (1922-)

PRIMARY

David Timms. *Philip Larkin.* New York: Barnes and Noble; Edinburgh: Oliver and Boyd, 1973. Pp. [vi], 138.

Pp. 132-135, primary bibliography. Form and genre arrangement. Books: place, publisher, date. Periods: date, page. Secondary bibliography, pp. 135-138.

Alan Brownjohn. *Philip Larkin.* Harlow, Essex: Longman Group (WTW 247), 1975. Pp. [38].

Pp. [33]-[34], primary and secondary bibliography. Books: place, date. Periods: date, pages.

Additions to Timms.

SECONDARY

Above, Timms, pp. 135-138; Brownjohn, pp. [33]-[34].

Lolette Kuby. *An Uncommon Poet for the Common Man.* The Hague: Mouton, 1974. Pp. 190.

P.[181], primary bibliography arranged chronologically (last date 1971). Books: place, publisher, date. Periods: volume, date, pages. Pp. 182-184, secondary bibliography arranged alphabetically by author.

GENERAL

Temple & Tucker; Adelman & Dworkin (Novel); Vinson-Poets; Drescher & Kahrmann; Stratford.

LASKI, MARGHANITA (1915-)

(Mrs. J. E. Howard).

Temple & Tucker.

LAVER, JAMES (1899-1975)

Millett; Temple & Tucker; Breed & Sniderman; NCBEL, IV, 1069-1070.

LAWRENCE, DAVID HERBERT (1885-1930)

PRIMARY

Edward D. McDonald. *A Bibliography of the Writings of D. H. Lawrence.* Philadelphia: Centaur Book Shop (Centaur Bibliographies No. 6), 1925. Pp. [154]. 500 copies. *The Writings of D. H. Lawrence, 1925-1930. A Bibliographical Supplement.* Philadelphia: Centaur Book Shop, 1931. [Not seen.] Reprinted in one volume (?Dawsons, 1970).

Primary first editions, British and American; secondary selected. Form arrangement. Primary books: transcribed TP, part collation, pagination, binding, date, contents, extensive bibliographical notes. Period contributions arranged by genre: dates, and titles of works in which collected. Pp. 131-145, secondary bibliography arranged by form. Books: place, date, publisher. Periods: date.

Most of the information in this first bibliography is reprinted in Roberts (below), but there are interesting notes here which should be consulted.

Warren Roberts. *A Bibliography of D. H. Lawrence.* London: Rupert Hart-Davis (Soho Bibliography No. 13), 1963. Pp. 399.

Primary first editions; secondary selected (books and pamphlets only). Form arrangement. Primary books: transcribed TP, part collation, binding, pagination, date, price, contents, number of copies of first printing, full bibliographical notes, some account of reprints and subsequent editions, list of reviews of the edition described. Translations of Lawrence listed under name of language: place, publisher, date, pages. List of MSS with brief description and location. Pp. 359-364, secondary bibliography.

The standard bibliography. Harry T. Moore, *Papers of the Bibliographical Society of America* 59 (1965): 75-77: "no serious studies of Lawrence from now on can be made without its help; the book is valuable for criticism as well as biography."

Additions to Roberts are provided by: James G. Hepburn. "Note 241. D. H. Lawrence's Plays: An Annotated Bibliography." *Book Collector* 14 (Spring, 1965): 78-81. Alphabetical list of play titles with dates of composition, of publication, and of production; reviews listed. Ample notes and list of 'lost' plays; and by Carole Ferrier. "D. H. Lawrence's Pre-1920 Poetry: A Descriptive Bibliography of Manuscripts, Typescripts, and Proofs." *D. H. Lawrence Review* 6 (1973): 333-359. Location and description of primary material with cross-references to Roberts. A guide to both primary and secondary material may be found in Mark Spilka, "Lawrence," in A. E. Dyson, ed. *The English Novel. Select Bibliographical Guides.* London: Oxford University Press, 1974, pp. 334-348. Survey and evaluation of texts, critical studies, biographies and letters, bibliographies, and background reading; also lists of titles (with date and place) arranged under these divisions.

SECONDARY

Above, McDonald; Roberts; Hepburn; Dyson.

William White. *D. H. Lawrence: A Checklist, 1931-1950.* Detroit: Wayne University Press, 1950. Pp. 46. 350 copies. Reprinted from *Bulletin of Bibliography* 19 (1948-1949): 174-177, 209-211, 235-239.

Primary; secondary selected. One chronological list. Books: place, publisher, date, pages, reviews of the book. Periods: volume, pages, date.

Maurice Beebe and Anthony Tommasi. "Criticism of D. H. Lawrence: A Selected Checklist with an Index to Studies of Separate Works," *Modern Fiction Studies* 5 (Spring, 1959): 83-98.

Arranged: General Writings, alphabetical by author. Studies of Separate Works of Fiction, alphabetical list of primary titles with studies listed under each. Books: place, publisher, date. Periods: volume, pages, date.

Richard D. Beards with G. B. Crump. "D. H. Lawrence: Ten Years of Criticism, 1959-1968: A Checklist," *D. H. Lawrence Review* 1 (1968): 245-285.

A supplement to Beebe and Tommasi (above). Arranged: General, Poetry, Studies of Individual Works of Fiction (titles alphabetically arranged), Studies of Non-Fiction Prose, Studies of the Drama. In each section, alphabetical by author. Books: place, publisher, date. Periods: volume, date, pages. Occasional brief annotations.

Supplements to this comprehensive secondary checklist appear annually in the *D. H. Lawrence Review* in the first number of each volume. Specialized checklists appear in other numbers; and the student of Lawrence should consider the bibliographical aids in the *Review* as the starting point for scholarly research. One should also note that the Annotated Secondary Bibliography Series on English Literature in Transition, Helmut E. Gerber, general editor, Northern Illinois University Press, is to include a volume on Lawrence.

GENERAL

Millett; Longaker & Bolles; Daiches; Temple & Tucker; Coleman & Tyler; Adelman & Dworkin, Palmer & Dyson; Breed & Sniderman; NCBEL, IV, 481-503; Bufkin.

LAWRENCE, FRIEDA VON RICHTHOFEN (1879-1956)

(Mrs. Ernest Weekley; *later* Mrs. D. H. Lawrence; *later* Mrs. Angelo Ravagli)

PRIMARY

Lois Hoffmann. "A Catalogue of the Frieda Lawrence Manuscripts in German at the University of Texas." *Library Chronicle of the University of Texas at Austin* NS6 (December, 1973): 87-105.

Description of the collection of letters by and to Frieda Lawrence with brief précis of contents of each.

Martin Green. *The Von Richthofen Sisters. The Triumphant and the Tragic Modes of Love. Else and Frieda von Richthofen, Otto Gross, Max Weber, and D. H. Lawrence in the years 1870-1970.* New York: Basic Books, Inc., 1974. Pp. xviii, 396.

No bibliography, but references in text, *passim,* to all of Frieda Lawrence's writings.

LAWRENCE, THOMAS EDWARD (1888-1935)

PRIMARY

T. German-Reed. *Bibliographical Notes on T. E. Lawrence's Seven Pillars of Wisdom and Revolt in the Desert.* London: W. and G. Foyle, Ltd., 1928. Pp. 16. 375 copies.

G. [Terence Ian Fytton Armstrong]. *Annotations on Some Minor Writings of 'T. E. Lawrence.'* London: Eric Partridge Ltd., 1935. Pp. 28. 500 copies.

Although less informative than Duval (below), these two books provide bibliographical details not in Duval.

Elizabeth W. Duval. *T. E. Lawrence: A Bibliography.* New York: Arrow Editions, 1938. Pp. 95. 500 copies.

Primary writings. Form arrangements. Books: transcribed TP, part collation, pagination, binding, date, all editions, reprints including foreign, notes. Includes books in which Lawrence's letters are quoted. Index.

The standard bibliography.

SECONDARY

Jeffrey Meyers. *T. E. Lawrence: A Bibliography.* New York and London: Garland Publishing, Inc., 1974. Pp. [iv], 48.

Pp. 2-7, primary bibliography. Pp. 7-48, secondary bibliography, arranged alphabetically by author. Books: place, date, relevant pages. Periods: volume, date, pages. Other bibliographies are listed on p. 1.

GENERAL

Millett; Longaker & Bolles; Daiches; Temple & Tucker; NCBEL, IV, 1181-1185.

LEAVIS, FRANK RAYMOND (1895-)

PRIMARY

Donald F. McKenzie and M. P. Allum. *Frank Raymond Leavis.*

A Check-List. 1924-1964. London: Chatto and Windus; Hamden, Connecticut: Shoe String Press, 1966. Pp. 87.

Primary complete, secondary select. Primary: chronological arrangement. Books: place, publisher, date, pages, contents; includes all editions and most subsequent impressions. Periods: volume, pages, date; reviews by Leavis include title and author of book reviewed. Pp. 57-69, secondary bibliography, arranged: Reviews; Articles; Books. Index for primary titles.

TLS, No. 3364 (18 August 1966), p. 738: severely critical of lack of information and of organization; adds important secondary bibliography entries.

SECONDARY

Above, McKenzie-Allum, pp. 57-69.

GENERAL

Millett; Daiches; Temple & Tucker; NCBEL, IV, 1070-1072.

LE CARRÉ, JOHN (1931-)

Pseudonym of David John Moore Cornwell.

Vinson-Novelists; Bufkin.

LEDWIDGE, FRANCIS (1891-1917)

PRIMARY

Henry Danielson. *Bibliographies of Modern Authors.* London: Bookman's Journal, 1921. Pp. [xii] , [212] .

Pp. 115-116, primary books. Chronological arrangement. Transcribed TP, part collation, pagination, binding, variants, miscellaneous bibliographical notes.

GENERAL

NCBEL, IV, 295-296.

LEE, LAURIE (1914-)

Daiches; Temple & Tucker; Vinson-Poets; NCBEL, IV, 296.

LEE, VERNON (1856-1935)

Pseudonym of Violet Paget.

PRIMARY

F. Elizabeth Libbey, *et al.* "Vernon Lee Papers" [at Colby Collegs] . *Colby Library Quarterly,* Third Series, 1952.

Not seen.

Carl J. Weber. "An Interim Bibliography of Vernon Lee." *Colby Library Quarterly,* Third Series, 8 (November, 1952): 123-127.

Not seen.

Peter Gunn. *Vernon Lee. Violet Paget, 1856-1935.* London: Oxford University Press, 1964. Pp. [xii] , 244.

Pp. 233-234, primary books, English first editions. Chronological arrangement. Place, publisher, date. Pp. 234-235, general secondary bibliography.

Of limited use, since the many periodical contributions are not included (some are mentioned, in passing, in the text).

GENERAL

Millett; Temple & Tucker; NCBEL, III, 1444-1446.

LEGALLIENNE, RICHARD (1866-1947)

PRIMARY

R. J. C. Lingel. *A Bibliographical Checklist of the Writings of Richard LeGallienne.* Metuchen, New Jersey: Charles F. Heartman for the Americana Collector, 1926. Pp. 95. 151 copies.

Primary books, first editions. Chronological arrangement. Transcribed TP, format, pagination, binding, occasional brief notes. Index of names and titles. Pp. 7-21, "Reminiscences by an Old Friend," by Temple Scott.

Richard Whittington-Egan and Geoffrey Smerdon. *The Quest of the Golden Boy. The Life and Letters of Richard LeGallienne.* London: The Unicorn Press, 1960. Pp. [xxiv], 580.

Pp. 553-561, "A Catalogue of the Writings of Richard LeGallienne." Primary books. Chronological arrangement. Date, place, publisher, number of copies of limited editions.

Neither of these two entries provides a list of LeGallienne's many periodical contributions, although its outlines are suggested in the text of the biography. Further unpublished primary writings (letters and a diary) are located by L. D. Jacobs, "*The Quest of the Golden Boy:* Richard LeGallienne and Some Unpublished Evidence," *English Literature in Transition* 10 (1967): 195-198.

SECONDARY

Wendell Harris and Rebecca Larsen. "Richard LeGallienne: A Bibliography of Writings about Him." *English Literature in Transition* 19 (1976):111-132.

Selected secondary bibliography, arranged alphabetically by author. Books: place, publisher, date, relevant pages. Periods: volume, date, pages. Annotated.

GENERAL

Longaker & Bolles; NCBEL, III, 1063-1064.

LEHMANN, ROSAMOND NINA (1904-)

PRIMARY

Margaret T. Gustafson. "Rosamond Lehmann: A Bibliography." *Twentieth Century Literature* 4 (1959): 143-147.

Primary, secondary selected. Genre arrangement. Books: place, publisher, date. Periods: volume, pages, date. Includes translations of primary writings.

SECONDARY

Above, Gustafson, p. 147.

Diana E. LeStourgeon. *Rosamond Lehmann.* New York: Twayne Publishers, Inc. (TEAS 16), 1965. Pp. 157.

Pp. 152-154, selected secondary bibliography. Books: place, publisher, date. Period: volume, pages, date.

GENERAL

Millett; Longaker & Bolles; Daiches; Temple & Tucker; Adelman & Dworkin (Novel); Vinson-Novelists; NCBEL, IV, 630; Bufkin.

LEHMANN, RUDOLPH JOHN FREDERICK (1907-)

Daiches; Temple & Tucker; Vinson-Poets, NCBEL, IV, 297.

LEONARD, HUGH (1926-)

Pseudonym of John Keyes Byrne.

Breed & Sniderman; Hogan; Vinson-Dramatists.

LEONARD, LIONEL FREDERICK: *see* LONSDALE, FREDERICK.

LERNER, DAVID LAURENCE (1925-)

Vinson-Poets; Vinson-Novelists.

LESLIE, SIR JOHN RANDOLPH SHANE (1885-1971)

PRIMARY

David J. Hall. "Some Uncollected Authors. XLVIII. Shane Leslie." *Book Collector* 24 (1975): 565-585.

Primary bibliography of books by, and of books edited or with prose contribution by. Books by: transcribed title page, pagination, physical form of book, size in inches, binding, date, price, printer; includes subsequent editions and references to later issues. Books with contributions: title, author or editor, place, date, pages of contribution. Bibliographical notes. See pp. 565-567 for notes on the restrictions of this list.

GENERAL

Millett; Temple & Tucker; NCBEL, IV, 1186-1187.

LESSING, DORIS (1919-)

PRIMARY

Selma R. Burkom, with Margaret Williams. *Doris Lessing. A Checklist of Primary and Secondary Sources.* Troy, N. Y.: Whitston Publishing Co., Inc., 1973. Pp. [x], 88.

Pp. [1]-30, primary bibliography. Form arrangement, including translations of the novels (alphabetical list according to country of origin). Books (all English-language first editions and translations): place, publisher, year, contents of collections, translator. Period: volume, date, pages. Pp. 33-76, secondary bibliography arranged by topic, including criticism of individual works: items listed under title of work criticized. Pp. 77-88, index of titles and names. A very useful listing of items appearing up to 1971. Later writings (through 1973), both primary and secondary, are found in Agate Nesaule Krouse. "A Doris Lessing Checklist." *Contemporary Literature* 14 (Special number on Doris Lessing) (1973), 590-597.

SECONDARY

Above, Burkom and Krouse.

GENERAL

Temple & Tucker; Breed & Sniderman; Adelman & Dworkin (Novel); Vinson-Novelists; Vinson-Dramatists; Drescher & Kahrmann; Bufkin.

LETTS, WINIFRED M. (1882-)

(Mrs. W. H. Verschoyle).

Longaker & Bolles.

LEVENSON, CHRISTOPHER (1934-)

Vinson-Poets.

LEVERSON, ADA (1862-1933)

NCBEL, IV, 630.

LEVI, PETER, S. J. (1931-)

Vinson-Poets.

LEVY, BENN WOLFE (1900-1973)

Daiches; Temple & Tucker; Salem; Breed & Sniderman; Vinson-Dramatists; NCBEL, IV, 960-961.

LEWIS, ALUN (1915-1944)

PRIMARY

John Stuart Williams. "Alun Lewis. A Select Bibliography." *Anglo-Welsh Review* 16 (Spring, 1967): 13-15.

Primary books. Chronological arrangement. Place, date, publisher. Secondary bibliography arranged Articles and Notices; Reviews.

SECONDARY

Above, Williams, pp. 14-15.

GENERAL

Longaker & Bolles; Daiches; Temple & Tucker; NCBEL, IV, 298.

LEWIS, CECIL DAY (1904-1972)

Pseudonym used: Nicholas Blake.

PRIMARY

Clifford Dyment. *Cecil Day Lewis.* London: Longmans, Green and Co. (WTW 62), 1955. Pp. 48.

Pp. 46-48, bibliography. Primary books, including books edited by Lewis and books published under his pseudonym Nicholas Blake. Chronological arrangement. Date, genre.

Geoffrey Handley-Taylor and Timothy D'Arch Smith. *C. Day-Lewis. The Poet Laureate. A Bibliography.* Chicago and London: St. James Press, 1968. Pp. xii, 42.

Primary books. Arranged: books and pamphlets by Lewis; books with contributions by Lewis; detective stories published under pseudonym Nicholas Blake. For the first two sections: transcribed TP without lineation bars, part collation, binding, date, price. For third section: date. Index. Pp. ix-x give details of omissions.

TLS, No. 3489 (9 January 1969); p. 44: [As to] "the value of the bibliography to students of Mr. Day-Lewis's work . . . it must be roundly stated that it has none." Includes additional bibliographical information and corrects errors.

SECONDARY

Joseph N. Riddel. *C. Day Lewis.* New York: Twayne Publishers, Inc. (TEAS 124), 1971. Pp. 162.

Pp. 154-158, secondary bibliography, annotated.

GENERAL

Millett; Longaker & Bolles; Temple & Tucker; Vinson-Poets; Stratford; Vinson-Novelists; NCBEL, IV, 253-256.

LEWIS, CLIVE STAPLES (1898-1963)

PRIMARY

Jocelyn Gibb, ed. *Light on C. S. Lewis.* London: Geoffrey Bles, 1965. Pp. 160.

Pp. 117-160, "A Bibliography of the Writings of C. S. Lewis," by Walter Hooper. Primary. Form and genre arrangement. Books: place, publisher, date, reprints, subsequent editions. Periods: volume, pages, date; title of volume in which collected, also revised titles. Includes reviews by Lewis with author and title of book reviewed and published letters by Lewis. Index of titles.

SECONDARY

Joe R. Christopher and Joan K. Ostling. *C. S. Lewis: An Annotated Checklist of Writings about Him and His Works.* Kent: Kent State University Press, 1974. Pp. [xiv] , [393] .

Arranged under numerous headings based on form, genre, and topic. Includes extensive list of reviews of primary books (this list adds primary titles to those given by Hooper in *Light on C. S. Lewis,* above); also lists of theses and dissertations on Lewis; indices. Books: place, publisher, date, pages. Period: volume, date, pages. Extensive annotations and cross-references.

This basic study of Lewis's critics includes all references before 1974 which the student may need, and he should not allow himself to be discouraged by the over-elaborate and sometimes baffling arrangement of the material. Another source of specialized checklists is the monthly *Bulletin* of the New York C. S. Lewis Society (1969–). Not seen.

GENERAL

Longaker & Bolles; Daiches; Temple & Tucker; NCBEL, IV, 1073-1078; Bufkin.

LEWIS, DOMINIC BEVAN WYNDHAM (1894-1969)

Temple & Tucker.

LEWIS, PERCY WYNDHAM (1884-1957)

PRIMARY

John Gawsworth [T. Fytton Armstrong] , *Apes, Japes, and Hitlerism: A Study and Bibliography of Wyndham Lewis.* London:

Unicorn Press, 1932. Pp. 100.

Pp. 83-100, bibliography. Form arrangement. Transcribed TP, full collation, pagination, binding, price, notes.

Geoffrey Wagner. *Wyndham Lewis. A Portrait of the Artist as the Enemy.* London: Routledge and Kegan Paul, 1957. Pp. 363.

Pp. 315-336, "Checklist of the Writings of Wyndham Lewis." Primary, secondary selected. Chronological arrangement, May 1909 to November 1956. Place, publisher, date, occasional notes. Some authors and titles of books reviewed by Lewis are identified; translations of Lewis include translator's name. Pp. 336-348, secondary bibliography, excluding reviews of Lewis, some of them being mentioned in text, *passim.*

Mary F. Daniels. *Wyndham Lewis, A Descriptive Catalogue of the Manuscript Material in the Department of Rare Books, Cornell University Library.* Ithaca, New York: Cornell University Library, 1972. Pp. viii, 171.

Primary MSS, documents, letters, and Lewisiana: library catalog cards for each item (pp. 1-123). Graphic materials, pp. 123-127. Pp. 128-171, alphabetical listing of other writers whose MSS and letters are in this collection.

Lewis's paintings, drawings, and watercolors are listed and illustrated in Walter Michel. *Wyndham Lewis. Paintings and Drawings.* Berkeley and Los Angeles: University of California Press; London: Thames and Hudson, 1971. Pp. 455.

SECONDARY

Above Wagner, pp. 336-348.

William H. Pritchard. *Wyndham Lewis.* New York: Twayne Publishers, Inc. (TEAS 65), 1968. Pp. 180.

Pp. 173-175, secondary bibliography. Alphabetical-by-author arrangement. Annotated.

GENERAL

Millett; Longaker & Bolles; Daiches; Temple & Tucker; NCBEL, IV, 631-634; Bufkin.

LIDDELL, JOHN ROBERT (1908-)

Temple & Tucker; Vinson-Novelists.

LINDSAY, DAVID (1876-1945)

NCBEL, IV, 634-635.

LINDSAY, JACK (1900-)

Vinson-Novelists; Drescher & Kahrmann; NCBEL, IV, 635-636.

LINDSAY, JOHN MAURICE (1918-)

Vinson-Poets.

LINDSAY, NORMAN ALFRED WILLIAM (1879-1969)

PRIMARY

George MacKaness. "Collecting Norman Lindsay." *American Book Collector* 7 (1956): i, 15-20; ii, 22-27; iii, 17-20.

Discursive essay mentioning many primary books, usually with place, publisher, format, binding, original and current prices. Much miscellaneous bibliographical information, including mention of secondary bibliography.

John Hetherington. *Norman Lindsay.* Melbourne: Lansdowne Press (AWTW), 1962. Pp. 48.

Pp. 47-48, primary books. Genre arrangement. Place, publisher, date. Includes selected secondary bibliography.

Harry F. Chaplin. *Norman Lindsay. His books, manuscripts and autograph letters in the library of, and annotated by, Harry F. Chaplin.* Sydney: Wentworth Press, 1969. Pp. vi, 90. Reproduced from typescript.

A checklist of primary material with extensive bibliographical annotations.

Together MacKaness, Hetherington, and Chaplin provide a fairly complete bibliography.

SECONDARY

Above, MacKaness and Hetherington.

LINKLATER, ERIC ROBERT RUSSELL (1899-1974)

PRIMARY

William Russell Aitken. "Eric Linklater (b. 1899): a checklist of his books." *Bibliotheck* (Glasgow) 5, vi. (1969): 190-197.

Primary books. Chronological arrangement. Publisher, date. Miscellaneous notes.

GENERAL

Daiches; Temple & Tucker; Vinson-Novelists; NCBEL, IV, 636-638, 806; Bufkin.

LITVINOFF, EMANUEL (1915-)

Vinson-Novelists.

LIVINGS, HENRY (1929-)

Breed & Sniderman; Vinson-Dramatists; Temple & Tucker.

LLEWELYN, RICHARD (?1907-)

Pseundonym of Richard Dafydd Vivian Llewellyn Lloyd.

NCBEL, IV, 638; Bufkin.

LLOYD, RICHARD DAFYDD VIVIAN: *see* LLEWELYN, RICHARD.

LOCKE, WILLIAM JOHN (1863-1930)

PRIMARY

Henry Danielson. "Bibliographies of Modern Authors. XVI. William J. Locke." *Bookman's Journal* 3 (1920-1921): 162, 183, 192, 214, 228, 245, 274, 286.

Primary books and pamphlets, 1895-1921. Chronological arrangement. Transcribed TP, part collation, pagination, binding, variants, bibliographical notes.

GENERAL

NCBEL, IV, 638-639

LODGE, DAVID (1935-)

Vinson-Novelists; Drescher & Kahrmann.

LOGUE, CHRISTOPHER (1926-)

Temple & Tucker; Vinson-Poets.

LONG, GABRIELLE MARGARET VERE CAMPBELL (1885-1952)

Pseudonyms used: Joseph Shearing, Marjorie Bowen, Robert Paye, George R. Preedy, John Winch.

PRIMARY

Edward Wagenknecht. "Bowen, Preedy, Shearing & Co., A Note in Memory and a Check List." *Boston University Studies in English* 3 (1957): 181-189.

Pp. 186-189, check list of approximately 150 books: date, publisher; nom de plume under which published.

GENERAL

NCBEL, IV, 535-538.

LONGLEY, MICHAEL (1939-)

Vinson-Poets.

LONSDALE, FREDERICK (1881-1954)

Pseudonym of Lionel Frederick Leonard.

PRIMARY

Frances Donaldson. *Freddy Lonsdale.* London: William Heinemann Ltd., 1957. Pp. 257.

Pp. 247-249, bibliography, primary plays. Chronological arrangement. Date of first performance, theatre, number of performances. No information concerning publication.

GENERAL

Millett; Longaker & Bolles; Temple & Tucker; Salem; Breed & Sniderman; NCBEL, IV, 961-962.

LOWBURY, EDWARD JOSEPH LISTER (1913-)

Vinson-Poets.

LOWNDES, MARIE ADELAIDE BELLOC (1868-1947)

NCBEL, IV, 639-640.

LUBBOCK, PERCY (1879-1965)

Millett; Daiches; Temple & Tucker; NCBEL, IV, 1079.

LUCAS, EDWARD VERRALL (1868-1938)

PRIMARY

Audrey Lucas. *E. V. Lucas: A Portrait.* London: Methuen and Co., Ltd., 1939. Pp. xiii, 159.

Pp. 158-159, primary books. Topical arrangement includes "Miscellaneous" and "Books Edited by Lucas." Titles only.

GENERAL

Millett; Longaker & Bolles; Batho & Dobrée; Temple & Tucker; NCBEL, III, 1099; NCBEL, IV, 1079-1080.

LUCAS, FRANK LAURENCE (1894-1967)

Millett; Daiches; Temple & Tucker; Breed & Sniderman; NCBEL, IV, 1082-1083.

LUCIE-SMITH, JOHN EDWARD MCKENZIE (1933-)

Vinson-Poets; Stratford.

LYLE, ROB (1920-)

Temple & Tucker.

LYND, ROBERT WILSON (1879-1949)

Millett; Longaker & Bolles; Temple & Tucker; NCBEL, IV, 1083-1084.

LYNNE, JAMES BROOM (1920-)

Pseudonym used: James Quartermain.

Vinson-Dramatists.

LYON, LILIAN HELEN BOWES (1895-1949)

Longaker & Bolles; Temple & Tucker; NCBEL, IV, 241.

MACAULAY, DAME EMILIE ROSE (1881-1958)

PRIMARY

Alice R. Bensen. *Rose Macaulay.* New York: Twayne Publishers, Inc. (TEAS 85), 1969. Pp. 184.

Pp. 175-176, primary books. Genre arrangement. British and American first editions. Place, publisher, date. Pp. 177-178, secondary bibliography, selected. Alphabetical by author arrangement, annotated. Also see text, *passim,* and notes for an additional 78 reviews of Dame Rose's books.

A basic checklist; there is no published list of the extensive journalism and periodical contributions.

SECONDARY

Above, Bensen, pp. 177-178, also notes and text.

"Rose Macaulay." *English Fiction* (later *English Literature*) *in Transition* 3, i (1960): 31; 3, ii (1960): 51; 4, i (1961): 25; 5, i (1962): 44; 6, i (1963): 52; 6, ii (1963): 108; 6 (1963): 235; 8 (1965): 119-121.

This continuing list of secondary studies, annotated, provides the most up-to-date account of studies of Dame Rose.

GENERAL

Millett; Longaker & Bolles; Daiches; Temple & Tucker; NCBEL, IV, 642-643; Bufkin.

MACBETH, GEORGE MANN (1932-)

Vinson-Poets; Stratford; Temple & Tucker.

MACCAIG, NORMAN ALEXANDER (1910-)

Daiches; Temple & Tucker; Vinson-Poets; NCBEL, IV, 298-299.

MCCARTHY, SIR DESMOND (1878-1952)

Millett; Daiches; Temple & Tucker; NCBEL, IV, 1084-1085.

MCCRACKEN, ESTHER HELEN (1902-1971)

NCBEL, IV, 962-963.

MACDIARMID, HUGH (1892-)

Pseudonym of Christopher Murray Grieve.

PRIMARY

William R. Aitken. "A Check List of Books and Periodicals–Written, Translated, Edited, Published, or Introduced by Christopher Murray Grieve (Hugh MacDiarmid)" in K. D. Duval and Sydney Goodsir Smith, eds. *Hugh MacDiarmid, A Festschrift.* Edinburgh: K. D. Duval, 1962. Pp. 221.

Pp. 213-221, "Check List." Primary. Chronological arrangement, with "Books introduced by Grieve" and "Periodicals edited by Grieve" in separate lists. Books: place, publisher, date, binding, bibliographical notes, reprints, illustrator: information varies with each entry. Periods: volume, pages, date.

Duncan Glenn. *Hugh MacDiarmid (Christopher Murray Grieve) and the Scottish Renaissance.* Edinburgh and London: W. and R. Chambers Ltd., 1964. Pp. x, 294.

Pp. 245-280, bibliography. Primary, secondary selected. Form and genre arrangement. Books: place, publisher, date, reprints, subsequent editions. Periods: volume, pages, date. Includes list of anthologies with contributions by Grieve. Pp. 256-257, also in text, *passim,* selected, uncollected prose contributions to periodicals. Pp. 263-280, secondary bibliography, including association material.

Glenn includes more titles than Aitken, while giving less information about individual titles. Together they provide fairly complete lists, with Aitken adding later items in the following:

William Russell Aitken. "Hugh MacDiarmid, (Christopher Murray Grieve, b. 1892): a second checklist." *Bibliotheck* (Glasgow) 5, vii-viii (1970): 253-263.

Primary books, secondary books. Additions to Aitken's list above. Chronological arrangement. Place, publisher, date. Miscellaneous notes.

William Russell Aitkin, "A Hugh MacDiarmid Bibliography," in *Hugh MacDiarmid: A Critical Survey,* ed. Duncan Glen. Edinburgh and London: Scottish Academic Press, 1972. Pp. [x], 241.

Pp. 228-241, primary books, all editions. Place, publisher, date, limitations of issue, place of original publication and of reprinting; miscellaneous bibliographical information. Important facts about the problems associated with MacDiarmid's bibliography are noted by Aitken, pp. 228-230.

SECONDARY

Above, Glenn, pp. 263-280; Aitken (1970).

William Russell Aitken. "C. M. Grieve/Hugh MacDiarmid." *Bibliotheck* (Glasgow) 1, iv (1958): 15-23.

Chronological arrangement of selected items.

Kenneth Buthlay. *Hugh MacDiarmid* (*Christopher Murray Grieve*). Edinburgh: Oliver and Boyd (Writers and Critics Series), 1964: Pp. 125.

P. 125, secondary bibliography.

GENERAL

Longaker & Bolles; Daiches; Temple & Tucker; Vinson-Poets; NCBEL, IV, 299-302.

MACDONAGH, DONAGH (1912-1968)

Breed & Sniderman; Hogan; NCBEL, IV, 963.

MAC DONAGH, THOMAS (1878-1916)

PRIMARY

Patrick Sarsfield O'Hegarty. "Bibliographies of 1916 and the Irish Revolution. No. 2. Thomas Mac Donagh." *Dublin Magazine* 7 (January-March, 1932): 26-29. (Also issued as a pamphlet).

Primary books. Chronological arrangement. Transcribed TP, part collation, pagination, binding, variant bindings, bibliographical notes.

Edd Winfield Parks and Aileen Wells Parks. *Thomas Mac Donagh. The Man, The Patriot, The Writer.* Athens: University of Georgia Press, 1967. Pp. xiv, 151.

Pp. 139-141, primary bibliography. Form arrangement. Books: place, publisher, year. Periods: volume, pages, date; reviews by Mac Donagh include title and author of book reviewed. Locates MSS.

O'Hegarty gives bibliographical details, and the Parks, inclusive lists; together they provide an ample bibliography.

SECONDARY

Above, Parks-Parks, pp. 142-145.

GENERAL

NCBEL, IV, 302-303.

MACDONELL, ARCHIBALD GORDON (1895-1941)

NCBEL, IV, 643.

MACDOUGALL, ROGER (1910-)

Temple & Tucker; NCBEL, IV, 963-964.

MCEVOY, CHARLES ALBERT (1879-1929)

Millett; NCBEL, IV, 964.

MCFADDEN, ROY (1921-)

Vinson-Poets.

MCFEE, WILLIAM (1881-1966)

PRIMARY

James T. Babb. *A Bibliography of the Writings of William McFee with an Introduction and Notes by William McFee.* Garden City, New York: Doubleday, Doran and Co., Inc., 1931. Pp. [xxvi], [127]. 360 copies.

Primary, secondary selected. Form arrangement. Books: transcribed TP, part collation, pagination, binding, date, number of copies, price, variants, reprints or subsequent editions, bibliographical notes. For each title, note by McFee concerning composition and publication. Periods: date (includes only uncollected writings). Pp. 109-112, secondary bibliography, excluding reviews. Index.

Book Collector's Quarterly, No. 8 (December, 1932), p. 60: "Comprehensive and excellent study."

Harold Sinclair. "William McFee: A Checklist Bibliography." *Reading and Collecting,* 1, vi (May, 1937): 6.

Primary books, including books with contributions by McFee. Place, date, binding, notes. Information additional to Babb.

SECONDARY

Above, Babb, pp. 109-112.

GENERAL

Longaker & Bolles; NCBEL, IV, 643-644.

MCGOUGH, ROGER (1937-)

Vinson-Poets.

MACHEN, ARTHUR LLEWELYN JONES (1863-1947)

PRIMARY

Henry Danielson. *Arthur Machen. A Bibliography with Notes by Arthur Machen.* London: Henry Danielson, 1923. Pp. 59. 500 copies. Reprinted Ann Arbor, Michigan: Plutarch Press, 1971.

Primary books. Chronological arrangement. Transcribed TP, part collation, pagination, binding, illustrator, full bibliographical notes.

Information additional to that in Goldstone and Sweetser (below).

Adrian Goldstone and Wesley Sweetser. *A Bibliography of Arthur Machen.* Austin: University of Texas Press, 1965. Pp. 180. 500 copies.

Primary, secondary. Form arrangement. Books: transcribed TP, part collation, binding, date, price, contents with account of previous publication for each, later editions, notes. Pp. 68-73, translations by Machen. Pp. 86-144, Machen's periodical contributions, listed under alphabetically arranged periodical titles: volume, pages, date.

S. A. Reynolds, *Book Collector* 15 (1966): 229-230: "Much less entertaining but far more informative [than Danielson's bibliography] . . . a really useful bibliography."

SECONDARY

Above, Goldstone-Sweetser, pp. 146-164.

Wesley Sweetser. "Arthur Machen. A Bibliography of Writings about Him." *English Literature in Transition* 11 (1968): 1-33.

Annotated. Mainly post-1965 additions to Goldstone and Sweetser. Continued in later issues.

GENERAL

Millett; Batho & Dobrée; Temple & Tucker; NCBEL, IV, 644-648.

MACINNES, COLIN (1914-)

Temple & Tucker; Vinson-Novelists; Drescher & Kahrmann; Bufkin.

MACINTYRE, JOHN (1869-1947)

Pseudonym used: John Brandane.

NCBEL, IV, 913-914.

MACKAIL, DENNIS GEORGE (1892-1971)

NCBEL, IV, 648-649.

MCKENNA, STEPHEN (1888-1967)

Daiches; NCBEL, IV, 649-650.

MACKENZIE, SIR EDWARD MONTAGUE COMPTON (1883-1972)

PRIMARY

Henry Danielson. *Bibliographies of Modern Authors.* London: Bookman's Journal, 1921. Pp. [xii] , [212] .

Pp. 119-124, primary books, 1907-1921. Chronological arrangement. Transcribed TP, part collation, pagination, binding, variants, miscellaneous bibliographical notes.

Kenneth Young. *Compton MacKenzie.* London: Longmans, Green and Co. (WTW 202), 1968. Pp. 32.

Pp. 29-32, primary books. Chronological arrangement. Date, genre. Includes list of "Children's Short Stories." P. 32, secondary bibliography (12 entries).

P. 29: "A bibliography . . . is being prepared by Mr. Eugene Edge III for the University of Texas. The University has most of Sir Compton's manuscripts."

SECONDARY

Above, Young, p. 32.

Helmut Gerber. "Compton MacKenzie." *English Fiction in Transition* 1 (Winter, 1957): 29-30.

D. J. Dooley. *Compton MacKenzie.* New York: Twayne Publishers, Inc. (TEAS 173), 1974. Pp. 171.

Pp. 161-162, selected primary books. Chronologically arranged under Novels and Other Prose. First British editions only. Place, publisher, date. Pp. 163-165, selected secondary bibliography, annotated. Additional critical material is given in the notes, pp. 148-160.

GENERAL

Millett; Longaker & Bolles; Daiches; Temple & Tucker; Vinson-Novelists; NCBEL, IV, 650-652; Bufkin.

MACKENZIE, RONALD (1903-1932)

NCBEL, IV, 964.

MACKINTOSH, ELIZABETH (1896-1952)

Pseudonym used: Gordon Daviot.

NCBEL, IV, 930-931.

MACLEOD, JOSEPH TODD GORDON (1903-)

Pseudonym used: Adam Drinan.

Vinson-Poets.

MACLIAMMÓIR, MICHÉAL (1899-)

Breed & Sniderman; Hogan; NCBEL, IV, 964-965.

MACMAHON, BRYAN (1909-)

PRIMARY

Joanne L. Henderson. "Checklist of Four Kerry Writers: . . . Bryan MacMahon (1909-). . ." *Journal of Irish Literature* 1 (May 1972): 112-118.

Primary, secondary. Form arrangement. Books: place, publisher, date; all English language editions; reviews of each book. Periods: volume, date, pages.

GENERAL

Hogan.

MCMANUS, CHARLOTTE ELIZABETH (1853-1944)

PRIMARY

Patrick Sarsfield O'Hegarty. "L. McManus. Obituary." *Dublin Magazine* 20 (January-March, 1945): 68.

Primary books listed in text. Publisher, year, occasionally brief annotations.

MACMULLAN, CHARLES WALDEN KIRKPATRICK: *see* MUNRO, CHARLES KIRKPATRICK.

MACNAMARA, BRINSLEY: *see* WELDON, JOHN.

MACNEICE, LOUIS (1907-1963)

PRIMARY

C. M. Armitage and Neil Clark. *A Bibliography of the Works of Louis MacNeice.* London: Kaye and Ward (Second edition), 1974. Pp. 136.

Primary complete, secondary selected. Form arrangement, including lists of manuscript collections, of BBC radio scripts, of gramophone recordings of MacNeice's poems, and an index of poems arranged alphabetically by title. Books: transcribed TP, full collation, full pagination, binding, date, price, number of copies, contents, notes on subsequent impressions and reprints, other bibliographical notes. Periods: date, pages, some reviews include title and author of book reviewed. Pp. 83-101, secondary bibliography, chronologically arranged.

The standard bibliography. Armitage contributed an abbreviated handlist of the forty primary books to Terence Brown and Alec Reid, editors. *Time Was Away. The World of Louis MacNeice.* Dublin: Dolmen Press, 1974, pp. 131-139, for which volume R. D. Smith compiled a chronological list of primary "Radio Scripts 1941-1963," pp. 141-148. Additional information, including reviews of primary books, is given by William T. McKinnon. "Louis MacNeice: A Bibliography." *Bulletin of Bibliography* 27 (1970): 51-52, 48, 79-84. An abbreviated version of this bibliography is included in McKinnon's *Apollo's Blended Dream. A Study of the Poetry of Louis MacNeice.* New York: Oxford University Press, 1971.

SECONDARY

Above, Armitage-Clark, pp. 83-101; McKinnon, pp. 80-82.

Elton Edward Smith. *Louis MacNeice.* New York: Twayne Publishers Inc. (TEAS 99), 1970. Pp. 232.

Pp. 218-224, secondary bibliography, annotated; additional entries in notes, pp. 207-213.

GENERAL

Longaker & Bolles; Daiches; Temple & Tucker; Coleman & Tyler; Breed & Sniderman; Vinson-Poets; NCBEL, IV, 303-305.

MCNEILE, HERMAN CYRIL: *see* SAPPER.

MACSWEENEY, BARRY (1948-)

Vinson-Poets.

MAC SWINEY, TERENCE JOSEPH (1879-1920)

PRIMARY

Patrick Sarsfield O'Hegarty. "Bibliographies of 1916 and the Irish Revolution. X. Terence Mac Swiney." *Dublin Magazine* 11 (October-December, 1936): 74-76.

Primary books. Chronological arrangement. Transcribed TP, part collation, pagination, binding, bibliographical and occasionally biographical notes.

MADGE, CHARLES HENRY (1912-)

Daiches; Temple & Tucker; Breed & Sniderman; Vinson-Poets; NCBEL, IV, 305-306.

MAGEE, WILLIAM KIRKPATRICK: *see* EGLINTON, JOHN.

MAHON, DEREK (1941-)

Vinson-Poets.

MALET, LUCAS (1852-1931)

Pseudonym of Mary St. Leger Kingsley (later Mrs. William Harrison).

NCBEL, III, 1066.

MALLESON, WILLIAM MILES (1888-1969)

Breed & Sniderman; NCBEL, IV, 966-967.

MALLOCK, WILLIAM HURRELL (1849-1923)

PRIMARY

Charles C. Nickerson. "A Bibliography of the Novels of W. H. Mallock." *English Literature in Transition* 6 (1963): 190-198.

Primary books. Chronological arrangement. Transcribed TP, full collation, pagination, binding, date, price, full notes. Brief account of subsequent editions.

GENERAL

NCBEL, III, 1066-1067.

MANKOWITZ, WOLF (1924-)

Vinson-Novelists; Vinson-Dramatists.

MANNING, FREDERIC (1882-1935)

NCBEL, IV, 652.

MANNING, OLIVIA ( )

(Mrs. R. D. Smith).

Daiches; Temple & Tucker; Adelman & Dworkin (Novel); Stratford; Vinson-Novelists; NCBEL, IV, 653; Bufkin.

MANSFIELD, KATHERINE (1888-1923)

Pseudonym of Kathleen Mansfield Beauchamp (later Mrs. J. Middleton Murry).

PRIMARY

Ruth Elvish Mantz. *The Critical Bibliography of Katherine Mansfield.* Introduction by J. M. Murry. London: Constable and Co., Ltd., 1931. Pp. xx, 204. 1000 copies.

Primary (pp. 27-105); secondary complete. Form arrangement. Books: transcribed TP, full collation, pagination, binding, date, price, subsequent editions and reprints (no descriptions of these). Contents listed with full account of previous publications. Periods: volume, pages, date. Includes uncollected periodical contributions; also lists periodicals to which Mansfield contributed. Secondary bibliography arranged under title of primary work studied. Various prefaces, biographical notes, appendices.

P. H. Muir, *Book Collector's Quarterly,* No. 5 (January-March, 1932), pp. 89-91; praise for the bibliography, which "almost serves as a model of its kind."

Mary Louise Bardas. "The State of Scholarship on Katherine Mansfield, 1950-1970." *World Literature Written in English* 11 (1972): 77-93.

Primary and secondary bibliography. Arranged: Bibliographies; Primary Editions (all editions: place, publisher, date, selected reviews, critical annotations); Secondary Bibliography, pp. 83-93, arranged Books; Theses; Articles (volume, date, pages).

A valuable supplement and correction to Mantz; very important comments on textual validity of the different primary editions.

SECONDARY

Above, Bardas, pp. 80-81, 83-93, and especially p. 79 for list of bibliographies providing material not included in Bardas.

Jeffrey Meyers. "Katherine Mansfield: A Bibliography of International Criticism, 1921-1977." *Bulletin of Bibliography* 34 (1977): 53-67.

Alphabetical by author. Books: place, date relevant pages. Periods: volume, date, pages. Includes over 635 books and articles.

GENERAL

Millett; Longaker & Bolles; Daiches; Temple & Tucker; NCBEL, IV, 653-659.

MARCUS, FRANK (1928-)

Vinson-Dramatists.

MARKIEVICZ, CONSTANCE GORE-BOOTH, COUNTESS DE (1868-1927)

PRIMARY

Patrick Sarsfield O'Hegarty. "Bibliographies of 1916 and the

Irish Revolution. VIII. Constance Gore-Booth, Countess de Markievicz." *Dublin Magazine* 11 (July-September, 1936): 57-59.

Primary books. Chronological arrangement. Transcribed TP, part collation, pagination, binding, bibliographical notes.

Jacqueline Van Voris. *Constance de Markievicz in the Cause of Ireland.* Amherst: University of Massachusetts Press, 1967. Pp. 384.

Pp. 361-363, primary bibliography. Chronological arrangement. Includes periodical contributions and unpublished writings. Dates for each item. A much more comprehensive listing than that in O'Hegarty, above.

SECONDARY

Above, Voris, pp. 353-361.

Ann Marreco. *The Rebel Countess. The Life and Times of Constance Markievicz.* London: Weidenfeld and Nicolson; Philadelphia: Chilton Books, 1967. Pp. [xiv], 330. Reprinted London: Corgi Books, 1969. Pp. 319.

[Philadelphia edition] Pp. 307-309, general bibliography: books only: author, title, date, place. Pp. 311-317, notes with specific references to secondary sources. Index.

MARLOW, LOUIS (1881-1966)

Pseudonym of Louis Umfreville Wilkinson.

NCBEL, IV, 659.

MARRIOTT, CHARLES (1869-1957)

Temple & Tucker.

MARSH, SIR EDWARD HOWARD (1872-1953)

PRIMARY

Christopher Hassall. Edward Marsh. *Patron of the Arts. A Biography.* London: Longmans. Pp. 732.

No bibliography. Index. The beginning point of bibliographical study of Marsh.

See above, BROOKE, RUPERT: John Schroder. *A Catalogue of Books and Manuscripts by Rupert Brooke, Edward Marsh and Christopher Hassall;* and HASSALL, CHRISTOPHER: *Ambrosia and Small Beer. The Record of a Correspondence between Edward Marsh and Christopher Hassall,* for additional bibliographical information.

GENERAL

Temple & Tucker.

MARSHALL, ARCHIBALD (1866-1934)

PRIMARY

"Bibliographies of Modern Authors: Archibald Marshall." *London Mercury* 2 (1920): 741.

Primary books, 1899-1920. Chronological arrangement. Publisher, year.

MARSHALL, BRUCE (1899-)

Vinson-Novelists.

MARTIN, VIOLET FLORENCE (1862-1915)

See: SOMERVILLE, EDITH ANNA ŒNONE.

MARTYN, EDWARD JOSEPH (1859-1923)

PRIMARY

Courtney, Sister Marie-Thérèse. *Edward Martyn and the Irish Theatre.* New York: Vantage Press, 1956. Pp. [ii], 188.

Pp. 172-173, primary bibliography. Genre arrangement. Books: place, publisher, date, pages. Periods: date. P. 170, first productions of plays. Secondary bibliography and other bibliographical information, pp. 152-166, 173-188.

SECONDARY

Above, Courtney.

GENERAL

Coleman & Tyler; Adelman & Dworkin; NCBEL, III, 1939; Breed & Sniderman.

MASEFIELD, JOHN EDWARD (1878-1967)

PRIMARY

Charles H. Simmons. *A Bibliography of John Masefield.* New York: Columbia University Press; London: Oxford University Press, 1930. Pp. xii, [1 leaf], 171. 800 copies.

Primary first editions, secondary selected. Form arrangement. Transcribed TP, full collation, binding, pagination, date, number of copies; contents with place and date of previous publication. Textual and bibliographical notes. Uncollected contributions to books and periodicals arranged alphabetically by titles. Books: transcribed TP, date, size, pages. Periods: place, date. Pp. 141-142, list of earlier bibliographies providing information not given in Simmons. Index of titles and names.

Drew (below), p. 188: "accurate, extensive, and attractively organized and presented."

Fraser Bragg Drew. "Some Contributions to the Bibliography of John Masefield." *Papers of the Bibliographical Society of America* 53 (1959): 188-196, 262-267.

Pp. 188-196; list of 318 book reviews by Masefield in the *Manchester Guardian:* date, title of review. Pp. 262-267: corrections and additions to Simmons.

Geoffrey Handley-Taylor. *John Masefield, O. M. The Queen's Poet Laureate. A Bibliography and Eighty-First Birthday Tribute.* London: Cranbrook Tower Press, 1960. Pp. 96.

Primary books, secondary books. Chronological arrangement for primary material; alphabetical for secondary. Primary books: date, place, publisher, number of copies, partial account of subsequent editions and reprints; miscellaneous notes. Pp. 19-24, brief account of seven collections of primary writings.

SECONDARY

Above, Simmons, pp. 141-153; Handley-Taylor, pp. 71-73.

Clarence E. Sherman. "John Masefield. A Contribution toward a Bibliography." *Bulletin of Bibliography* 8 (1915): 158-160.

Includes many early periodical reviews of Masefield.

GENERAL

Millet; Longaker & Bolles; Batho & Dobrée; Daiches; Temple & Tucker; Coleman & Tyler; Salem; Breed & Sniderman; NCBEL, IV, 306-313; Bufkin.

MASON, ALFRED EDWARD WOODLEY (1865-1948)

PRIMARY

Roger Lancelyn Green. *A. E. W. Mason.* London: Max Parrish, 1952. Pp. 272.

Pp. 267-268, primary bibliography. Genre and form arrangement. Dates. Additional items are suggested in text, *passim.*

GENERAL

Temple & Tucker; NCBEL, IV, 660-661.

MASSINGHAM, HAROLD WILLIAM (1932-)

Vinson-Poets.

MASTERS, JOHN (1914-)

Temple & Tucker; Vinson-Novelists.

MATHIAS, ROLAND GLYN (1915-)

Vinson-Poets.

MAUGHAM, ROBIN CECIL ROMER, LORD MAUGHAM (1916-)

PRIMARY

Robin Maugham. *Escape from the Shadows. An Autobiography.* New York: McGraw-Hill Book Co., 1973. Pp. [xiv], 273.

Pp. 239-245, "Select Bibliography of Robin Maugham's Work," by Peter Burton. Genre arrangement. Books: place, publisher, and date of all editions and translations. Occasional bibliographical notes. There are references here and in the text to the periodicals to which Maugham contributed; also list of eight series of periodical articles and list of film scripts by Maugham with name of owner of script.

GENERAL

Vinson-Novelists.

MAUGHAM, WILLIAM SOMERSET (1874-1965)

PRIMARY

Raymond Mander and Joe Mitchenson, *Theatrical Companion to Maugham.* London: Rockliff, 1955. Pp. [xii], [308].

Pp. 299-302, published plays: titles, place, publisher, date. Important details of performances, *passim.*

J. Terry Bender. *A Comprehensive Exhibition of the Writings of W. S. Maugham.* [May-August, 1958]. Stanford: Stanford University Library, 1958. 1000 copies.

Pages unnumbered. Includes important association material, locates MSS, and provides additions to Stott (below).

W. H. Henry, Jr. *A French Bibliography of W. S. Maugham. A List of his works published in France, his contributions to French periodicals, the Swiss, Belgian, and French criticism of his books, plays, and films.* Charlottesville: Bibliographical Society of the University of Virginia, 1967. Pp. [viii], 133.

Primary and secondary bibliography, providing complete bibliographical information for all aspects of French criticism and appreciation of Maugham. Note Table of Contents, pp. v-vii, and Index of Names and Titles, pp. 127-133.

Raymond Toole Stott. *A Bibliography of the Works of W. Somerset Maugham.* London: Kaye and Ward, 1973 (revised and extended edition). Pp. 320.

Primary first editions. Form arrangement, including Plays novelised or Books Dramatised by Others. Transcribed TP, full collation, pagination, binding, date, number of copies, descriptions of selected later editions and issues; extensive bibliographical notes. Periods: chronological arrangement: dates, notes including details of reprinting in other periodicals or in book form and changes of titles. Index of titles. Appendices, pp. [266]-315, include locations of manuscripts and letters with summaries of contents and bibliographical descriptions; a list of unpublished plays by Maugham; and a list of unpublished plays adapted by other writers. Selected secondary bibliography arranged chronologically under Books (pp. 222-247) and Periodicals (pp. 250-264) including important comments on these critics.

The standard bibliography.

See below, Sanders, pp. 3-8.

SECONDARY

See above, Mander and Mitchenson, *passim;* Stott, pp. 222-264; Bender, *passim;* Henry, *passim.*

Charles Sanders, ed. *W. S. Maugham An Annotated Bibliography of Writings about Him.* DeKalb, Illinois: Northern Illinois University Press, 1970. Pp. x, 436.

Pp. 3-8, primary books. Genre arrangement. Place and date of British and American editions, contents of collections. Pp. 14-381, secondary bibliography. Chronological arrangement. Books: place, publisher, date. Periods: volume, pages, date. Précis of each of the 2355 entries (1897-1968). Indices of authors, of titles of secondary works, of periodicals and newspapers, of foreign languages, and of primary titles. Includes (especially pp. v-viii) references to earlier primary and secondary bibliographies that list additional material.

The beginning point for locating studies and reviews of Maugham. Supplementary items are listed by Sanders in *English Literature in Transition* 15 (1972): 168-173.

Edward Halim Mikhail. "Somerset Maugham and the Theatre." *Bulletin of Bibliography* 27 (1970): 42-48.

Arranged: Bibliographies, Books, Periodicals, Reviews, Unpublished Material. Alphabetical by author or title in each section. Books: place, publisher, date. Periods: volume, pages, date.

The selectivity and arrangement of this specialized checklist make it a valuable addition to Sanders.

GENERAL

Millett; Longaker & Bolles; Daiches; Temple & Tucker; Coleman & Tyler; Adelman & Dworkin; Salem; Palmer & Dyson; Breed & Sniderman; NCBEL, IV, 661-668; Bufkin.

MAVOR, OSBORNE HENRY: *see* BRIDIE, JAMES.

MAXWELL, WILLIAM BABINGTON (1866-1938)

NCBEL, IV, 668-669.

MAYNE, ETHEL COLBURN (187?-1941)

Millett; Daiches; NCBEL, IV, 669.

MAYNE, RUTHERFORD (1878-)

Pseudonym of Samuel Waddell.

NCBEL, III, 1941; Breed & Sniderman; Hogan.

MEAD, MATTHEW (1924-)

Vinson-Poets.

MENEN, SALVATOR AUBREY CLARENCE (1912-)

Temple & Tucker; Vinson-Novelists; Bufkin.

MERCER, CECIL WILLIAM: *see* YATES, DORNFORD.

MERCER, DAVID (1928-)

Vinson-Dramatists.

MERRICK, LEONARD (1864-1938)

PRIMARY

Henry Danielson. *Bibliographies of Modern Authors.* London: Bookman's Journal, 1921. Pp. [xii] , [212] .

Pp. 159-166, primary books. Chronological arrangement. Transcribed TP, part collation, pagination, binding, variants, miscellaneous bibliographical notes.

The Works of Leonard Merrick. London: Hodder and Stoughton, 1918-1922. 14 volumes.

A fairly complete collection, each volume having a critical introduction by various authors.

SECONDARY

"Leonard Merrick." *English Fiction in Transition* 1, i (1957): 32; 1, ii (1958): 33; 3, i (1960): 32.

Miscellaneous references to secondary writings.

GENERAL

Millett; Batho & Dobrée; NCBEL, III, 1068-1069.

MEW, CHARLOTTE MARY (1870-1928)

PRIMARY

Charlotte Mew. *Collected Poems,* ed. Alida Monro. London: Gerald Duckworth and Co., Ltd., 1953. Pp. 80.

No bibliography, but the biographical memoir by Monro provides bibliographical information and suggestions.

T. E. M. Boll. "The Mystery of Charlotte Mew and May Sinclair: An Inquiry." *Bulletin of the New York Public Library* 74 (1970): 445-453.

An important essay on Mew, indicating sources of both primary and secondary writings, and explaining some of the covert references in Monro's memoir (above).

GENERAL

Millett; Longaker & Bolles; Daiches; Temple & Tucker; Stratford; NCBEL, IV, 313.

MEYERSTEIN, EDWARD HARRY WILLIAM (1889-1952)

PRIMARY

E. H. W. Meyerstein. Poet and Novelist. A Bibliography. Bristol: Bristol Public Libraries, 1938. One printed sheet, folded.

Primary books. Genre arrangement. Title, date, publisher.

E. H. W. Meyerstein. *Some Poems,* ed. Maurice Wollman. London: Neville Spearman, 1960. Pp. 168.

Pp. 167-168, chronological list of primary books. Arranged: lyrical poetry; narrative and dramatic poetry; translations. Title, year.

GENERAL

Temple & Tucker.

MEYNELL, ALICE CHRISTIANA THOMPSON (1847-1922)

(Mrs. Wilfrid Meynell).

PRIMARY

C. A. and H. W. Stonehill. *Bibliographies of Modern Authors* (Second Series). London: John Castle, 1925. Pp. [xiv], 162. 750 copies.

Pp. 79-125, primary bibliography. Form arrangement (but mainly books). Transcribed TP, full collation, pagination, binding, price, number of copies, variants, notes.

Anne Kimball Tuell. *Mrs. Meynell and Her Literary Generation.* New York: E. P. Dutton and Co., 1925. Pp. 286.

Pp. 259-271, "Bibliographical Notes." Primary selected. Form and genre arrangement. Place, publisher, date. Essays in collections listed with date and place of original publication. Includes short list of essays not reprinted. Limitations of the bibliography described, p. 259.

Sir Francis Meynell. Alice Meynell, 1847-1922. *Catalogue of the Centenary Exhibition.* London: National Book League, [1947]. Pp. 45.

Includes books, MSS, letters, portraits. Information varies; generally for books: place, publisher, date.

Terence L. Connolly, S. J. ed. *Alice Meynell Centenary Tribute.* Boston: Bruce Humphries, Inc., 1948. Pp. 72.

Pp. 41-72, "A Short-Title List of Poetry, Essays, Miscellaneous Works, Anthologies, Translations, Editings, and Introductions with Data on some of the volumes in the complete collection at Boston College." Chronological arrangement under each of the above divisions. Place, publisher, date, number of copies, binding.

These four bibliographies together provide a fairly complete list of primary writings, although there are many unsigned or pseudonymous writings which can likely never be identified.

GENERAL

Millett; Longaker & Bolles; Batho & Dobrée; Temple & Tucker; NCBEL, III, 638-639.

MEYNELL, SIR FRANCIS (1891-1975)

PRIMARY

Francis Meynell. *My Lives.* London: Bodley Head, 1971. Pp. 331.

An autobiography from which some bibliographical details can be deduced.

MEYNELL, VIOLA (1886-1956)

(Mrs. John Dallyn).

Millett; Temple & Tucker; NCBEL, IV, 669-670.

MIDDLETON, JOHN CHRISTOPHER (1926-)

Vinson-Poets; Temple & Tucker.

MIDDLETON, RICHARD BARHAM (1882-1911)

PRIMARY

Henry Danielson. *Bibliographies of Modern Authors.* London: Bookman's Journal, 1921. Pp. [xii] , [212] .

Pp. 171-172, primary books. Chronological arrangement. Transcribed TP, part collation, pagination, binding, variants, miscellaneous bibliographical notes.

GENERAL

Batho & Dobrée; NCBEL, IV, 670.

MIDDLETON, STANLEY (1919-)

Vinson-Novelists; Drescher & Kahrmann; Bufkin.

MILLAR, RONALD (1919-)

Vinson-Dramatists; NCBEL, IV, 967.

MILLETT, NIGEL (-)

Pseudonym used: Richard Oke.

NCBEL, IV, 687.

MILNE, ALLAN ALEXANDER (1882-1956)

PRIMARY

John R. Payne. "Four Children's Books by A. A. Milne." *Studies in Bibliography* 23 (1970): 127-139.

Primary books. Chronological arrangement. Transcribed TP, full collation, pagination, description of paper and of illustrations, binding, variants, subsequent editions and reprints, number of copies, detailed bibliographical notes. Includes suggestions of sources of other primary writings.

Thomas Burnett Swann. *A. A. Milne.* New York: Twayne Publishers, Inc. (TEAS 113), 1971. Pp. 153.

Pp. 141-143, primary bibliography. Genre arrangement. Books (selected editions): place, publisher, date. Period: volume, date, pages. Pp. 145-148, secondary bibliography, annotated.

There is no list of Milne's periodical contributions, but Swann does name in his text many of the periodicals and newspapers in which Milne's writings appeared.

SECONDARY

Above, Swann.

GENERAL

Millett; Longaker & Bolles; Temple & Tucker; Adelman & Dworkin; Salem; Palmer & Dyson; NCBEL, IV, 671-673.

MILNE, CHARLES EWART (1903-)

Vinson-Poets.

MITCHELL, ADRIAN (1932-)

Vinson-Poets; Vinson-Novelists.

MITCHELL, CHARLES JULIAN (1935-)

Vinson-Novelists; Drescher & Kahrmann.

MITCHELL, JAMES LESLIE (1901-1935)

Pseudonym used: Lewis Grassic Gibbon.

PRIMARY

Geoffrey Wagner. "James Leslie Mitchell/Lewis Grassic Gibbon. A Chronological Checklist of his Writings." *Bibliotheck* (Glasgow) 1, i (1956): 3-21.

Primary complete, secondary selected. Primary, chronological arrangement; secondary, alphabetical by author. Books: place, publisher, date, contents, subsequent editions and reprints. Periods: volume, date, pages. Name under which published. Miscellaneous notes; includes list of books dedicated to Mitchell.

W. R. Aitken. "Further Notes on the Bibliography of James Leslie Mitchell/Lewis Grassic Gibbon." *Bibliotheck* (Glasgow) 1, ii (1956): 34-35.

Additions to the primary and secondary bibliography by Wagner (above). Further primary and secondary additions are made in the *Bibliotheck* by Douglas F. Young, "James Leslie Mitchell/Lewis Grassic Gibbon: a chronological checklist. Additions I," 5, v (1969): 169-173; and by James Kidd, ". . .Additions II," 5, v (1969): 174-177.

Ian S. Munro. *Leslie Mitchell: Lewis Grassic Gibbon.* Edinburgh and London: Oliver and Boyd, 1966. Pp. 224.

Pp. 223-224, bibliography. Form and genre arrangement. Place, date.

Secondary bibliography in footnotes, *passim.*

SECONDARY

Above, Munro, footnotes, *passim.*

GENERAL

Daiches; NCBEL, IV, 588-589; Bufkin.

MITCHELL, SUSAN LANGSTAFF (1866-1926)

PRIMARY

Richard M. Kain. *Susan L. Mitchell.* Lewisburg: Bucknell University Press (Irish Writers Series), 1972. Pp. 103.

Pp. 97-103, selected primary bibliography. Chronologically arranged. Books: place, publisher, date. Extensive textual and bibliographical notes locating MSS collections and citing references to the author in other works.

MITCHISON, NAOMI MARY MARGARET HALDANE (1897-)

(Lady Mitchison)

Millett; Daiches; Temple & Tucker; Vinson-Novelists; NCBEL, IV, 673-674; Bufkin.

MITFORD, HON. NANCY FREEMAN (1904-1973)

Daiches; Temple & Tucker; Adelman & Dworkin (Novel); Vinson-Novelists; NCBEL, IV, 674; Bufkin.

MOLE, JOHN (1941-)

Vinson-Poets.

MONCRIEFF, CHARLES KENNETH SCOTT (1889-1930)

PRIMARY

J. M. Scott Moncrieff and L. W. Lunn, eds. *C. K. Scott Moncrieff. Memories and Letters.* London: Chapman and Hall, 1931. Pp. 242.

No bibliography, but on p. [ii] a list of titles translated by Moncrieff, while the letters themselves point to some of his periodical contributions and other literary work.

MONKHOUSE, ALLAN NOBLE (1858-1936)

Millett; Longaker & Bolles; Batho & Dobrée; Temple & Tucker; NCBEL, IV, 968.

MONRO, HAROLD EDWARD (1879-1932)

PRIMARY

Joy Grant. *Harold Monro and the Poetry Bookshop.* London: Routledge and Kegan Paul, 1967. Pp. x, 286.

Pp. 276-279, bibliography. Primary books, secondary selected. Arranged: published works (including books, pamphlets, periodicals edited by Monro); unpublished works (including brief account of three main collections of MSS); selected criticism and reminiscences of Monro. Publisher, place, date. Additional primary and secondary bibliography in footnotes.

GENERAL

Millett; Longaker & Bolles; Batho & Dobrée; Daiches; Temple & Tucker; NCBEL, IV, 313-314; Stratford.

MONSARRAT, NICHOLAS JOHN TURNEY (1910-)

Temple & Tucker; Vinson-Novelists; NCBEL, IV, 674-675; Bufkin.

MONTAGUE, CHARLES EDWARD (1867-1928)

PRIMARY

Margaret Stapleton. "A Bibliography of Writings by and about Charles Edward Montague." *Bulletin of Bibliography* 16 (1938-1939): 135-136, 157-158.

Primary, secondary selected. Form arrangement. Books: place, publisher, later editions, brief description of contents. Periods: volume, pages, date. "Miscellaneous Writings" gives contents of books listed alphabetically by title with place of first publication. P. 158, secondary bibliography. Arranged alphabetically by author with reviews listed under title of book reviewed.

GENERAL

Millett; Longaker & Bolles; NCBEL, IV, 675-676; Bufkin.

MOORE, GEORGE (1852-1933)

PRIMARY

Jean C. Noël. *George Moore. L'homme et l'œuvre (1852-1933).* Paris: Marcel Didier (Etudes Anglaises No. 24), 1966. Pp. 706.

Pp. 555-647, bibliography. Primary, secondary selected. Form and genre arrangement. Primary books: transcribed TP, part collation, binding, pagination, occasional notes. Periods: volume, dates, pages. Pp. 604-647, secondary bibliography. Arranged by topic and by language, including many general references. [In French].

While Gilcher (below) provides the more authoritative primary bibliography, Noël is a useful cross-check and often helpful.

Edwin Gilcher. *A Bibliography of George Moore.* DeKalb, Illinois: Northern Illinois University Press, 1970. Pp. xiv, 274.

Primary bibliography. Form arrangement. Books (new editions): transcribed TP, full collation, price, pagination, binding, contents, full notes. Other primary books: place, publisher, date, notes. Periods: chronologically arranged, dates, notes on inclusion of item in later writings or collections; author and title of books reviewed by Moore identified; unsigned writings by Moore identified. Translations of Moore listed under language in which translated. Index.

A model of bibliographic completeness. See pp. ix-xiv for Gilcher's statement of bibliographical principles and pp. 243-246 for his acknowledgement of assistance, both providing clues to the secondary bibliography and to further research.

SECONDARY

Above, Noël, pp. 604-647.

Helmut E. Gerber. "George Moore: An Annotated Bibliography of Writings about Him." *English Fiction in Transition* 2, ii (1959): 1-91.

Alphabetical by author arrangement. Books: place, publisher, date. Periods: volume, pages, date. Annotations.

This basic checklist of secondary writings is supplemented in almost every issue of *English Fiction* (later *English Literature*) *in Transition,* particularly lengthy or otherwise important installments being as follows: 1, i (1957): 32-35; 3, ii (1960): 34-46; 4, ii (1961): 30-42; 4, iii (1961): 52-53; 5, iv (1962): 33-35; 14 (1971): 75-83; 16 (1973): 154-161; 17 (1974): 49-53; 18 (1975): 63-70.

Through the efforts of Noël, Gilcher, and Gerber, Moore has received almost as much bibliographical attention as he would have considered his due.

GENERAL

Millett; Longaker & Bolles; Batho & Dobrée; Temple & Tucker; NCBEL, III, 1014-1019; Breed & Sniderman.

MOORE, GEORGE EDWARD (1873-1958)

PRIMARY

Emerson Buchanan and G. E. Moore. "Bibliography of the Writings of G. E. Moore to November, 1942." In *The Philosophy of G. E. Moore,* ed. Paul Arthur Schilp. Evanston and Chicago: Northwestern University Press (Library of Living Philosophers, IV), 1942. Pp. 717.

Pp. 681-689, bibliography. Primary, secondary selected. Chronological arrangement. Books: place, publisher, date, pages, subsequent editions, translations, reprints; reviews of primary writings listed under primary title. Periods: volume, pages, date.

E. D. Klemke, ed. *Studies in the Philosophy of G. E. Moore.* Chicago: Quadrangle Books, 1969. Pp. [x], 306.

Pp. 299-302, "Bibliography, Compiled with the assistance of G. Moore." Primary writings, chronologically arranged. Secondary arranged alphabetically by author. Books: place, publisher, date. Periods: volume, date, pages.

SECONDARY

Above, Buchanan-Moore, *passim;* Klemke, pp. 301-302.

GENERAL

Batho & Dobrée; NCBEL, IV, 1277-1278.

MOORE, NICHOLAS (1918-)

Daiches; Temple & Tucker; Vinson-Poets; NCBEL, IV, 314-315.

MOORE, THOMAS STURGE (1870-1944)

PRIMARY

Frederick L. Gwynn. *Sturge Moore and the Life of Art.* Lawrence: Kansas University Press, 1951. Pp. 159.

Pp. 125-135, bibliography. Primary, secondary selected. Chronological arrangement, with years subdivided: Prose and Verse. Books: publisher, date, reviews of the book. Periods: volume, pages, date. Chronological list of "Printed Wood-Engravings." Pp. 134-135, secondary bibliography.

GENERAL

Millett; Longaker & Bolles; Daiches; Batho & Dobrée; Temple & Tucker; Breed & Sniderman; NCBEL, IV, 315-316.

MORAES, DOMINIC FRANK (1938-)

Vinson-Poets; Stratford.

MORE, ADELYNE: *see* RICHARDS, IVOR ARMSTRONG.

MORGAN, CHARLES LANGBRIDGE (1894-1957)

PRIMARY

Gilbert H. Fabes. *The First Editions of A. E. Coppard, A. P. Herbert, and Charles Morgan, with Values and Bibliographical Points.* London: Myers and Co., 1933. Pp. 154.

Transcribed TP, binding, variants, value in sterling. A book for dealers or collectors.

Henry Charles Duffin. *The Novels and Plays of Charles Morgan.* London: Bowes and Bowes, 1959. Pp. 221.

No bibliography; index lists Morgan's novels and plays. There appears to be no account of Morgan's journalism.

GENERAL

Millett; Longaker & Bolles; Daiches; Temple & Tucker; Adelman & Dworkin; Breed & Sniderman; Adelman & Dworkin (Novel); NCBEL, IV, 676-677; Bufkin.

MORGAN, EDWIN GEORGE (1920-)

Vinson-Poets.

MORGAN, ROBERT (1921-)

Vinson-Poets.

MORLEY, ROBERT (1908-)

Salem.

MORRISON, ARTHUR (1863-1945)

PRIMARY

Jocelyn Bell. "A Study of Arthur Morrison" in *Essays and Studies 1952* (NS 5), ed. Arundell Esdaile for The English Association. London: John Murray, 1952. Pp. 77-89.

A survey of Morrison's literary œuvre which provides titles and dates for his books and suggestions for locating his other writings.

Vincent Brome. *Four Realist Novelists.* London: Longmans, Green, and Company (WTW 183), 1963. Pp. 36.

P. 33, primary books. Place, date, genre. P. 36, general secondary bibliography, selected.

SECONDARY

Above, Brome, p. 36.

Helmut E. Gerber. "Arthur Morrison." *English Fiction in Transition* 1, i (1957): 35; 4, ii (1961): 58; 4, iii (1961): 53.

A total of five entries, annotated.

GENERAL

Batho & Dobrée; NCBEL, III, 1069-1070.

MORRISON, NANCY AGNES BRYSSON (-)

Daiches; NCBEL, IV, 677-678.

MORTIMER, JOHN CLIFFORD (1923-)

Breed & Sniderman; Vinson-Dramatists.

MORTIMER, PENELOPE RUTH (1918-)

Vinson-Novelists; Drescher & Kahrmann; Bufkin.

MORTON, HENRY CANOVA VOLLAM (1892-)

NCBEL, IV, 1322-1323.

MORTON, JOHN CAMERON ANDRIEU BINGHAM MICHAEL (1893-)

NCBEL, IV, 1088-1089.

MOSLEY, NICHOLAS, LORD RAVENSDALE (1923-)

Vinson-Novelists; Drescher & Kahrmann; Temple & Tucker.

MOTTRAM, RALPH HALE (1883-1971)

PRIMARY

Gilbert H. Fabes. *The First Editions of Ralph Hale Mottram.* London: Myers and Co., 1934. Pp. 128. 300 copies.

Primary books, including books with contributions by Mottram. Chronological arrangement. Transcribed TP, full collation, pagination, binding, notes.

GENERAL

Millett; Longaker & Bolles; Daiches; Temple & Tucker; NCBEL, IV, 678-679; Bufkin.

MUIR, EDWIN (1887-1959)

PRIMARY

Elgin W. Mellown. *Bibliography of the Writings of Edwin Muir.* University: University of Alabama Press, 1964; Reprinted with corrections and additions., London: Nicholas Vane Ltd., 1966.

Pp. 144. 1964 edition reissued with Mellown's *Supplement to the Bibliography . . . Incorporating Additional Entries Compiled by Peter Hoy.* University: University of Alabama Press, [1971]. Pp. 28.

Primary bibliography, complete. Form arrangement. Books: transcribed TP, part collation, pagination, binding, date, price, miscellaneous notes, contents. Periods: volume, pages, date; some reviews by Muir include author and title of book reviewed. Index of titles provides history of individual publication. London edition includes selected secondary criticism with reviews listed under book titles, also additional primary bibliography. Supplement arranged in the form of the 1964 edition.

With the *Supplement* this bibliography provides a virtually complete list of the primary writings.

SECONDARY

Above, Mellown, (1966), pp. 138-144.

Peter C. Hoy and Elgin W. Mellown. *A Checklist of Writings about Edwin Muir.* Troy, New York: Whitston Publishing Co., Inc., 1971. Pp. [iv], 80.

Form arrangement, including list of previous primary and secondary bibliographies. Brief annotations identify type of criticism.

GENERAL

Millett; Daiches; Temple & Tucker; Stratford; NCBEL, IV, 316-319.

MUIR, WILLA (1890-1970)

Née Wilhelmina Johnstone Anderson.

[For translations by Willa Muir *see* Mellown, *Bibliography of the Writings of Edwin Muir* (above), pp. 121-125.]

NCBEL, IV, 679-680.

MUNRO, CHARLES KIRKPATRICK (1889-1973)

Pseudonym of Charles Walden Kirkpatrick Macmullan.

Millett; Daiches; Temple & Tucker; Salem; NCBEL, IV, 969.

MUNRO, HECTOR HUGH (1870-1916)

Pseudonym used: Saki.

PRIMARY

George James Spears. *The Satire of Saki.* New York: Exposition Press, 1963. Pp. 127.

Pp. [123]-127, primary selected, secondary selected bibliography. Genre arrangement. Books: place, publisher, date, pages, brief critical annotations and bibliographical evaluations. Periods: volume, pages, date. Includes reviews of primary books.

While the secondary bibliography is limited, it includes works omitted by Gillen (below); and the primary bibliography gives details not in Gillen.

Charles H. Gillen. *Hector Hugh Munro (Saki).* New York: Twayne Publishers (TEAS 102), 1969. Pp. 178.

Pp. 171-172, primary books: Place, publisher, date. Pp. 172-175, secondary bibliography. Arranged: alphabetical by author. Periods: volume, pages, date. Each entry annotated. Other secondary references in notes, pp. 161-169.

Spears and Gillen together provide a starting point for compiling the definitive bibliography. It appears that no one has ever listed the journalism.

SECONDARY

Above, Spears and Gillen.

Robert Drake, "Saki: Some Problems and a Bibliography," *English Fiction in Transition* 5 (1962): 12-26. [See later issues of

English Fiction (later *English Literature*) *in Transition* for continuation by various compilers] .

Annotations.

GENERAL

Millett; Longaker & Bolles; Batho & Dobrée; Temple & Tucker; NCBEL, IV, 727-728; Bufkin.

MURDOCH, JEAN IRIS (1919-)

(Mrs. J. O. Bayley).

PRIMARY

Thomas T. Tominaga and Wilma Schneidermeyer. *Iris Murdoch and Muriel Spark: A Bibliography.* Metuchen, N. J.: Scarecrow Press, Inc., 1976. Pp. xvi, 237.

Pp. 3-39, primary bibliography. Form and genre arrangement, alphabetical arrangement within each division. Books (all first editions and translations): place, publisher, date, translator, and reviews of the book. Periods: volume, date, pages. Reviews by Miss Murdoch include title and author of book reviewed. Occasional annotations. Pp. 41-97, secondary bibliography arranged under six headings, including (pp. 95-97) primary and secondary bibliographies. Pp. 193-237, indices of authors, titles, and subjects (Murdoch and Spark listed together). Pp. xi-xiii, biographical and publications chronology.

SECONDARY

Above, Tominaga and Schneidermeyer, pp. 3-39, reviews of primary books; pp. 41-97, other critical writings.

Ann Culley, with John Feaster. "Criticism of Iris Murdoch: A Selected Checklist," *Modern Fiction Studies* 15 (1969): 449-457.

Primary selected, secondary selected. Arranged: general studies, criticism of individual novels (under title of novel); primary writings subdivided novels, critical works and essays, interviews. Books: place, publisher, date. Periods: volume, pages, date.

Frank Baldanza. *Iris Murdoch.* New York: Twayne Publishers, Inc. (TEAS 169), 1974. Pp. [189].

Pp. 180-184, selected secondary bibliography with evaluative annotations.

GENERAL

Temple & Tucker; Adelman & Dworkin (Novel); Vinson-Novelists; Vinson-Dramatists; Drescher & Kahrmann; Bufkin.

MURRAY, GEORGE GILBERT AIMÉ (1866-1957)

PRIMARY

"Bibliographies of Modern Authors: George Gilbert Aimé Murray," *London Mercury* 3 (1921): 326-327.

Primary books. Genre arrangement. Publisher, date, notes.

J. A. K. Thomson and A. J. Toynbee, eds. *Essays in Honour of Gilbert Murray.* London: Allen and Unwin Ltd., 1936. Pp. [310].

Pp. [309-310], primary books published by Allen and Unwin.

Gilbert Murray. *An Unfinished Autobiography,* ed. Jean Smith and Arnold Toynbee. London: Allen and Unwin Ltd., 1960. Pp. [228].

Pp. [227-228], primary books published by Allen and Unwin; see "Introduction" by E. R. Dodds (pp. 13-19) for references to other titles.

GENERAL

Millett; Longaker & Bolles; Temple & Tucker; NCBEL, IV, 1089-1092.

MURRAY, THOMAS CORNELIUS (1873-1959)

Millett; Adelman & Dworkin; Salem; NCBEL, III, 1944-1945; Breed & Sniderman; Hogan.

MURRY, JOHN MIDDLETON (1889-1957)

PRIMARY

George Lilley. *A Bibliography of John Middleton Murry 1889-1957.* Folkestone: Dawsons of Pall Mall, 1974; Toronto: University of Toronto Press, 1975. Pp. 226.

Primary. Form arrangement (books by, books with contributions by, contributions to periodicals, articles signed "Journeyman"). Books: title, place, publisher, date, pages, height in inches, genre, contents with citation of any previous publication, notice of other editions and reprints. Bibliographical notes. Periods: volume, date, pages; reviews include title and author of book reviewed, cross references to books in which collected and to other publications of the same article. Pp. 179-226, useful indices. Pp. 7-19, important introduction in which Lilley defines the scope of the bibliography.

The authoritative bibliography, praised by R. J. Roberts, *Book Collector* 25 (1976): 117-118.

SECONDARY

Ernest G. Griffin. *John Middleton Murry.* New York: Twayne Publishers, Inc. (TEAS 72), 1969. Pp. 182.

Pp. 173-175, primary writings. Books, British and American editions, chronologically arranged: place, publisher, year, subsequent editions. Periodical contributions: ten uncollected items: volume, pages, date. Pp. 175-177, secondary bibliography. Annotated. Other primary and secondary references in notes, pp. 159-172.

GENERAL

Millett; Longaker & Bolles; Daiches; Temple & Tucker; NCBEL, IV, 1092-1096.

MYERS, LEOPOLD HAMILTON (1881-1944)

PRIMARY

Geoffrey Herman Bantock. *L. H. Myers. A Critical Study.* Leicester: University College, and London: Jonathan Cape, 1956. Pp. [x], 157.

Little or no bibliographical information as such, yet titles and dates of Myers' books are given, along with letters both to and from him referring to his writings.

GENERAL

Millett; Daiches; Temple & Tucker, NCBEL, IV, 680; Bufkin.

NAIPAUL, VIDIADHAR SURAJPRASAD (1932-)

PRIMARY

Paul Theroux. *V. S. Naipaul. An Introduction to His Work.* New York: Africana Publishing Co., 1972. Pp. 144.

Pp. 142-144, selected primary bibliography. Books, first British edition: place, publisher, date. Selected periodical contributions arranged chronologically, 1957-1972: volume, date, pages.

SECONDARY

Robert D. Hamner. *V. S. Naipaul.* New York: Twayne Publishers, Inc. (TWAS 258), 1973. Pp. 81.

Selected primary bibliography, pp. 167-168. Form arrangement. Books: place, publisher, date. Periods: volume, date, pages. Pp. 168-174, reviews of Naipaul's books listed under title of book reviewed. Pp. 174-177, general criticism of Naipaul, annotated.

GENERAL

Vinson-Novelists; Bufkin.

NASH, PAUL (1889-1946)

See BOTTOMLEY, GORDON.

NAUGHTON, BILL (1910-)

Vinson-Novelists; Vinson-Dramatists.

NESBIT, EDITH (1858-1924)

(Mrs. Hubert Bland, later Mrs. Tucker).

PRIMARY

Doris Langley Moore. *E. Nesbit. A Biography.* (Revised with New Material). Philadelphia and New York: Chilton Books, 1966. Pp. [xxxiii], [315].

Pp. 302-306, bibliography. Primary books, first English editions. Chronological arrangement. Place, publisher, year, format, occasionally pages, and occasionally names of illustrators. Anthologies and periodicals are excluded from this list, but many of them are mentioned in the text, *passim,* as are secondary criticisms and references to Hubert Bland's literary carrer.

GENERAL

Batho & Dobrée; NCBEL, III, 641-642.

NEVINSON, HENRY WOODD (1856-1941)

PRIMARY

Henry W. Nevinson. *Visions and Memories,* ed. Evelyn Sharp. London: Oxford University Press, 1944. Pp. 199.

P. 188, bibliography. Primary books. Genre arrangement. Dates. See p. vi for selected list of periodicals to which Nevinson contributed.

GENERAL

Millett; NCBEL, IV, 1197-1198.

NEWBOLT, SIR HENRY JOHN (1862-1938)

PRIMARY

"Bibliographies of Modern Authors: Sir Henry John Newbolt." *London Mercury* 2 (1920): 115.

Primary books, 1892-1918. Publisher, date, brief notes.

Margaret Newbolt, ed. *The Later Life and Letters of Sir Henry Newbolt.* London: Faber and Faber, 1942. Pp. 426.

Pp. 413-414, "A Short Bibliography." Primary books. Publisher, date. References to writings not included in this bibliography will be found in the text, *passim;* and also in Newbolt's memoirs, *My World in My Time.* London: Faber and Faber, 1932. Pp. 321.

GENERAL

Millett; Longaker & Bolles; Temple & Tucker; NCBEL, III, 642-643.

NEWBY, PERCY HOWARD (1918-)

PRIMARY

E. C. Bufkin. *P. H. Newby.* Boston: Twayne Publishers, G. K. Hall & Co. (TEAS 176), 1975. Pp. 144.

Pp. 137-140, selected primary bibliography. Arranged: fiction; other prose; selected reviews by Newby with titles and authors of books reviewed. Books (British and American first editions): place, publisher, date. Periods: date, pages. Pp. 140-142, selected secondary criticism, annotated. Additional secondary criticism and bibliographical details are given in the Notes and References, pp. 129-135.

SECONDARY

George Sutherland Fraser. *P. H. Newby*. London: Longman Group (WTW 235), 1974. Pp. 34.

Pp. 32-34, selected secondary bibliography, including reviews of Newby's books listed under the book title. Dates only.

GENERAL

Daiches; Temple & Tucker; Adelman & Dworkin (Novel): Vinson-Novelists; Drescher & Kahrmann; NCBEL, IV, 680-681; Bufkin.

NICHOLS, JOHN BEVERLEY (1899-)

Temple & Tucker; NCBEL, IV, 681-682.

NICHOLS, PETER RICHARD (1927-)

Vinson-Dramatists; Temple & Tucker.

NICHOLS, ROBERT MALISE BOWYER (1893-1944)

PRIMARY

Robert Nichols. *Robert Nichols*. London: Ernest Benn Ltd. (Augustan Books of Poetry), 1932. Pp. [32].

P. [32], bibliography. Primary books, first editions. Genre arrangement. Publisher, date.

John Gawsworth. *Ten Contemporaries. Notes Toward their Definitive Bibliography* [First Series]. London: Ernest Benn Ltd., 1932. Pp. 224.

Pp. 118-131, primary books, first editions, 1915-1932. Chronological arrangement. Transcribed TP, full collation, pagination, binding, date, bibliographical notes.

Montrose J. Moses and Oscar J. Campbell, eds. *Dramas of Modernism and Their Forerunners.* Boston: Little, Brown and Co., 1941. Pp. xvi, 946.

Pp. 925, 941, bibliography. Primary selected, secondary selected. One alphabetical list. Books: place, publisher, date. Periods: volume, pages, date. Studies or reviews of *Wings over Europe* listed thereunder.

No complete list of all of Nichol's writings is available.

SECONDARY

Above, Moses and Campbell.

GENERAL

Millett; Longaker & Bolles; Temple & Tucker; Salem; Breed & Sniderman; NCBEL, IV, 319-320.

NICHOLSON, NORMAN CORNTHWAITE (1914-)

PRIMARY

Philip Gardner. *Norman Nicholson.* New York: Twayne Publishers, Inc. (TEAS 153), 1973. Pp. 181.

Pp. 170-176, bibliography. Primary selected, secondary selected. Form and genre arrangement. Books: place, publisher, year. Periods: date. Notes, pp. 162-169, provide additional primary titles and secondary criticism.

SECONDARY

Above, Gardner.

GENERAL

Daiches; Temple & Tucker; Breed & Sniderman; Vinson-Poets; NCBEL, IV, 320-321; Stratford.

NICOLSON, HON. SIR HAROLD GEORGE (1886-1968)

PRIMARY

Margaret L. Stapleton. "Sir Harold Nicolson (1886-1968) A Bibliography." *Bulletin of Bibliography* 31 (1974): 45-49.

Selected primary, selected secondary. Form arrangement. Books (British and American editions): place, publisher, date. Periods: volume, date, pages. Pp. 48-49, secondary bibliography includes reviews of only the *Diaries and Letters*.

SECONDARY

Above, Stapleton, pp. 48-49.

GENERAL

Millett; Daiches; Temple & Tucker; NCBEL, IV, 1198-1199.

NOONAN, ROBERT (1870-1911)

Pseudonym used: Robert Tressell.

NCBEL, IV, 751.

NORMAN, JOHN FRANK (1930-)

Vinson-Dramatists.

NORRIS, LESLIE (1921-)

Vinson-Poets.

NORRIS, WILLIAM EDWARD (1847-1925)

NCBEL, IV, 682-683.

NORWAY, N. S.: *see* SHUTE, NEVIL.

NOTT, KATHLEEN CECILIA (-)

Vinson-Novelists; Vinson-Poets.

NOVELLO, IVOR (1893-1951)

Formerly David Ivor Davies.

NCBEL, IV, 970.

NOYES, ALFRED (1880-1958)

PRIMARY

Walter C. Jerrold. *Alfred Noyes.* London: Harold Shaylor (Modern Writers Series, ed. Thomas Moult), 1930. Pp. 251.

Pp. 247-251, bibliography of primary books, including books edited or introduced by Noyes. Place, publisher, date.

Catherine Merrick Neale. "Contemporary Catholic Authors: Alfred Noyes, Litteratur." *Catholic Library World* 13 (October, 1941): 3-8.

Not seen.

James E. Tobin. "Alfred Noyes: A Corrected Bibliography." *Catholic Library World* 15 (March, 1944): 181-184, 189.

Revisions to Neale (above). Not seen.

GENERAL

Millett; Longaker & Bolles; Batho & Dobrée; Temple & Tucker; NCBEL, IV, 321-323.

NUTTALL, JEFF (1933-)

Vinson-Poets.

NYE, ROBERT (1939-)

Vinson-Poets; Vinson-Novelists.

OAKES, PHILIP (1928-)

Vinson-Poets.

O'BRIEN, EDNA (1930-)

PRIMARY

Grace Eckley. *Edna O'Brien.* Lewisburg: Bucknell University Press (Irish Writers Series), 1974. Pp. 88.

Pp. 85-87, selected primary bibliography. Form and genre arrangement of British and American first editions. Books: place, publisher, date. Period: volume, date, pages. Screenplays: director, producer, company, date, actors.

GENERAL

Temple & Tucker; Bufkin.

O'BRIEN, FLANN: *see* O'NOLAN, BRIAN.

O'BRIEN, FLORENCE ROMA MUIR WILSON: *see* WILSON, ROMER.

O'BRIEN, KATE (1897-1974)

Daiches; NCBEL, IV, 683-684; Bufkin.

O'CASEY, SEAN (1884-1964)

PRIMARY

I. M. Levidova and V. M. Parchevskaia. *Sean O'Casey Bibliographic Guide.* Moscow: Kniga Publishing House (Writers of Foreign Countries Series), 1964. Pp. [100]. In Russian.

Primary complete, secondary complete. Form and genre arrangement. Books: place, publisher, date, reprints, subsequent editions; translations listed separately. Periods: pages, date. Secondary bibliography includes reviews; brief annotations.

Particularly strong on O'Casey's Russian publications.

William A. Armstrong. *Sean O'Casey.* London: Longmans, Green and Co. (WTW 198), 1967. Pp. 39.

Pp. 35-39, bibliography. Primary; secondary books. Chronological arrangement. Books: place, date, genre, occasional annotations. Periods: dates.

Not complete--but easy to use.

Ronald Ayling, ed. *Sean O'Casey. Modern Judgements.* London: Macmillan (Modern Judgements Series), 1969. Pp. 274.

Pp. 261-269, bibliography. Primary books, secondary selected. Genre arrangement. Books: date, place, publisher (both British and American editions). Periods: volume, date, pages. Annotations.

An easy-to-use list with helpful evaluations; see also comments in the "Introduction," pp. 11-41.

Bernard Benstock, *Sean O'Casey.* Lewisburg: Bucknell University Press (Irish Writers Series), 1970: Ayling provides "the best and most current bibliography of secondary material" (p. 122).

SECONDARY

Above, Levidova and Parchevskaia; Ayling, pp. 263-269.

Otto Brandstädter, "Ein O'Casey-Bibliographie." *Zeitschrift fur Anglistik and Amerikanistik* [Berlin], 2 (1954), 240-254.

Pp. 244-254, secondary bibliography. Books arranged alphabetically by author (place, publisher, date). Periodicals arranged chronologically (volume, pages, date).

Armstong, p.35: ". . . detailed, but not always accurate."

E. H. Mikhail. *Sean O'Casey: A Bibliography of Criticism.* With introduction by Ronald Ayling. London: Macmillan Press Ltd., 1972. Pp. xii, 152.

Secondary. Arrangement: Bibliographies; Reviews of Books; Books; Periodicals; Reviews of Plays; [other critical writings]. Books: place, publisher, date. Periods: volume, date, pages. Brief annotations. Indices.

On p. ix Mikhail evaluates previous bibliographies. While he does not include in this volume all material listed in the earlier bibliographies, he provides the starting point for study of criticism of O'Casey.

GENERAL

Millett; Longaker & Bolles; Daiches; Temple & Tucker; Coleman & Tyler; Adelman & Dworkin; Salem; Palmer & Dyson; Breed & Sniderman; Hogan; NCBEL, IV, 879-885.

O'CONNOR, FRANK (1903-1966)

Pseudonym of Michael Francis O'Donovan. Other pseudonym: Ben Mayo.

PRIMARY

Maurice Sheehy, ed. *Michael/Frank. Studies on Frank O'Connor With a Bibliography of His Writing.* Dublin: Gill and Macmillan; London: Macmillan and Co., 1969. Pp. viii, [204].

Pp. [168]-199, "Towards a Bibliography of Frank O'Connor's Writing." Genre and topic arrangement, including writings for television and the theatre, radio broadcasts, recordings, in English, German and Danish. Books: place, publisher, date. Periods: dates. Each item numbered. Pp. 189-198, alphabetical by title list of short stories: title and date of periodical publication, number of book in which collected. Pp. 198-199, secondary bibliography.

The beginning of a complete bibliography, although difficult to use because of the eccentric arrangement.

SECONDARY

Above, Sheehy, pp. 198-199.

Gerry Brenner. "Frank O'Connor, 1903-1966: A Bibliography." *West Coast Review* 2, ii (1967): 55-64.

Pp. 55-62, primary bibliography. Pp. 62-64, secondary bibliography, including book reviews listed under title of book reviewed.

GENERAL

Temple & Tucker; NCBEL, IV, 684-685; Breed & Sniderman; Hogan.

O'DONNELL, PEADAR (1893-)

PRIMARY

Paul A. Doyle. "Peadar O'Donnell: A Checklist." *Bulletin of Bibliography* 28 (1971): 3-4.

Primary selected. Genre arrangement. Books (British and American editions): place, publisher, date. Periods: volume, date, pages.

O'DONOVAN, MICHAEL: *see* O'CONNOR, FRANK.

O'DUFFY, EIMAR ULTAN (1893-1935)

PRIMARY

Alf MacLochlainn. "Eimar O'Duffy. A Bibliographical Biography." *Irish Book*, 1 (Winter, 1959-1960): 37-46.

Essay with bibliographical information in text. For books, usually date, notice of later editions, publisher; some account of contributions to periodicals.

Robert Hogan. *Eimar O'Duffy*. Lewisburg: Bucknell University Press (Irish Writers Series), 1972. Pp. 84.

Pp. 82-84, selected primary and secondary bibliography. Chronologically arranged. Books: place, publisher, date. References to O'Duffy's other writings, published and unpublished, will be found in the text, *passim.*

O'FAOLAIN, SEAN (1900-)

PRIMARY

Maurice Harmon. *Sean O'Faolain. A Critical Introduction.* Notre Dame and London: University of Notre Dame Press, 1967. Pp. xix, 221.

Pp. 203-213, bibliography. Primary. Form arrangement. Books: place, publisher, date. Periods: volume, pages, date. Pp. 216-217, secondary bibliography.

Paul A. Doyle. *Sean O'Faolain.* New York: Twayne Publishers, Inc. (TEAS 70), 1968. Pp. 156.

Pp. 143-147, primary bibliography. Chronological arrangement. Books: place, publisher, date; includes both British and American editions. Periods: volume, pages, date, annotations. Pp. 148-152, secondary bibliography. Additional primary and secondary items in notes, pp. 131-141.

Doyle provides a more complete list of titles (especially of primary periodical contributions) than does Harmon and also gives additional information about editions and a longer secondary bibliography; yet Harmon includes entries which Doyle omits; and both should be consulted.

SECONDARY

Above, Harmon, pp. 216-217; Doyle, pp. 148-152, 131-141.

GENERAL

Millett; Daiches; Temple & Tucker; Hogan; Vinson-Novelists; NCBEL, IV, 685-686; Bufkin.

O'FLAHERTY, LIAM (1896-)

PRIMARY

John Gawsworth. *Ten Contemporaries. Notes Toward Their Definitive Bibliography. (Second Series).* London: Joiner and Steele, 1933. Pp. 240. 1000 copies.

Pp. 144-160, primary first editions, 1923-1932. Chronological arrangement. Transcribed TP, full collation, pagination, binding, date, bibliographical notes.

Paul A. Doyle. *Liam O'Flaherty: An Annotated Bibliography.* Troy, New York: Whitston Publishing Co., Inc., 1972. Pp. [viii], 68.

Pp. 1-33, primary bibliography. Form and genre arrangement. Books (all editions): place, publisher, date, bibliographical notes. Period: volume, pages, date. Précis given for each non-fiction item. Pp. 34-59, selected secondary bibliography. Arranged alphabetically by author. Fully annotated. Pp. 61-68, index.

Doyle attempts "to present a thorough listing of [O'Flaherty's] literary efforts . . . as well as a survey of the highlights of his work in non-fiction and the basic articles and books of analysis dealing with his life and career" (p. i).

SECONDARY

Above, Doyle.

GENERAL

Millett; Daiches; Temple & Tucker; Vinson-Novelists; NCBEL, IV, 686-687; Bufkin.

O'GRADY, STANDISH (1846-1928)

PRIMARY

Patrick Sarsfield O'Hegarty. *A Bibliography of Books written by*

Standish O'Grady. Dublin: For the author, 1930. Pp. 8. 25 copies. [Reprint of "Bibliographies of Irish Authors. No. 2. Standish O'Grady." *Dublin Magazine* 5 (April-June, 1930): 49-56].

Primary books. Chronological arrangement. Transcribed TP, part collation, pagination, binding, date, bibliographical notes.

John R. McKenna. "The Standish O'Grady Collection at Colby College: A Check List," *Colby Library Quarterly,* 4 (1958): 291-303.

Not seen.

Philip L. Marcus. *Standish O'Grady.* Lewisburg: Bucknell University Press (Irish Writers Series), 1970. Pp. 92.

Pp. 90-91, primary books. Chronological arrangement. Place, publisher, date, all editions. Pp. 91-92, secondary selected. Information as for primary.

There appears to be no account of O'Grady's journalism and contributions to periodicals.

SECONDARY

Above, Marcus, pp. 91-92.

GENERAL

NCBEL, III, 1892-1894.

O'HANRAHAN, MICHAEL (-1916)

PRIMARY

Patrick Sarsfield O'Hegarty. "Bibliographies of 1916 and the Irish Revolution. IX. Micheál O'Hannracháin." *Dublin Magazine* 11 (July-September, 1936): 59.

Primary books. Chronological arrangement. Transcribed TP, part collation, pagination, binding, bibliographical notes.

O'HIGGINS, KEVIN CHRISTOPHER (1892-1927)

PRIMARY

Patrick Sarsfield O'Hegarty. "Bibliographies of 1916 and the Irish Revolution. XIV. Kevin O'Higgins." *Dublin Magazine* 12 (January-March, 1937): 67.

Primary books. Chronological arrangement. Transcribed TP, part collation, pagination, binding, bibliographical and biographical notes.

OKE, RICHARD: *see* MILLETT, NIGEL.

O'KELLY, SEUMAS ([?1875-1878]-1918)

PRIMARY

George Brandon Saul. *Seumas O'Kelly.* Lewisburg: Bucknell University Press (Irish Writers Series), 1971. Pp. 101.

Pp. 81-99, primary bibliography. Form arrangement. Books: place, publisher, date, contents with notes on previous publication, extensive bibliographical and textual notes. Periods: date. Pp. 99-101, selected secondary bibliography. See Saul's note, p. 98, concerning the omission of O'Kelly's journalism.

P. 81, Editor's Note: "this invaluable annotated bibliography. . .is definitive and comprehensive." Additional bibliographical details concerning bindings and pagination will be found in Patrick Sarsfield O'Hegarty. "Bibliographies of 1916 and the Irish Revolution. IV. Seumas O'Kelly." *Dublin Magazine* 9 (October-December, 1934): 47-51.

SECONDARY

Above, Saul.

GENERAL

Breed & Sniderman; NCBEL, IV, 687-688.

OLIVER, GEORGE: *see* ONIONS, OLIVER.

OLIVIER, EDITH MAUD (?1879-1948)

Millett; NCBEL, IV, 688.

OMAN, CAROLA MARY ANIMA (1897-)

(Lady Lenanton).

Millett; NCBEL, IV, 688-689.

ONIONS, OLIVER (1873-1961)

Pseudonym of George Oliver.

PRIMARY

John Gawsworth. *Ten Contemporaries. Notes Toward Their Definitive Bibliography (Second Series).* London: Joiner and Steele, 1933. Pp. 240. 1000 copies.

Pp. 170-188, primary first editions, 1900-1931. Chronological arrangement. Transcribed TP, full collation, pagination, binding, date, bibliographical notes. Pp. 167-169, list of collections of primary books and MSS.

Apparently the only primary bibliography. NB: a complete collection (as of 1931) was given to the Widener Library, Harvard, by Randolph Edgar.

SECONDARY

(Although *English Literature in Transition* lists Onions as an author whose works will be listed by its compilers, up to 1976 no material relating to him had been published).

GENERAL

Millett; Daiches; Temple & Tucker, NCBEL, IV, 689-670; Bufkin.

O'NOLAN, BRIAN (1912-1966)

Pseudonyms used: Flann O'Brien, Myles na Gopaleen, and others.

PRIMARY

David Powell. "A Checklist of Brian O'Nolan." *Journal of Irish Literature* 3, 1 (1974): 104-112.

Primary, secondary selected. Form arrangement. Books (all editions): place, publisher, date, genre, name used by author, extensive list of reviews and articles concerning the book. Periods: volume, date, pages, pseudonym employed, genre. Secondary bibliography, p. 112 and 104-108.

Powell here lists works published under the author's own name or under "Brian Nolan" and under the two main pseudonyms, while pointing out that O'Nolan may have employed more than one hundred other pseudonyms for his not yet identified writings. Many of the periodical citations merely point to long runs of contributions under a common title without providing specific bibliographical details.

The beginning of an obviously difficult-to-compile bibliography.

GENERAL

NCBEL, IV, 683; Hogan; Temple & Tucker; Bufkin.

OPPENHEIM, EDWARD PHILLIPS (1866-1946)

PRIMARY

Hulings C. Brown. "Oppenheim and his Ninety Novels." *Boston Evening Transcript.* 4 May 1923.

Primary books. British and American titles, publisher, date, genre, nom de plume under which published.

Grant Overton. *Cargoes for Crusoes.* New York: D. Appleton and Co., 1924. Pp. 416.

Pp. 138-141, bibliography. Primary books. Chronological arrangement. British and American titles, nom de plume under which published, date. Secondary bibliography, pp. 126-138; also see text, *passim.*

Robert Standish. *The Prince of Storytellers. The Life of E. Phillips Oppenheim.* London: Peter Davies, 1957. Pp. 253.

Pp. 247-253, "1887-1943. The Harvest of Fifty-six Years' Writing." Primary books. Genre arrangement. British and American titles, date. P. 247, note concerning contributions to periodicals and American piracies.

SECONDARY

Above, Overton.

O'RIORDAN, CONAL HOLMES O'CONNELL (1874-1950)

Millet; Longaker & Bolles; Breed & Sniderman; NCBEL, III, 1065.

ORMOND, JOHN (1923-)

Vinson-Poets.

ORTON, JOE (1933-1967)

Temple & Tucker.

ORWELL, GEORGE (1903-1950)

Pseudonym of Eric Blair.

PRIMARY

Zoltan G. Zeke and William White. "Orwelliana." *Bulletin of Bibliography* 23 (1961): 110-114, 140-144, 166-168.

Primary. Genre arrangement, chronological in each section. Books: title, place, publisher, year, pages, subsequent editions, name used. Periods: volume, pages, date; reviews include title and author of book reviewed. Pp. 140-144, secondary bibliography. Form arrangement. Reviews of Orwell listed under title of book. Pp. 166-168, continuation of reviews; p. 168, addenda to all sections.

M. Jennifer McDowell. "George Orwell: Bibliographical Addenda." *Bulletin of Bibliography* 23 (1963): 224-229; 24 (1963): 19-24, 36-40.

Pp. 224-229, additional primary bibliography; also letters of reply to Orwell in periodicals. Pp. 19-24, 36-40, additional secondary bibliography and supplemental addenda for all sections.

Ian R. Willison and Ian Angus. "George Orwell: Bibliographical Addenda." *Bulletin of Bibliography* 24 (1965): 180-187.

Additional primary bibliography and letters of reply.

George Orwell. *The Collected Essays, Journalism and Letters of George Orwell,* ed. Sonia Orwell and Ian Angus. London: Secker and Warburg; New York: Harcourt, Brace and World, 1968. Four volumes.

Chronologically arranged primary material. Important bibliographical footnotes, *passim,* indicate date and place of publication of essays and reviews, the latter including author and title of book reviewed. Other information.

SECONDARY

Above, Zeke and White; McDowell; Willison and Angus.

Jeffrey and Valerie Meyers. *George Orwell. An Annotated Bibliography of Criticism.* New York and London: Garland Publishing, Inc., 1977. Pp. [xx] , 132.

Alphabetically-by-author arranged list, annotated. Books: place, date, Periods: volume, date, pages. Previously published in *Bulletin of Bibliography* 31 (1974): 117-121 and *Modern Fiction Studies* 21 (Spring, 1975): 133-136, this list supplements the earlier *Bulletin of Bibliography* checklists cited above.

GENERAL

Longaker & Bolles; Daiches; Temple & Tucker; Adelman & Dworkin (Novel); NCBEL, IV, 690-696; Bufkin.

OSBORNE, JOHN JAMES (1929-)

PRIMARY

Cameron Northouse and Thomas P. Walsh. *John Osborne: A Reference Guide.* Boston: G. K. Hall and Co., 1974. Pp. [x] . 158.

Pp. 1-5, primary bibliography. Form and genre arrangement of British and American first editions. Books: place, publisher, date. Periods: volume, date, pages. Pp. 7-138, secondary bibliography. Chronological arrangement, subdivided by form. Précis of each entry. Pp. 140-158, index of authors and of primary titles.

Additional bibliographical details are provided by Alan Carter. *John Osborne.* Edinburgh: Oliver and Boyd (Biography and Criticism, 14), 1969, pp. 184-187; and by Simon Trussler. *The Plays of John Osborne. An Assessment.* London: Victor Gollancz Ltd., 1969, pp. 247-249.

SECONDARY

Above, Northouse and Walsh, pp. 7-138; Carter, pp. 187-191; and Trussler, pp. 249-252.

Shirley Jean Bailey. "John Osborne: A Bibliography." *Twentieth Century Literature* 7 (October, 1961): 118-120.

A useful list of reviews of the plays listed under title of the play.

GENERAL

Temple & Tucker; Coleman & Tyler; Adelman & Dworkin; Salem; Palmer & Dyson; Breed & Sniderman; Vinson-Dramatists.

O'SULLIVAN, SEUMAS (1879-1958)

Pseudonym of James Sullivan Starkey.

PRIMARY

Alan Denson. "The Books of Seumas O'Sullivan (James Sullivan Starkey, 1879-1958) A Bibliographical Check-List," in *Retrospect,* ed. Liam Miller. Dublin: Dolmen Editions, 1973. Pp. [104]. 750 copies.

Pp. 98-103, primary books and pamphlets, including those with contributions by O'Sullivan. Chronological arrangement. Place, publisher, date, pages, binding, number of copies (information varies for each entry). P. 98, a note points out that this checklist is extracted from "Denson's forthcoming complete *Bibliography* . . . to be published . . . in 1973."

GENERAL

Longaker & Bolles; NCBEL, IV, 323-324.

O'SULLIVAN, VINCENT (1872-1940)

PRIMARY

George Sims. "Some Uncollected Authors. XV. Vincent O'Sullivan." *Book Collector* 6 (1957): 395-402.

Primary. Arranged: Books; Contributions to Books. Chronological in both sections. Transcribed TP, format, binding, date; also date of first American edition. Bibliographical notes.

OWEN, ALUN DAVIES (1926-)

Coleman & Tyler; Breed & Sniderman; Vinson-Dramatists.

OWEN, WILFRED EDWARD SALTER (1893-1918)

PRIMARY

Joseph Cohen. "Wilfred Owen: Fresher Fields than Flanders." *English Literature in Transition* 7 (1964): 1-7.

An important essay on the various publications of Owen's writings.

William White. *Wilfred Owen (1893-1918): A Bibliography.* Kent: Kent State University Press (Serif Series, 1), 1967. Pp. 41.

Primary, secondary. Form arrangement. Books: place, publisher, pages, contents, subsequent editions and reprints. Periods: volume, pages, date. Includes translations of Owen's poems. Reviews of primary books listed under title of book.

Additions are given by White in "Wilfred Owen: Bibliographical Notes and Addenda." *Serif* 7, i (1970): 25-27, and by Dominic Hibberd. *Wilfred Owen.* Harlow: Longman Group Ltd. (WTW 246), 1975, pp. 40-41.

SECONDARY

Above, White, pp. 25-37, biography and general criticism; pp. 38-41, reviews.

GENERAL

Millett; Longaker & Bolles; Daiches; Temple & Tucker; NCBEL, IV, 324-326.

OXENHAM, JOHN: *see* DUNKERLEY, WILLIAM ARTHUR.

PAGET, VIOLET: *see* LEE, VERNON.

PAIN, BARRY ERIC ODELL (1864-1928)

NCBEL, IV, 697-699.

PALMER, HERBERT EDWARD (1880-1961)

PRIMARY

John Gawsworth. *Ten Contemporaries. Notes Toward their Definitive Bibliography* [First Series]. London: Ernest Benn Ltd., 1932. Pp. 224.

Pp. 141-148, primary first editions, 1918-1931. Chronological arrangement. Transcribed TP, full collation, pagination, binding, date, bibliographical notes; occasionally number of copies.

GENERAL

Daiches; NCBEL, IV, 326-327.

PALMER, JOHN LESLIE (1885-1944)

Pseudonyms used: Francis Beeding, Christopher Haddon; and, with Hilary St. George Saunders, David Pilgrim.

PRIMARY

Hilary St. George Saunders, "John Palmer, 1885-1944, A Memoir." In David Pilgrim, *The Emperor's Servant.* London: Macmillan and Co., 1946. Pp. 124.

Pp. ix-xxxiv, essay account of Palmer's literary activities. No actual list of writings.

GENERAL

Millett.

PARKER, LOUIS NAPOLEON (1852-1944)

Salem; NCBEL, IV, 971-972.

PARSONS, CLERE TREVOR JAMES HERBERT (1908-1931)

NCBEL, IV, 327.

PATTEN, BRIAN (1946-)

Vinson-Poets.

PATTERSON, PETER: *see* TERSON, PETER.

PAYE, ROBERT: *see* LONG, GABRIELLE.

PEACH, LAWRENCE DU GARDE (1890-)

NCBEL, IV, 973-975.

PEAKE, MERVYN (1911-1968)

PRIMARY

G. A. J. Farmer. "Mervyn Peake, Book Illustrator, and a Checklist of his Works." *Australian Library Journal* 8 (July, 1959): 134-137.

Arranged: Books by; Books and Periodicals with illustrations by; Secondary. Books: place, publisher, date, subsequent editions. Periods: volume, date, pages. Occasional notes.

Maeve Gilmore. *A World Away. A Memoir of Mervyn Peake.* London: Victor Gollancz, 1970. Pp. 157.

P. [149], "Principal Works." Primary books only: place, publisher, date. Pp. [150]-[151]. books illustrated by Peake.

GENERAL

NCBEL, IV, 699.

PEARSE, PADRAIC HENRY (1879-1916)

PRIMARY

Patrick Sarsfield O'Hegarty. "Bibliographies of 1916 and the Irish Revolution. I. Padraic Henry Pearse." *Dublin Magazine* 6 (July-September, 1931): 44-49.

Primary books. Chronological arrangement. Transcribed TP, part collation, pagination, binding, bibliographical notes; occasionally textual notes and description of contents.

Raymond J. Porter. *P. H. Pearse.* New York: Twayne Publishers, Inc. (TEAS 154), 1973. Pp. 168.

Pp. 155-158, primary bibliography. Books: place, publisher, date, description of contents. Periods: volume, date, pages, contents. Pp. 158-162, secondary bibliography, annotated. Additional primary and secondary items are referred to in the Notes and References, pp. 141-154.

SECONDARY

Above, Porter, pp. 158-162.

PERTWEE, ROLAND (1885-1963)

NCBEL, IV, 975.

PHILLIPS, STEPHEN (1868-1915)

PRIMARY

Edward Everett Hale, Jr. *Dramatists of Today.* London: George Bell and Sons, 1906. Pp. 236.

P. 220, plays by Phillips: title, theatre and date of first performances in England, America, and on the Continent. Brief annotations.

Clara A. Milliken. "Reading List on Modern Dramatists: Stephen Phillips." *Bulletin of Bibliography* 5 (1907): 51.

Primary books. Alphabetical arrangement. Date, place, publisher, pages, format, price, précis; reviews. Secondary criticism arranged alphabetically by author: date, pages.

GENERAL

Longaker & Bolles; Batho & Dobrée; Temple & Tucker; Salem; NCBEL, III, 1194-1196.

PHILLPOTTS, EDEN (1862-1960)

PRIMARY

Percival Hinton. *Eden Phillpotts. A Bibliography of First Editions.* Birmingham: Greville Worthington, 1931. Pp. 164. 350 copies.

Primary books, 1888-1931. Chronological arrangement. Transcribed TP, full collation, pagination, binding, number of copies, bibliographical notes. P. v, important note on periodical contributions excluded and their location; pp. x-xiii, chronological list of book titles; pp. xiv-xvi, books classified by subject matter. P. 158, books with contributions by Phillpotts: author or editor, year, title of contribution. Pp. 159-161, chronological list of American first editions. Index.

Book Collector's Quarterly. No. 5 (January-March, 1932), p. 111: "one of the best printed bibliographies ever produced."

Waveney Girvan. *Eden Phillpotts. An Assessment and a Tribute.* London: Hutchinson, 1953. Pp. 159.

Pp. 153-159, English first editions, 1888-1953. Chronological arrangement. Publisher, genre.

Girvan supplements Hinton's list of book titles, but even Hinton and Girvan together do not provide a complete primary list.

Percival F. Hinton. "Note 226. A Ghost Laid." *Book Collector* 13 (1964): 350-351.

Notes on a spurious edition.

GENERAL

Millett; Temple & Tucker; NCBEL, IV, 699-704.

PICKARD, TOM (1946-)

Vinson-Poets.

PICKTHALL, MARMADUKE WILLIAM (1875-1936)

PRIMARY

Anne Fremantle. *Loyal Enemy.* London: Hutchinson and Co., 1938. Pp. 448.

A biography with many references, *passim,* to primary books and other writings. Index of names, only.

GENERAL

Millett.

PILGRIM, DAVID: *see* PALMER, JOHN LESLIE.

PINERO, SIR ARTHUR WING (1855-1934)

PRIMARY

Edward Everett Hale, Jr. *Dramatists of Today.* London: George Bell and Sons, 1906. Pp. 236.

Pp. 212-227, plays by Pinero, 1877-1904. Title, theatre and date of first performance in England, in America, and on the Continent. Brief annotations.

Frank K. Walter. "Reading List on Arthur Wing Pinero." *Bulletin of Bibliography* 6 (1912): 298-300.

Primary books. Alphabetical arrangement. Place, publisher, format, pages, price, précis; reviews. Secondary bibliography arranged alphabetically by author: volume, pages, date, brief annotations.

Walter Lazenby. *Arthur Wing Pinero.* New York: Twayne Publishers, Inc. (TEAS 150), 1972. Pp. 173.

Pp. 165-167, primary bibliography. Arranged: Published Plays, Unpublished Plays with location of MSS, Other Works. Books: date of composition, place, publisher, date of publication. Period: volume, pages, date. Pp. 167-168, secondary bibliography of nine items, annotated. Other secondary items in Notes, pp. 157-163.

SECONDARY

Above, Walter and Lazenby.

GENERAL

Millett; Longaker & Bolles; Batho & Dobrée; Temple & Tucker; Coleman & Tyler; Adelman & Dworkin; Salem; Palmer & Dyson; NCBEL, III, 1166-1169; Breed & Sniderman.

PINTER, HAROLD (1930-)

PRIMARY

Martin Esslin. *The Peopled Wound: The Work of Harold Pinter.* Garden City, New York: Doubleday and Co., Inc., 1970. Pp. [xii], 270.

Pp. 255-261, primary bibliography. Arranged: Plays, Other Writings, Interviews, and Translations. Books: British and American editions, place, publisher, date (NB: p. 255, important note concerning textual changes in different editions). Periods: date. Translations listed under name of language (13 different languages listed). Pp. 262-265, secondary bibliography selected, excluding reviews. Form arrangement.

The best primary bibliography, and a basic list of secondary studies.

William Baker and Stephen Ely Tabachnick. *Harold Pinter.* Edinburgh: Oliver and Boyd (Modern Writers Series), 1973. Pp. [viii], 156.

Pp. 151-153, supplementary primary bibliography.

SECONDARY

Herman T. Schroll. *Harold Pinter: A Study of His Reputation (1958-1969) and a Checklist.* Metuchen, N. J.: Scarecrow Press, Inc., 1971. Pp. 153.

Pp. 95-143, secondary bibliography. Form and genre arrangement including reviews of productions listed under title of production. Books: place, publisher, date, pages, Period: volume, date, pages. Index of names and play titles.

The bibliography section on p. 95 omits David S. Palmer, "A Harold Pinter Checklist," *Twentieth Century Literature* 16 (1970): 287-297. Useful annotations are provided by Steven H. Gale in "Harold Pinter. An Annotated Bibliography 1957-1971." *Bulletin of Bibliography* 29 (1972): 46-56.

Rüdiger Imhof. "Forschungsberichte und Bibliographien zu Harold Pinter." *Anglia* 93 (1975): 413-423, evaluates Schroll's work, points to the numerous bibliographies which preceded Schroll, and lists (pp. 419-423) pre-1969 items omitted by Schroll.

Austin E. Quigley. *The Pinter Problem.* Princeton: Princeton University Press, 1975. Pp. [xx], [295].

Pp. 279-289, secondary bibliography including items for 1969-1971. Steven H. Gale, *Journal of Modern Literature* 5 (1977): 786: "The 'Bibliography' has a British bias and is limited. . .(G. K. Hall is publishing an extensive annotated Pinter bibliography in 1977)."

GENERAL

Temple & Tucker; Coleman & Tyler; Adelman & Dworkin; Salem; Palmer & Dyson; Breed & Sniderman; Vinson-Dramatists.

PITTER, RUTH (1897-)

Longaker & Bolles; Daiches, Temple & Tucker; Vinson-Poets; NCBEL, IV, 327-328.

PLOMER, WILLIAM CHARLES FRANKLYN (1903-1973)

PRIMARY

John Robert Doyle, Jr. *William Plomer.* New York: Twayne Publishers, Inc. (TWAS 54), 1969. Pp. 183.

Pp. 175-176, "A Complete Chronological List of Books by William Plomer and Books Which He Has Edited or Introduced." Arranged: English Editions; American Editions; Books Edited or Introduced. Place, publisher, date. No details of Plomer's periodical contributions.

GENERAL

Millett; Daiches; Temple & Tucker; Stratford; NCBEL, IV, 704-705; Vinson-Poets; Vinson-Novelists; Bufkin.

PLUNKETT, EDWARD JOHN MORETON DRAX, LORD DUNSANY: *see* DUNSANY.

PLUNKETT, JOSEPH MARY (1887-1916)

PRIMARY

Patrick Sarsfield O'Hegarty. "Bibliographies of 1916 and the Irish Revolution. III. Joseph Mary Plunkett." *Dublin Magazine* 7 (January-March, 1932): 30.

Primary books. Chronological arrangement. Transcribed TP, part collation, pagination, binding, bibliographical notes.

PORTER, ALAN (1899-1942)

NCBEL, IV, 328.

PORTER, PETER (1929-)

Stratford; Temple & Tucker.

POTOCKI, GEOFFREY WLADISLAS VAILE (1903-)

?Count De Montalk.

PRIMARY

A Letter from Richard Aldington, and a Summary Bibliography of Count Potocki's Published Works. Draguignan (Var), France: Melissa Press, [1961], [1963]. Four leaves.

P. IV_r, primary books. Place, date (1927-1947).

Rigby Graham. "A Tentative Checklist of the Work of Geoffrey Count Potocki." *Private Libraries* 8 (1967): 23-26.

Primary writings. Chronological arrangement. Date, place, publisher, annotations.

POTTER, DENNIS CHRISTOPHER GEORGE (1935-)

Vinson-Dramatists.

POTTER, HELEN BEATRIX (1866-1943)

(Mrs. William Heelis).

PRIMARY

Jane Quinby. *Beatrix Potter: A Bibliographical Checklist.* New York: The Author, 1954. 250 copies.

Not seen.

Marcus Crouch. *Beatrix Potter.* London: Bodley Head (Bodley Head Monograph), 1960. P. 19: Quinby's "work is clearly incomplete . . . [but] . . . it is indispensable."

Leslie Linder. *Beatrix Potter, 1966-1943, Centenary Catalogue, 1966.* London: National Book League, [1966]. Pp. 109.

Not seen.

Described in the essay by Laurie Deval, *Book Collector* 15 (1966): 454-459.

--*A History of the Writings of Beatrix Potter including Unpublished Work.* London and New York: Frederick Warne and Co. Ltd., 1971. Pp. xxvi, 446;

Essays on all aspects of all primary writings, published and unpublished, arranged under headings: Letters to Children; Peter Rabbit Books; Painting Books; Plays; Music Books; Fairy Caravan; Sister Anne; Wag-by-Wall; Tale of the Faithful Dove; Miscellaneous Writings including journalism and election work. Appendices provide tabulated information for books and illustrations, including part collation, date, number of copies in first edition, price. Lavish illustrations, many of MSS here first reproduced. Text of many writings also provided. Index.

TLS, No. 3610 (7 May 1971): 535: "a most detailed and careful examination of the provenance of Beatrix Potter's written work, and a valuable contribution to the bibliography of her published books . . . With the publication of this massive compilation, Beatrix Potter becomes almost the best documented writer of the century."

POTTER, STEPHEN MEREDITH (1900-1969)

Daiches; Temple & Tucker; NCBEL, IV, 1104-1105.

POWELL, ANTHONY DYMOKE (1905-)

PRIMARY

Neil Brennan. *Anthony Powell.* New York: Twayne Publishers, Inc. (TEAS 158), 1974. Pp. 231.

Pp. 221-223, selected primary bibliography. Form arrangement. Books, British and American editions: place, publisher, date. Periods: [listed only in notes, pp. 209-219] volume, date, pages. Pp. 223-225, annotated secondary bibliography; other entries in Notes.

P. 223: "Articles and reviews by Powell published in periodicals number in the thousands and cannot be given here. The curious should check especially the London *Daily Telegraph* (1936, 1958-72), the *Spectator* (1937-39, 1946), and *Punch* (1953-58)."

GENERAL

Daiches; Temple & Tucker; Adelman & Dworkin (Novel); Vinson-Novelists; Drescher & Kahrmann; NCBEL, IV, 705-706; Bufkin.

POWYS, JOHN COWPER (1872-1963)

PRIMARY

Lloyd Emerson Siberell. *A Bibliography of the First Editions of John Cowper Powys.* Cincinnatti: Ailanthus Press, 1934. Pp. 53. 350 copies.

Primary first editions. Form arrangement. Transcribed TP, part collation, pagination, binding, date, bibliographical notes. P. 49, titles of books with introductions by Powys. Pp. 50-52, articles by Powys: chronological arrangement. Dates; poems are identified.

R. C. Churchill. *The Powys Brothers.* London: Longmans, Green and Co. (WTW 150), 1962. Pp. 40.

Pp. 32-34, primary books. Date, place, genre, miscellaneous notes.

Derek Langbridge. *John Cowper Powys. A Record of Achievement.* London: Library Association, 1966. Pp. 256.

Pp. 74-229, bibliography. Primary, secondary. Chronological arrangement, with works by Powys on verso (books: place, publisher, date, pages, quotations; and periods: volume, date, pages), and on the facing recto, reviews of, comments about, and reprints of Powys. Pp. 233-256, indices.

An accurate and virtually complete list, arranged so eccentrically as to prevent one's using it (see comments of R. J. Roberts, *Book Collector* 17 [1968] : 103).

Arthur J. Anderson. "John Cowper Powys: A Bibliography." *Bulletin of Bibliography* 25 (1967): 73-78, 94.

Primary, secondary selected. Chronological arrangement in both parts. Books: place, publisher, date. Periods: volume, date, pages. Excludes reviews of Powys.

Less informative than Langbridge, but much simpler to use.

SECONDARY

Above, Churchill, pp. 39-40; Langbridge, *passim;* Anderson, pp. 77-78, 94.

GENERAL

Millett; Daiches; Longaker & Bolles; Temple & Tucker; NCBEL, IV, 706-710; Bufkin.

POWYS, LLEWELLYN (1884-1939)

PRIMARY

A Catalogue of the Llewellyn Powys Manuscripts. Hurst, Berks, G. F. Sims (Rare Books), n.d. [ca. 1953] .

200 plus items in this bookseller's catalogue.

Kenneth Hopkins, ed. *Llewellyn Powys.* New York: Horizon Press, 1961. Pp. 318.

Pp. 311-316, "A Check List of Books by Llewellyn Powys." Publisher, place, date, short description of contents. Separate entry for each edition. Pp. 317-318, books relating to Powys.

R. C. Churchill. *The Powys Brothers.* London: Longmans, Green and Co. (WTW 150), 1962. Pp. 40.

Pp. 34-36, primary books. Date, place, genre, miscellaneous notes.

SECONDARY

Above, Hopkins, pp. 317-318; Churchill, pp. 39-40.

GENERAL

Millett; Daiches; Longaker & Bolles; NCBEL, IV, 1105-1107.

POWYS, THEODORE FRANCIS (1875-1953)

PRIMARY

Henry Coombes. *Theodore Francis Powys.* London: Barrie and Rockliff, 1960. Pp. 173.

Pp. 167-169, primary books. Place, publisher, date.

R. C. Churchill. *The Powys Brothers.* London: Longmans, Green and Co. (WTW 150), 1962. Pp. 40.

Pp. 36-38, primary books. Date, place, genre, miscellaneous notes.

Peter Riley. *A Bibliography of Theodore Francis* Powys. Hastings: R. A. Brimmell, 1967. Pp. 72.

Primary first editions, secondary selected. Form arrangement. Transcribed TP, full collation, pagination, binding, date, price, list of later editions, contents, bibliographical and textual notes. Includes lists of uncollected contributions to periodicals and anthologies. Pp. 68-69, literary studies of Powys, excluding reviews.

The standard bibliography. R. J. Roberts, *Book Collector* 17 (1968): 103: "virtues of orthodoxy . . . sensible and competent."

SECONDARY

Above, Riley, pp. 68-69.

GENERAL

Millett; Longaker & Bolles; Daiches; Temple & Tucker; NCBEL, IV, 710-712; Bufkin.

PREEDY, GEORGE R.: *see* LONG, GABRIELLE.

PRESCOTT, HILDA FRANCES MARGARET (1896-1972)

Vinson-Novelists; Bufkin.

PRIESTLEY, JOHN BOYNTON (1894-)

PRIMARY

Lucetta J. Teagarden. "The J. B. Priestley Collection" [at the University of Texas]. *Library Chronicle of the University of Texas* 7, iii (1963): 27-32.

A descriptive essay of this extensive collection.

Alan Edwin Day. "J. B. Priestley: A Checklist." *Bulletin of Bibliography* 28 (1971): 42-48.

Primary selected, secondary selected. Arranged: Collected Editions, Separate Works, Contributions to Books and Pamphlets (British editions only). Books: place, publisher, date. Secondary bibliography, pp. 47-48. Exclusions from this list (primarily Priestley's journalism) are described on p. 42.

There is no complete listing of Priestley's writings.

SECONDARY

Above, Day, pp. 47-48.

Gareth L. Evans. *J. B. Priestley--The Dramatist.* London: Heinemann, 1964. Pp. 230.

Pp. 226-227, secondary bibliography.

GENERAL

Millett; Longaker & Bolles; Daiches; Temple & Tucker; Coleman & Tyler; Adelman & Dworkin; Salem; Palmer & Dyson; Breed & Sniderman; Adelman & Dworkin (Novel); Vinson-Novelists; Vinson-Dramatists; NCBEL, IV, 712-717; Bufkin.

PRINCE, FRANK TEMPLETON (1912-)

Daiches; Temple & Tucker; Vinson-Poets; NCBEL, IV, 328-329; Stratford.

PRICHETT, VICTOR SAWDON (1900-)

Daiches; Temple & Tucker; Vinson-Novelists; NCBEL, IV, 717; Bufkin.

PRYS-JONES, ARTHUR GLYN (1888-)

Vinson-Poets.

PUDNEY, JOHN SLEIGH (1909-)

Longaker & Bolles; Temple & Tucker; Vinson-Poets; Vinson-Novelists.

PUGH, EDWIN WILLIAM (1874-1930)

PRIMARY

Theophilus E. M. Boll. *The Works of Edwin Pugh (1874-1930).* Philadelphia: University of Pennsylvania Dissertation, 1934. Pp. 104.

P. [97], bibliography. Primary books, English editions. Genre arrangement. Publisher, date, reprints.

Vincent Brome. *Four Realist Novelists.* London: Longmans, Green and Co. (WTW 183), 1965. Pp. 36.

Pp. 33-34, primary books. Date, place, genre.

GENERAL

NCBEL, IV, 717-718.

PULLEIN-THOMPSON, DENNIS: *see* CANNAN, DENIS.

PYM, BARBARA MARY CRAMPTON (1913-)

NCBEL, IV, 718.

QUARTERMAIN, JAMES: *see* LYNNE, JAMES BROOM.

QUENNELL, PETER COURTNEY (1905-)

Millett; Daiches; Temple & Tucker; NCBEL, IV, 1107-1108.

QUILLER-COUCH, SIR ARTHUR THOMAS (1863-1944)

PRIMARY

"Bibliographies of Modern Authors. Sir Arthur Thomas Quiller-Couch." *London Mercury* 4 (1921): 532-533.

Primary books, 1881-1920. Chronological arrangement. Publisher, year, brief notes.

Fred Brittain. *Arthur Quiller-Couch. A Biographical Study of Q.* Cambridge: University Press, 1947. Pp. 174.

Pp. 159-166, "Chronological List of Q's Publications, including a selection from his contributions to periodical literature." Books: date, genre. Periods: date. Also mention of Q's contributions to books.

Brittain gives details of four books in "Four 'Q' Rarities," *Book Handbook* II, i (March, 1951): 27-35. Transcribed TP, part collation, binding, bibliographical notes, reproduction of the four title pages.

GENERAL

Millett; Longaker & Bolles; Batho & Dobrée; Temple & Tucker; NCBEL, III, 1071-1073.

RACKHAM, ARTHUR (1867-1939)

PRIMARY

Frederick Coykendall. *Arthur Rackham. A List of Books Illustrated by Him.* New York: Privately Printed, 1922. Pp. 22. 175 copies.

Pp. 15-22, list of titles with author, date, place, publisher.

Sarah Briggs Latimore and Grace Clark Haskell. *Arthur Rackham A Bibliography.* Los Angeles: Suttonhouse, 1936. Pp. 112. 550 copies. Reprinted: New York: Burt Franklin, 1970.

Primary bibliography. Form arrangement. Books: Transcribed TP, binding, description of Rackham's illustration, bibliographical notes. Periods: date, author and title of work illustrated, description of illustrations.

Roland Baughman, *Book Collector* 10 (Summer, 1961): 236: "the definitive bibliography of Rackham . . . " But see Dorothy Colman's review in *Reading and Collecting* 1 (December, 1936): 11, 24, for corrections of errors and numerous additional items.

Bretram Rota, "The Printed Work of Arthur Rackham," in Derek Hudson, *Arthur Rackham,* London: William Heinemann Ltd.; New York: Charles Scribner's Sons, 1960 [also available as separate offprint]. Pp. 181.

Pp. 164-181, bibliography. A simplified listing of all items in Latimore and Haskell, with a number of additional items.

Latimore and Haskell provide the most details, while Rota must be checked for his complete list of illustrations.

RAFFALOVICH, MARK ANDRÉ (1864-1934)

PRIMARY

Father Brocard Sewell, ed. *Two Friends, John Gray and André Raffalovich. Essays Biographical and Critical.* Aylesford: St. Albert's Press, 1963. Pp. 193.

Pp. 188-189, "Checklist of Raffalovich," by Alan Anderson. Primary. Form, place, publisher, date. Secondary bibliography in text, *passim.*

RAINE, KATHLEEN JESSIE (1908-)

Daiches; Temple & Tucker; Vinson-Poets; NCBEL, IV, 329; Stratford.

RANSOME, ARTHUR MICHELL (1884-1967)

PRIMARY

Anthony Rota. "Some Uncollected Authors. XXI. Arthur Ransome." *Book Collector* 8 (1959): 289-293.

Primary first editions. Publisher, date, format, binding. Occasional miscellaneous notes.

Hugh Shelley. *Arthur Ransome.* London: Bodley Head (Bodley Head Monograph), 1960. Pp. 72.

Pp. 71-72, primary bibliograpny. Books: dates. Books translated by, edited by, or with contributions by Ransome ("not exhaustive"): main author or editor, date, identification of Ransome's contribution.

GENERAL

NCBEL, IV, 718-719.

RATTIGAN, SIR TERENCE MERVYN (1911-1977)

Daiches; Temple & Tucker; Coleman & Tyler; Adelman & Dworkin; Salem; Palmer & Dyson; Breed & Sniderman; Vinson-Dramatists; NCBEL, IV, 976-977.

RAVEN, SIMON ARTHUR NOEL (1927-)

Vinson-Novelists; Drescher & Kahrmann; Temple & Tucker.

RAYMOND, ERNEST (1888-1974)

Vinson-Novelists.

RAWORTH, THOMAS MOORE (1938-)

Vinson-Poets.

READ, SIR HERBERT EDWARD (1893-1968)

PRIMARY

Francis Berry. *Herbert Read.* London: Longmans, Green and Co. (WTW 45), 1961. Pp. 43.

Pp. 41-43, bibliography of primary books. Place, date, genre.

Henry Treece, ed. *Herbert Read: An Introduction to his Work by Various Hands.* London: Faber and Faber, 1944. Pp. 120.

Pp. 116-120, bibliography of primary books, first editions. Chronological arrangement. Transcribed TP, place, publisher, date, size in inches.

Robin Skelton, ed. *Herbert Read: A Memorial Symposium.* London: Methuen and Co., Ltd., 1970. Pp. 264.

Pp. 192-258, "A Checklist of the Herbert Read Archive in the McPherson Library of the University of Victoria" [based upon Read's private papers], by Howard Gerwing. Primary. Form arrangement. Books, arranged alphabetically by title: place, publisher, date, pages, contents, subsequent editions, miscellaneous notes. Lists of unique typescripts and manuscripts by Read with suggestions concerning place of publication; lists of letters to Read (with name of writer, number of letters, holograph or type) and by him.

This checklist, with a three-page addenda (pp. 69-71), has been separately published by the University of Victoria, Victoria, B. C., 1969, pp. 71. It and Treece (above) provide a start toward the definitive bibliography.

GENERAL

Millett; Daiches; Longaker & Bolles; Temple & Tucker; NCBEL, IV, 1108-1113.

REDGROVE, PETER WILLIAM (1932-)

Vinson-Poets.

REED, HENRY (1914-)

Vinson-Poets; NCBEL, IV, 330.

REEVES, JAMES (1909-)

Pseudonym of John Morris Reeves.

Vinson-Poets; NCBEL, IV, 330-331; Stratford.

REID, ALASTAIR (1926-)

Vinson-Poets.

REID, FORREST (1875-1947)

PRIMARY

Russell Burlingham. *Forrest Reid A Portrait and a Study.* London: Faber and Faber, 1953. Pp. 259.

Pp. 227-250, primary, secondary bibliography. Form arrangement. Books: date, place, publisher, part collation, dedication, price, binding, contents listed with details of previous publication. Bibliographical and textual notes include references to reprints. Periods: volume, pages, dates, title of book in which reprinted. Pp. 249-250, secondary bibliography.

Forrest Reid. An Exhibition of Books and Manuscripts held in the Museum and Art Gallery, Belfast. September, 1953. City and County Borough of Belfast, 1954. Pp. xxxv. 200 copies.

Checklist of Reid's printed work in this collection. Arranged: Books; Contributions to Books and Periodicals; Letters; Other Items. Locates Reid's manuscripts and letters.

SECONDARY

Above, Burlingham, pp. 249-250.

GENERAL

Daiches; Temple & Tucker; NCBEL, IV, 719-720; Bufkin.

RENAULT, MARY (1905-)

Pseudonym of Mary Challans.

PRIMARY

Peter Wolfe. *Mary Renault.* New York: Twayne Publishers, Inc. (TEAS 98), 1969. Pp. 198.

Pp. 193-194, "Selected Bibliography." Primary, secondary. Books: place, publisher, date. Periods: volume, date, pages. Additional secondary criticism in text, *passim.*

GENERAL

Temple & Tucker; Bufkin.

REYNOLDS, STEPHEN SYDNEY (1881-1919)

NCBEL, IV, 720.

RHYS, JEAN (1894-)

(Mrs. Max Hamer).

PRIMARY

Elgin W. Mellown. "A Bibliography of the Writings of Jean Rhys with a Selected List of Reviews and Other Critical Writings." *World Literature Written in English* 16 (1977): 179-202.

Primary writings, selected secondary. Form arrangement. Books (British and American first editions): transcribed TP, part collation, binding, date, contents; listing of all editions, impressions, and translations (place, publisher, date, and translator for books other than first editions). Periods: volume, date, pages. Reviews of primary books listed under title of book.

SECONDARY

Above, Mellown, pp. 180-198 (reviews), pp. 200-202 (studies).

GENERAL

NCBEL, IV, 720; Vinson-Novelists; Stratford; Temple & Tucker.

RICHARDS, IVOR ARMSTRONG (1893-)

Pseudonym of Richards and C. K. Ogden: Adelyne More.

PRIMARY

Jerome P. Schiller. *I. A. Richards' Theory of Literature.* New Haven and London: Yale University Press, 1969. Pp. [xiv], 189.

Pp. 177-180, primary bibliography. Form arrangement, alphabetical by title in each section. Books: place, publisher, date. Periods: volume, date, pages. Pp. 180-184, secondary bibliography. Form arrangement, alphabetical by author in each section. Information as for primary.

SECONDARY

Above, Schiller, pp. 180-184.

GENERAL

Millett; Daiches; Temple & Tucker; Vinson-Poets; NCBEL, IV, 1113-1116.

RICHARDSON, DOROTHY MILLER (1873-1957)

(Mrs. Alan Odle).

PRIMARY

John Gawsworth. *Ten Contemporaries. Notes Toward their Definitive Bibliography (Second Series).* London: Joiner and Steele, 1933. Pp. 240. 1000 copies.

Pp. 199-207, primary books, first editions, 1913-1932. Chronological arrangement. Transcribed TP, full collation, pagination, binding, occasional bibliographical notes. Includes books translated by Richardson.

Joseph Prescott, "A Preliminary Checklist of the Periodical Publications of Dorothy M. Richardson" in A. Dayle Wallace and Woodburn O. Ross, eds. *Studies in Honor of John Wilcox.* Detroit: Wayne State University Press, 1958. Pp. xiv, 269.

Pp. 219-225, primary periodical contributions. Chronological arrangement. Volume, date, pages, genre.

Caesar R. Blake. *Dorothy Richardson.* Ann Arbor: University of Michigan Press, 1960. Pp. 208.

Pp. 201-202, primary selected bibliography. Books: place, publisher, date. Periods: volume, pages, date. Pp. 202-207, secondary bibliography.

Gloria Glikin. "Checklist of Writings by Dorothy M. Richardson." *English Literature in Transition* 8 (1965): 1-11.

Primary. Genre arrangement. Books: place, publisher, date, notes on later editions and reprints. Periods: volume, pages, date.

The most complete primary bibliography.

SECONDARY

Above, Blake, pp. 202-207.

Gloria Glikin. "Dorothy M. Richardson: An Annotated Bibliography of Writings about Her." *English Literature in Transition* 8 (1965): 12-35; 14 (1971): 84-88.

Alphabetical by author arrangement, annotated. Continued in later issues.

GENERAL

Millett; Longaker & Bolles; Daiches; Temple & Tucker; NCBEL, IV, 721-722; Bufkin.

RICKWORD, JOHN EDGELL (1898-)

Millett; Temple & Tucker; Vinson-Poets; Stratford.

RIDGE, WILLIAM PETT (1860-1930)

PRIMARY

Vincent Brome. *Four Realist Novelists.* London: Longmans, Green and Co. (WTW 183), 1956. Pp. 36.

Pp. 35-36, bibliography. Primary books. Chronological arrangement. Date, place, genre. P. 36, brief secondary bibliography.

SECONDARY

Above, Brome, p. 36.

GENERAL

Millett; Batho & Dobrée; NCBEL, IV, 722-723.

RIDLER, ANNE BARBARA BRADBY (1912-)

(Mrs. Vivian Ridler).

Daiches; Temple & Tucker; Breed & Sniderman; Vinson-Poets; NCBEL, IV, 331-332; Vinson-Dramatists.

ROBERTS, CECIL EDRIC MORNINGTON (1892-)

NCBEL, IV, 723-724.

ROBERTS, MICHAEL (1902-1949)

PRIMARY

T. W. Eason and R. Hamilton. *A Portrait of Michael Roberts.* Chelsea: College of S. Mark and S. John, 1949. Pp. 72.

Pp. 65-72, "Select Bibliography of the Published Writings of Michael Roberts," by R. Hamilton. Primary first editions. Genre arrangement. Books: publisher, date. Periods: volume, pages. Reviews by Roberts include title and author of book reviewed. P. 65, important note on limitations of bibliography.

Michael Roberts. *Collected Poems.* With Introductory Memoir by Janet Roberts. London: Faber and Faber, 1958. Pp. 226.

Bibliographical information additional to Hamilton (above) is given on pp. 7-8, 13-40.

GENERAL

Daiches; Temple & Tucker; NCBEL, IV, 332-333.

ROBERTS, MORLEY CHARLES (1857-1942)

PRIMARY

Storm Jameson. "Morley Roberts: The Last of the True Victorians." *Library Chronicle* (University of Pennsylvania) 27 (1961): 93-127.

A biographical appreciation, followed on pp. 124-125 by "Check-List" of primary books. Genre arrangement. Title and date. Pp. 125-127, description and location by Jameson and T. E. M. Boll of primary and secondary MSS, letters, and association items.

GENERAL

Millett.

ROBINSON, ESMÉ STUART LENNOX (1886-1958)

PRIMARY

Kaspar Spinner. *Die Alte Dame Sagt: Nein! Drei Irische Dramatiker. Lennox Robinson. Sean O'Casey. Denis Johnston.* Bern. Francke Verlag (Schweizer Anglistische Arbeiten 52), 1961. Pp. 210.

Pp. 207-208, bibliography of primary books. Genre arrangement. Publisher, date; date of first performance for plays.

Michael J. O'Neill. *Lennox Robinson.* New York: Twayne Publishers, Inc. (TEAS 9), 1964. Pp. 192.

Pp. [15]-[21], chronological table includes primary books and plays: date, theatre of first performance or publisher. Pp. 181-184, annotated secondary bibliography arranged alphabetically by author. Books: place, publisher, date. Periods: volume, pages, date.

SECONDARY

Above, O'Neill, pp. 181-184.

GENERAL

Millett; Longaker & Bolles; Temple & Tucker; Salem; NCBEL, III, 1943. Breed & Sniderman; Hogan.

ROBSON, JEREMY (1939-)

Vinson-Poets.

ROCHE, PAUL (1928-)

Vinson-Poets.

RODGERS, WILLIAM ROBERT (1909-1969)

PRIMARY

Darcy O'Brien. *W. R. Rodgers (1909-1969).* Lewisburg: Bucknell University Press (Irish Writers Series), 1970. Pp. 103.

P. 103, primary books, British and American first editions. Place, publisher, date, other information concerning unpublished primary writings. Also see "Chronology," pp. 11-12, and text, *passim,* for suggestions of primary periodical contributions and secondary bibliography.

GENERAL

Daiches; Temple & Tucker; NCBEL, IV, 333.

ROHMER, SAX (1883-1959)

Pseudonym of Arthur Henry Ward.

PRIMARY

Bradford M. Day. *Sax Rohmer. A Bibliography.* Denver, New York: Science Fiction and Fantasy Publications, 1963. Pp. 34 (mimeographed sheets).

Pp. 5-19, primary books, arranged alphabetically by title. Information varies, but usually place, publisher, date of various editions, account of previous publication of contents, binding. Pp. 20-31, stories published in magazines, chronologically arranged. Date and title of book in which collected.

A great amount of information, haphazardly presented.

Cay Van Ash and Elizabeth Sax Rohmer. *Master of Villainy: A Biography of Sax Rohmer.* [With bibliography by Robert E. Briney] Bowling Green, Ohio: Bowling Green University

Popular Press, 1972. Pp. x, 312.

Pp. 299-303, "Chronological Bibliography of the Books of Sax Rohmer." British and American first editions: place, publisher, date, contents of anthologies. Bibliographical suggestions concerning periodical contributions, and reprints and later editions are given in the text of this "popular" biography.

ROLFE, FREDERICK WILLIAM SERAFINO AUSTIN LEWIS MARY (1860-1913)

?Baron Corvo

PRIMARY

George Frederick Sims. *A Catalogue of Letters, Manuscript Papers and Books of Frederick Rolfe (Baron Corvo)*. Harrow: Sims (Booksellers), 1949. Pp. 24. 600 copies.

Extensive descriptions of 88 items.

Cecil Woolf. *A Bibliography of Frederick Rolfe Baron Corvo.* London: Rupert Hart-Davis (Soho Bibliography No. 7), 1957. Pp. 136. Revised Edition, 1970. Pp. 196. [Not seen].

Primary. Form arrangement. Transcribed TP, part collation, pagination, binding, date, all British and foreign editions; extensive bibliographical and textual notes. Books with contributions by Rolfe described like first editions. Periods: date, pages, notes. Chronology of Rolfe's writings. Index.

The most complete bibliography, but not without flaws: see reviews of both editions in the *Library* 12 (1957), 135-137 and 28 (1973), 167; and also the *Private Library* 5 (1972), 159-166.

Cecil Woolf and Timothy d'Arch Smith. *Frederick William Rolfe, Baron Corvo. A Catalogue.* Marylebone Central Public Library Exhibition, October 19 - November 12, 1960. Seven mimeographed sheets (eleven sides).

Catalogue of the Centenary exhibition, listing many association items.

Cecil Woolf. *A Corvo Library.* London: C. Woolf, 1965. Pp. 23.

Detailed description of Rabbi Bertram Korn's collection offered for sale by Woolf.

SECONDARY

Above, Woolf and Smith.

Robert John Bayer. "About Rolfe." *Reading and Collecting* 1 (February, 1937): 6.

Books and periodicals about Rolfe. Place, Date. Brief annotations.

GENERAL

Batho & Dobrée; Temple & Tucker; NCBEL, IV, 724-725; Bufkin.

ROOK, WILLIAM ALAIN (1909-)

Vinson-Poets.

ROS, AMANDA MCKITTRICK (1861-1939)

PRIMARY

Jack Loudan. *O Rare Amanda! The Life of Amanda McKittrick Ros.* London: Chatto and Windus, 1954. Pp. 200.

Pp. 195-200, bibliography by T. Stanley Mercer. Primary books. Chronological arrangement. Transcribed TP, part collation, binding, date, variant bindings, bibliographical notes, subsequent editions.

ROSE, CHRISTINE BROOKE (1923-)

(Mrs. Jerzy Peterkiewicz).

Temple & Tucker; Bufkin; Vinson-Novelists; Drescher & Kahrmann.

ROSENBERG, ISAAC (1890-1918)

PRIMARY

Gordon Bottomley and Denys Harding, eds. *The Collected Poems of Isaac Rosenberg.* London: Chatto and Windus, 1949. Pp. 240.

Pp. 1-2, description of primary books: date, publisher, place, pages. Important omissions and errors in this volume are listed by Joseph Cohen, "Isaac Rosenberg: The Poet's Progress in Print." *English Literature in Transition* 6 (1963), 142-146.

Jon Silkin and Maurice de Sausmarez, eds. *Isaac Rosenberg, 1890-1918. A Catalogue of an Exhibition held at Leeds University May-June, 1959, together with the text of unpublished material.* Leeds: University of Leeds with Partridge Press, 1959. Pp. 36.

Best checklist of Rosenberg's writings and other artistic activities. Arranged: pp. 4-20, texts of unpublished writings; pp. 21-23, poetry MSS; p. 24, MSS letters; p. 25, printed works; pp. 26-27, association material; pp. 28-36, paintings and drawings by Rosenberg. A checklist of the art works is provided by Jean Liddiard. *Isaac Rosenberg: The Half Used Life.* London: Victor Gollancz Ltd., 1975. Pp. [277]-282; and Rosenberg's manuscripts are located by Joseph Cohen. *Journey to the Trenches. The Life of Isaac Rosenberg 1890-1918.* London: Robson Books Ltd., 1975, pp. [188]-189.

SECONDARY

Above, Liddiard, pp. [271]-275; Cohen, pp. [209]-216.

GENERAL

Longaker & Bolles; Daiches; Temple & Tucker; Breed & Sniderman; NCBEL, IV, 333-334.

ROSS, ALAN (1922-)

Temple & Tucker; Vinson-Poets; NCBEL, IV, 334-335; Stratford.

ROSS, MARTIN: *see* SOMERVILLE, EDITH ANNA OENONE.

ROSS, SIR RONALD (1857-1932)

PRIMARY

Rodolphe L. Mégroz. *Ronald Ross, Discoverer and Creator.* London: Allen and Unwin, 1931. Pp. 282.

Pp. 263-273, bibliography. Arranged: Medical; Related Material by Others; Mathematics; Literature. Books: publisher, place, date, brief annotations.

John Gawsworth. *Ten Contemporaries. Notes Toward their Definitive Bibliography* [First Series]. London: Benn, 1931. Pp. 224.

Pp. 158-165, "The Literary Work of Sir Ronald Ross." Primary first editions, selected, 1883-1928. Chronological arrangement. Transcribed TP, full collation, pagination, binding, date, bibliographical and textual notes.

ROWSE, ALFRED LESLIE (1903-)

Daiches; Temple & Tucker; Vinson-Poets; NCBEL, IV, 1210-1211.

ROYDE-SMITH, NAOMI GWLADYS (-1964)

(Mrs. Ernest Milton).

Millett; Temple & Tucker; NCBEL, IV, 725-726.

RUBINSTEIN, HAROLD FREDERICK (1891-)

NCBEL, IV, 977-978.

RUDDOCK, MARGOT (1907-1951)

NCBEL, IV, 335.

RUSSELL, COUNTESS: *see* ELIZABETH.

RUSSELL, BERTRAND ARTHUR WILLIAM, LORD RUSSELL (1872-1970)

PRIMARY

Gertrude Jacob. "Bertrand Russell. An Essay toward a Bibliography." *Bulletin of Bibliography* 13 (1929): 198-199; 14 (1930): 28-30.

Primary, secondary selected. Form and subject arrangement. Books: place, publisher, date, pages, brief annotations.

Periods: volume, date, pages. Reviews by Russell include title and author of book reviewed. Pp. 29-30, secondary bibliography. Continued by Ruja (below).

Harry Ruja. "Bertrand Russell. A Classified Bibliography, 1929-1967." *Bulletin of Bibliography* 25 (1968): 182-190, 192; 26 (1969): 29-32.

Information and arrangement as in Jacob (above), except that reviews of Russell's books are included in the primary title entry.

Lester E. Denonn. "Bibliography of the Writings of Bertrand Russell to 1962" in Paul Arthur Schilp, ed., *The Philosophy of Bertrand Russell.* New York: Harper and Row (Harper Torchbooks, The Academy Library), 1963. Two volumes.

II, 746-825, bibliography. Pp. 746-789, writings to 1944; pp. 790-811, writings 1944-1962; pp. 812-825, addenda and revisions. Primary. Chronological arrangement. Books: publisher, place, date, pages, contents, reprints and subsequent editions. Periods: volume, pages, date. Reviews by Russell include author and title of book reviewed.

Harry Ruja. "A Selective, Classified Bertrand Russell Bibliography" in D. F. Pears, ed., *Bertrand Russell. A Collection of Critical Essays.* Garden City, N. Y.: Doubleday and Co., Inc. (Anchor Books), 1972.

Pp. 357-387, selected primary and secondary bibliography of writings on philosophy. Topical arrangement, each section subdivided: primary books, primary period contributions, and secondary criticism. Books: place, publisher, date. Periods: volume, date, pages. P. 366, other bibliographies; pp. 363-364, obituary notices.

A continuation of Jacob, Ruja, and Denonn.

SECONDARY

Above, Jacob, pp. 29-30; Ruja, *passim.*

Alan Dorward. *Bertrand Russell. A Short Guide to his Philosophy.* London: Longmans, Green and Co. (Supplement to British Book News No. 10), 1951. Pp. 44.

P. 40, books about Russell.

GENERAL

Millett; Daiches; Batho & Dobrée; Temple & Tucker; NCBEL, IV, 1283-1291.

RUSSELL, GEORGE WILLIAM (AE) (1867-1935)

PRIMARY

Alan Denson. *Printed Writings by George William Russell (AE) A Bibliography with some notes on his pictures and portraits.* Evanston, Illinois: Northwestern University Press, 1961. Pp. [256], plus additional 4 pp. "Corrigenda and Addenda" (issued separately).

Primary, secondary selected. Form arrangement. Primary books: transcribed TP, part collation, pagination, binding, date, price, variants and reprints, occasionally number of copies and contents with details of earlier publication; numerous notes, especially in reference to specific copies. Periodicals arranged alphabetically by title, Russell's contribution being listed chronologically under each title: volume, pages, date, various notes. Divisions of material include: Letters and MSS; Oral Evidence to Parliamentary Committees; Public Sales; Books Dedicated To AE; Portraits by AE; Printed Reproductions; and others. Also essays concerning AE; chronology of his life; chronology of main publications; index.

M. O. N. Walsh, *Irish Book* 2 (Spring, 1963): 63-64: "There can be no doubting Mr. Denson's accuracy and comprehensiveness . . . "

SECONDARY

Above, Denson, pp. 182-205.

GENERAL

Millett; Longaker & Bolles; Temple & Tucker; NCBEL, III, 1912-1916.

RUSSELL, IRWIN PETER (1921-)

Vinson-Poets.

RYAN, WILLIAM PATRICK (1867-1942)

PRIMARY

Partick Sarsfield O'Hegarty. "Obituary." *Dublin Magazine* 18 (July-September, 1943): 72-73.

P. 73, primary books. Chronological arrangement. Date.

SACKVILLE-WEST, EDWARD CHARLES, LORD SACKVILLE (1901-1965)

Millett; Daiches; Temple & Tucker; NCBEL, IV, 726; Bufkin.

SACKVILLE-WEST, HON. VICTORIA MARY (1892-1962)

(Lady Nicolson).

PRIMARY

Florence Boochever. "A Selected List of Writings by and about Victoria Sackville-West." *Bulletin of Bibliography* 16 (1938):

93-94, 113-115.

Primary first editions (either British or American, but not both), secondary selected. Genre arrangement. Books: place, publisher, date, pages, précis. Periods: volume, pages, date, précis. P. 115, secondary bibliography.

Michael Stevens. *V. Sackville-West. A Critical Biography.* Stockholm: [Uppsala University Dissertation], 1972; New York: Scribner's, 1974. Pp. [136].

Pp. 120-124, primary bibliography. Genre arrangement. Books: place, publisher, date. Periods: date. Includes title of book in which period contribution is collected. Includes some but not all period contributions. Pp. 125-126, 129-131, secondary bibliography includes reviews of books. Additional primary and secondary references and bibliographical notes are given in the text, *passim.*

Sara Ruth Watson. *V. Sackville-West.* New York: Twayne Publishers, Inc. (TEAS 134), 1972. Pp. 164.

Pp. 151-157, selected primary and secondary writings. Books: place, publisher, date. Periods: volume, date, pages. Additional secondary material in notes, pp. 145-150.

There appears to be no complete list of all the primary writings.

SECONDARY

Above, Boochever, Stevens, and Watson.

GENERAL

Millett; Longaker & Bolles; Daiches; Temple & Tucker; NCBEL, IV, 335-337; Bufkin.

SADLEIR, MICHAEL THOMAS HARVEY (1888-1957)

PRIMARY

Simon Nowell-Smith. "Michael Sadleir A Handlist," *Library,* 5th

Series, 13 (June, 1958): 132-138.

Primary selected. Two chronological sections: works wholly by Sadleir; selected list of his contributions to books and periodicals, including unsigned reviews by him in the *TLS*. British first and revised editions only (unless American edition is first). Books: date, brief identification or note on contents, occasionally place and publisher. Periods: dates. Reviews by Sadleir include title and author of book reviewed.

GENERAL

Daiches; NCBEL, IV, 1116-1118.

SAINTSBURY, GEORGE EDWARD BATEMAN (1845-1933)

PRIMARY

John W. Oliver, ed. *George Saintsbury. A Last Vintage.* London: Methuen and Co., Ltd., 1950. Pp. 255.

Pp. 244-255, "A Saintsbury Bibliography," by W. M. Parker. Primary books. Arranged: Literary Histories; Biographical and Critical Works; Miscellaneous (including Translations); Introductions; Prefaces; Edited Matter. Publisher, date, occasional notes concerning reprints.

Leuba (below), p. 120: "a fairly complete check list."

Walter Leuba. *George Saintsbury.* New York: Twayne Publishers, Inc. (TEAS 56), 1967. Pp. 129.

Pp. 120-122, primary books and pamphlets (51). Chronological arrangement. Place, publisher, date. Pp. 122-126, annotated secondary bibliography. Alphabetical by author. Books: as for primary. Periods: volume, date, pages. Additional primary and secondary references in notes, pp. 105-119. P. 120, evaluation of previous bibliographies.

SECONDARY

Above, Leuba, pp. 105-119, 122-126.

GENERAL

Longaker & Bolles; Batho & Dobrée; Temple & Tucker; NCBEL, III, 1451-1453.

SAKI: *see* MUNRO, HECTOR HUGH.

SALMON, ARTHUR LESLIE (1865-[deceased])

PRIMARY

Arthur Leslie Salmon. London: Ernest Benn Ltd. (Augustan Books of Poetry), 1932. Pp. 32.

P. 31, bibliography of primary books. Genre arrangement. Publisher, date, price.

SANSOM, WILLIAM (1912-1976)

Daiches; Adelman & Dworkin (Novel); Vinson-Novelists; Drescher & Kahrmann; NCBEL, IV, 728-729; Bufkin.

SAPPER (1888-1937)

Pseudonym of Herman Cyril McNeile.

PRIMARY

Richard Usborne. *Clubland Heroes.* London: Constable, 1953. Pp. 217.

Some details of the primary writings can be obtained from pp. 143-202.

GENERAL

NCBEL, IV, 729-730.

SASSOON, SIEGFRIED LORAINE (1886-1967)

PRIMARY

Geoffrey Keynes. *A Bibliography of Siegfried Sassoon.* London: Rupert Hart-Davis (Soho Bibliography No. 10), 1962. Pp. [200].

Primary complete. Form arrangement. Books: transcribed TP, full collation, pagination, binding, date, price, subsequent editions, translations, reprints, contents, number of copies, full notes. Periods: volume, pages, date, references to later publication. Reviews by Sassoon include title and author of book reviewed. Indices of titles and of first lines locate all publications of individual pieces. Includes many unsigned and pseudonymous writings by Sassoon.

R. J. Roberts, *Book Collector* 11 (1962): 518: "a definitive bibliography"; offers corrections and additions.

David Farmer. "Addenda to Keyne's Bibliography of Siegfried Sassoon." *Papers of the Bibliographical Society of America* 63 (1969): 310-317.

Important additions and corrections.

SECONDARY

Michael Thorpe. *Siegfried Sassoon. A Critical Study.* Leiden: Leiden University Press; London: Oxford University Press, 1966. Pp. [xi], 318.

Pp. 301-302, secondary bibliography. Alphabetical-by-author arrangement. Books: place, publisher, date, annotations. Periods: date. Additional secondary bibliography in notes, *passim.*

GENERAL

Millett; Longaker & Bolles; Daiches; Temple & Tucker; NCBEL, IV, 337-340; Bufkin.

SAUNDERS, HILARY ST. GEORGE: *see* PALMER, JOHN LESLIE.

SAUNDERS, JAMES A. (1925-)

Vinson-Dramatists.

SAVAGE, DEREK STANLEY (1917-)

Temple & Tucker.

SAVORY, GERALD (1909-)

NCBEL, IV, 978.

SAYERS, DOROTHY LEIGH (1893-1957)

(Mrs. Atherton Fleming).

PRIMARY

James Sandoe. "Contribution toward a Bibliography of Dorothy L. Sayers." *Bulletin of Bibliography* 18 (1944): 76-81.

Primary first editions, British and American. Genre and form arrangement. Books: place, publisher, date, bibliographical notes, contents. Periods: volume, date, pages.

The best available checklist of writings to 1943.

Dorothy L. Sayers. *The Poetry of Search and the Poetry of Statement and Other Posthumous Essays on Literature, Religion and Language.* London: Victor Gollancz Ltd., 1963. Pp. [287].

P. [287], list of original sources or places where these 12 essays were published or delivered.

Dorothy L. Sayers, ed. Roderick Jellema. *Christian Letters to a Post-Christian World. A Selection of Essays.* Grand Rapids: William B. Eerdmans Publishing Company, 1969. Pp. [xiv], 236.

Pp. vii-xiii, "Introduction," and p. [iv] provide some bibliographical assistance.

These two posthumous collections appear to provide all of the available bibliographical information for the later primary writings.

Joe Randell Christopher. "A Sayers Bibliography." *Unicorn* [Brooklyn, New York] . Not seen.

Annotated primary and secondary bibliography published in parts, Part 5 appearing in 3, ii (1974) and Part 6 in 3, iii (1976).

GENERAL

Daiches; Temple & Tucker; Breed & Sniderman; NCBEL, IV, 730-731.

SCANNELL, VERNON (1922-)

Vinson-Poets; Vinson-Novelists; Stratford.

SCARFE, FRANCIS HAROLD (1911-)

Longaker & Bolles; Daiches; Temple & Tucker.

SCHIFF, SYDNEY ALFRED: *see* HUDSON, STEPHEN.

SCOTT, ALEXANDER (1920-)

Daiches; Vinson-Poets.

SCOTT, GEOFFREY (1886-1928)

Daiches; NCBEL, IV, 1118.

SCOTT, JOHN DICK (1917-)

Daiches; Vinson-Novelists; Drescher & Kahrmann; NCBEL, IV, 732; Bufkin.

SCOTT, PAUL MARK (1920-)

Vinson-Novelists; Drescher & Kahrmann; Bufkin.

SCOTT, TOM (1918-)

Daiches; Vinson-Poets.

SCOVELL, EDITH JOY (1907-)

Vinson-Poets; NCBEL, IV, 340.

SCUPHAM, JOHN PETER (1933-)

Vinson-Poets.

SEAMAN, SIR OWEN (1861-1936)

Millett; Batho & Dobrée; NCBEL, IV, 340.

SELBOURNE, DAVID (1937-)

Vinson-Dramatists.

SERGEANT, HERBERT HOWARD (1914-)

Vinson-Poets.

SEYMOUR, BEATRICE KEAN STAPLETON (-1955)

(Mrs. William Kean Seymour).

Millett; NCBEL, IV, 732.

SEYMOUR-SMITH, MARTIN (1928-)

Vinson-Poets.

SHAFFER, PETER LEVIN (1926-)

Pseudonym used with Anthony Shaffer: Peter Anthony.

PRIMARY

John Russell Taylor. *Peter Shaffer.* Harlow: Longman Group Ltd. (WTW 244), 1974. Pp. 34.

P. 33, primary books. Place, date, genre, collaborators. Pp. 33-34, secondary.

GENERAL

Coleman & Tyler; Adelman & Dworkin; Salem; Breed & Sniderman; Vinson-Dramatists; Temple and Tucker.

SHAIRP, ALEXANDER MORDAUNT (1887-1939)

Salem; Breed & Sniderman; NCBEL, IV, 978.

SHANKS, EDWARD BUXTON (1892-1953)

Millett; Longaker & Bolles; Daiches; Temple & Tucker; NCBEL, IV, 341.

SHARP, MARGERY (1905-)

(Mrs. Geoffrey Castle).

Vinson-Novelists.

SHAW, GEORGE BERNARD (1856-1950)

PRIMARY

Geoffrey H. Wells. *A Bibliography of the Books and Pamphlets of George Bernard Shaw.* London: Bookman's Journal, 1928. Pp. 46. [Reprinted from *Bookman's Journal* 11 (March, 1925);

12 (April, 1925).]

Primary books. Chronological arrangement (two lists: books by Shaw and books with contributions by Shaw). Books: transcribed TP, part collation, pagination, binding, date, bibliographical notes. Books with contributions: title, place, publisher, date, page numbers, identification of Shaw's contribution.

An early work, designed mainly for the collector of first editions.

C. Lewis Broad and Violet M. Broad. *Dictionary to the Plays and Novels of Bernard Shaw, with Bibliography of his Works and of the Literature concerning him with a Record of the principal Shavian Play Productions.* London: A. and C. Black; New York: Macmillan Co., 1929. Pp. [xii], [231].

Primary selected, secondary selected. Form arrangement. Pp. 87-100, Chronological list of primary books: date, British and American publishers, very brief annotations. Pp. 101-112, chronological lists of other writings and of reported speeches: dates and titles of periodicals in which published. Pp. 209-231, Play productions: alphabetical by title, including place, date, cast. Pp. 114-131, secondary criticism.

Useful mainly to the general reader.

Sir Maurice Holmes. *Some Bibliographical Notes on the Novels of G. B. Shaw.* London: Dulau and Co., 1929. Pp. [20]. 500 copies.

An essay on the bibliographical "points" of the four novels; pp. 17-[20], descriptions: transcribed TP, full collation, binding, pagination, notes.

F. E. Loewenstein. *The Rehearsal Copies of Bernard Shaw's Plays.* London: Reinhardt and Evans, 1950. Pp. 36.

Primary bibliography of the play-rehearsal-copies or "First-prints." Chronological arrangement. Transcribed TP, part collation, binding, date, extensive bibliographical, textual, and historical notes. P. 36, alphabetical index of titles.

Alfred C. Ward. *Bernard Shaw.* London: Longmans, Green and

Co., Ltd. (WTW 1), 1951. Pp. 56.

Pp. 41-56, bibliography and indices. Arranged: First Performances of Principal Plays (date, place, theatre); Primary Books (date, genre, contents); Indices of Plays, Prefaces, and Essays with titles of volumes in which collected.

Particularly useful for the listing of contents and locating of individual pieces.

Shaw Bulletin, I-II (1951-1959); title changed to *Shaw Review,* III (1960)- to date.

A feature of each issue is "A Continuing Check-List of Shaviana" by various editors; Part I lists "Works by Shaw" with title, place, publisher, date, notes and annotations.

A basic source of primary and secondary bibliographical information.

Lawrence C. Keough. "George Bernard Shaw, 1946-1955: A Selected Bibliography." *Bulletin of Bibliography* 22 (1959): 224-226; 23 (1960), 20-24, 36-41.

Primary and secondary. Genre arrangement. Books: place, publisher, date. Periodicals: date, volume and page numbers. Secondary, alphabetical by author under general topics.

SECONDARY

Above, Broad and Broad, pp. 114-131; Keough, pp. 20-24, 36-41.

Clara A. Milliken. "Reading List of Modern Dramatists . . . Shaw . . ." *Bulletin of Bibliography* 5 (October, 1907): 52-53.

Reviews and studies listed under title of the work criticized. Date; volume and page number, or place and publisher.

Earl Farley and Marvin Carlson. "George Bernard Shaw: A Selected Bibliography (1945-1955)." *Modern Drama* 2 (1959): 188-202, 295-325.

Books listed alphabetically by author: place, publisher, date, page references. Periodical contributions listed alphabetically by author under "General" or under title of appropriate play: date, volume and page numbers.

Shaw Review (formerly *Shaw Bulletin,* 1951-1959), 1960--to date. Practically every issue of the *Shaw Review* contains bibliographical checklists of primary and secondary material, as well as checklists of works on a specific topic (Shaw and Woman, for example). The secondary bibliography in each issue is arranged as follows: Books and Pamphlets (place, publisher, date, pages, annotations), Periodicals (date, volume, pages, annotations), Dissertations (brief entries taken from *Dissertations Abstracts*). The "Cumulative Index to *The Shaw Review* Vols. I-XVIII (1950-1975)," compiled by Shirley Rader, *Shaw Review* 18 (1975): 110-124, gives the volume, date, and pages of these checklists; and this "Index" and the relevant issues of the *Review* are perhaps the most valuable of all Shavian research tools. Helpful surveys of secondary work, including the bibliographies of such secondary work, are provided by Arthur O. Lewis, Jr., and Stanley Weintraub. "Bernard Shaw--Aspects and Problems of Research." *Shaw Review* 3 (1960): 18-26; and by Betty Hoyenga Richardson. "Anatomizing GBS: A Survey of Recent Shaw Scholarship." *Papers on Language and Literature* 8 (1972): 211-223.

GENERAL

Millett; Batho & Dobrée; Longaker & Bolles; Temple & Tucker; Coleman & Tyler; Adelman & Dworkin; Salem; Palmer & Dyson; NCBEL, III, 1169-1182; Breed & Sniderman.

SHAW, ROBERT ARCHIBALD (1927-)

Vinson-Novelists; Drescher & Kahrmann; Bufkin.

SHEARING, JOSEPH: *see* LONG, GABRIELLE.

SHELDON, RICHARD: *see* BURN, WILLIAM LAURENCE.

SHERRIFF, ROBERT CEDRIC (1896-)

Daiches; Temple & Tucker; Palmer & Dyson; Salem; Breed & Sniderman; Vinson-Dramatists; NCBEL, IV, 979.

SHIEL, MATTHEW PHIPPS (1865-1947)

PRIMARY

John Gawsworth. *Ten Contemporaries. Notes Toward their Definitive Bibliography* [First Series]. London: Ernest Benn Ltd., 1932. Pp. 224.

Pp. 174-191, primary books, first editions, 1895-1930. Chronological arrangement. Transcribed TP, full collation, pagination, binding, date, bibliographical notes. (This information is reprinted in Morse, below).

A. Reynolds Morse. *The Works of M. P. Shiel. A Study in Bibliography.* Los Angeles: Fantasy Publishing Co., Inc., 1948. Pp. 170. 1000 copies.

Primary. Form arrangement. Pp. 24-28, checklist of book titles. Pp. 32-113, books: short essay about or précis of each title; for each edition, transcribed TP, full collation, pagination, binding, bibliographical notes. Pp. 114-124, list of shorter writings and periodical contributions; pp. 125-136, description of MSS; pp. 137-154, collaborations (described like primary books). Also includes biographical essay, list of books in Shiel's library, and index.

A very informative, if idiosyncratically arranged, work.

Harold W. Billings. "Matthew Phipps Shiel: A Collection and Comments." *Library Chronicle of the University of Texas 6,* ii (1958): 34-43.

A discursive essay mentioning many primary books with place, publisher, date, and bibliographical notes.

GENERAL

NCBEL, IV, 732-733.

SHIELS, GEORGE (1886-1949)

Salem; Breed & Sniderman; NCBEL, IV, 979-980.

SHOVE, FREDEGOND (1889-1945)

Née Fredegond Maitland.

NCBEL, IV, 342.

SHUTE, NEVIL (1899-1960)

Pseudonym of Nevil Shute Norway.

PRIMARY

Julian Smith. *Nevil Shute (Nevil Shute Norway).* Boston: Twayne Publishers, G. K. Hall and Co. (TEAS 190), 1976. Pp. 166.

Pp. 159-161, primary bibliography of books and manuscripts. Books (British and American editions): place, publisher, date. Description of manuscript collections. P. 161, secondary bibliography, annotated. Additional secondary material is given in the Notes, pp. 151-157.

Further information about published primary works and manuscripts in the Syracuse University Library is provided by Howard L. Applegate. "Preliminary Calendar of the Nevil Shute Norway Manuscripts Microfilm." *Courier* 9 (October 1971): 14-20 [not seen].

GENERAL

Temple & Tucker; NCBEL, IV, 734.

SIDGWICK, ETHEL (1877-1970)

Millett; Temple & Tucker; NCBEL, IV, 734-735.

SIGERSON, DORA MARY (1866-1918)

(Mrs. Clement Shorter).

PRIMARY

E. O. S. [?Edith Oenone Somerville]. "Bibliography of Dora Sigerson Shorter." *Studies* (Dublin) 7 (March, 1918): 144-145.

Primary books. Chronological arrangement. Place, publisher, date, brief summary of contents, occasionally binding, brief notes.

GENERAL

NCBEL, III, 1911-1912.

SILKIN, JON (1930-)

Temple & Tucker; Vinson-Poets.

SILLITOE, ALAN (1928-)

PRIMARY

Allen Richard Penner. *Alan Sillitoe.* New York: Twayne Publishers, Inc. (TEAS 141), 1972. Pp. 156.

P. 151, primary books and articles, 1957-1969. Books, British and American first editions: place, publisher, date. Periods: volume, pages, date. Pp. 152-154, secondary bibliography, annotated. Other secondary items in notes, pp. 147-150.

SECONDARY

Above, Penner.

GENERAL

Temple & Tucker; Adelman & Dworkin (Novel); Vinson-Poets; Vinson-Novelists; Drescher & Kahrmann; Bufkin.

SIMMONS, JAMES STEWART ALEXANDER (1933-)

Vinson-Poets.

SIMPSON, JOHN FREDERICK NORMAN HAMPSON (1901-1955)

Pseudonym used: John Hampson.

NCBEL, IV, 596.

SIMPSON, NORMAN FREDERICK (1919-)

Adelman & Dworkin; Salem; Breed & Sniderman; Vinson-Dramatists; Temple & Tucker.

SINCLAIR, ANDREW ANNANDALE (1935-)

Vinson-Novelists; Bufkin.

SINCLAIR, MAY (1865-1946)

Pseudonym of Mary Amelia St. Clair Sinclair.

PRIMARY

T. E. M. Boll. "May Sinclair: A Check List." *Bulletin of the New York Public Library* 74 (1970): 454-467.

Pp. 454-458, introductory, biographical essay. Pp. 459-467, primary writings. Arranged by genre, topic, and form in 24 sections. Books: place, publisher and date for all editions. Periods: dates. Cross-references to show reprintings.

A complete list of Miss Sinclair's varied writings, the arrangement serving as annotation on the entries. A simplified version of this bibliography, limited primarily to books, is given by Boll in his *Miss May Sinclair: Novelist. A Biographical and Critical Introduction.* Rutherford, N. J.: Fairleigh Dickinson University Press, 1973, pp. 317-321. Boll's essay "On the May Sinclair Collection." *Library Chronicle* (University of Pennsylvania) 27 (1961): 1-15, describes the important Sinclair primary and secondary materials in the Pennsylvania Library; Boll also provides many references to secondary criticism.

SECONDARY

Above, Boll, *Library Chronicle, passim.*

Kenneth A. Robb. "May Sinclair: An Annotated Bibliography of Writings about Her." *English Literature in Transition* 16 (1973): 177-231.

Arranged alphabetically by author. Books: place, publisher, date, relevant pages. Periods: volume, date, pages. Continued in later issues.

Hrisey Dimitrakis Zegger. *May Sinclair.* Boston: Twayne Publishers, G. K. Hall and Co. (TEAS 192), 1976. Pp. 176.

Pp. 165-168, primary bibliography. Pp. 168-172, secondary bibliography, arranged alphabetically by author. Useful annotations. Additional critical material is provided in the notes, pp. 149-164.

GENERAL

Millett; Batho & Dobrée; Temple & Tucker; NCBEL, IV, 735-736; Bufkin.

SISSON, CHARLES HUBERT (1914-)

Vinson-Poets.

SITWELL, DAME EDITH LOUISA (1887-1964)

PRIMARY

Richard Fifoot. *A Bibliography of Edith, Osbert and Sacheverell Sitwell.* Second Edition, Revised. London: Rupert Hart-Davis (Soho Bibliography No. 11); [Hamden, Conn.] : Archon Books, 1971. Pp. 432.

Pp. 17-141, bibliography of Edith Sitwell. Primary first editions. Form arrangement. Books: transcribed TP, part collation, pagination, binding, date, price, contents, selected later editions and issues (Fifoot's Preface, p. 9, explains selection), number of copies, bibliographical and textual notes. Periods: volume, pages, date; title and author of books reviewed by Dame Edith. Lists of translations of her writing (translator, place, publisher, date), of recordings by her, and of musical settings of works by her. Pp. 395-432, index for the entire volume indicates the inclusion of individual pieces in later collections.

The standard bibliography. Reviewed by B. C. Bloomfield, *The Library* 28 (1973): 76-77.

SECONDARY

Lois D. Rosenberg. "Edith Sitwell: A Critical Bibliography, 1915-1950." *Bulletin of Bibliography* 21 (1953-1954): 40-43, 57-60. Supplemented by John W. Ehrstine and Douglas D. Rich. "Edith Sitwell: A Critical Bibliography 1951-1973." *Bulletin of Bibliography* 31 (1974): 111-116.

Arranged: [Selected] Critical Writings by Dame Edith (concerning her own works] ; Bibliography, Biography and Criticism; Reviews (listed under title of book reviewed). Books: place, publisher, date. Periods: volume, pages, date. Brief annotations.

GENERAL

Millett; Longaker & Bolles; Daiches; Temple & Tucker; NCBEL, IV, 342-346.

SITWELL, SIR FRANCIS OSBERT SACHEVERELL (1892-1969)

PRIMARY

Roger Fulford. *Osbert Sitwell.* London: Longmans, Green and Co. (WTW 16), 1951. Pp. 44.

Pp. 37-40, selected primary and secondary bibliography. Date, genre. Pp. 41-44, Index to Essays and Short Stories. Alphabetical list of titles with title of volume in which collected.

Richard Fifoot. *A Bibliography of Edith, Osbert and Sacheverell Sitwell.* Second Edition, Revised. London: Rupert Hart-Davis (Soho Bibliography No. 11); [Hamden, Conn.] : Archon Books, 1971. Pp. 432.

Pp. 145-269, bibliography of Osbert Sitwell. Primary first editions. Form arrangement. Books: transcribed TP, part collation, pagination, binding, date, price, contents, selected later editions and issues (Fifoot's Preface, p. 9, explains selection), number of copies, bibliographical and textual notes. Periods: volume, pages, date; title and author of books reviewed by Sir Osbert. Listings of translations of Sir Osbert (translator, place, publisher, date), of recordings by him, and of musical settings of works by him. Pp. 395-432, index for the entire volume indicates the inclusion of individual pieces in later collections.

The standard bibliography.

SECONDARY

Above, Fulford, p. 39.

GENERAL

Millett; Longaker & Bolles; Temple & Tucker; NCBEL, IV, 346-349.

SITWELL, SIR SACHEVERELL (1897-)

PRIMARY

Richard Fifoot. *A Bibliography of Edith, Osbert and Sacheverell Sitwell.* Second Edition, Revised. London: Rupert Hart-Davis (Soho Bibliography No. 11); [Hamden, Conn.] : Archon Books, 1971. Pp. 432.

Pp. 273-391, bibliography of Sacheverell Sitwell. Primary first editions. Form arrangement. Books: transcribed TP, part collation, pagination, binding, date, price, contents, selected later editions and issued (Fifoot's Preface, p. 9, explains selection), number of copies, bibliographical and textual notes. Periods: volume, pages, date; title and author of books reviewed by Sir Sacheverell. Lists of translations of his writings (translator, place, publisher, date), of recordings by him, and of musical settings of works by him. Pp. 395-432, index for the entire volume indicates the inclusion of individual pieces in later collections.

The standard bibliography.

SECONDARY

Rodolphe L. Mégroz. *The Three Sitwells.* London: Richards Press, 1927.

P. 333, bibliography.

GENERAL

Millett; Longaker & Bolles; Temple & Tucker; Vinson-Poets; NCBEL, IV, 349-351.

SKEFFINGTON, FRANCIS SHEEHY (-1916)

PRIMARY

Patrick Sarsfield O'Hegarty. "Bibliographies of 1916 and the Irish Revolution. XI. Francis Sheehy Skeffington." *Dublin Magazine* 11 (October-December, 1936): 76-78.

Primary books. Chronological arrangement. Transcribed TP, part collation, pagination, binding, bibliographical and occasionally biographical notes.

SKELTON, ROBIN (1925-)

Vinson-Poets.

SMITH, DODIE [DOROTHY GLADYS] (1896-)

Psuedonym used to 1935: C. L. Anthony.

(Mrs. A. M. Beesley).

Salem; Breed & Sniderman; NCBEL, IV, 980-981.

SMITH, ERNEST BRAMAH: *see* BRAMAH, ERNEST.

SMITH, FRANCIS SLADEN (1886-)

NCBEL, IV, 981.

SMITH, IAIN CRICHTON (1928-)

Vinson-Novelists; Vinson-Poets.

SMITH, JOHN (1924-)

Vinson-Poets.

SMITH, KENNETH JOHN (1938-)

Vinson-Poets.

SMITH, LLOYD LOGAN PEARSALL (1865-1946)

PRIMARY

"Bibliographies of Modern Authors. Logan Pearsall Smith." *London Mercury* 4 (1921): 436.

Primary books, 1895-1920. Chronological arrangement. Publisher, year, notes.

Robert Gathorne-Hardy. *Recollections of Logan Pearsall Smith* London: Constable, 1949. Pp. 259.

No bibliography. Bibliographical information in text, *passim,* especially for the post-1928 period.

GENERAL

Temple & Tucker; NCBEL, IV, 1119-1120.

SMITH, STEVIE [FLORENCE MARGARET] (1902-1971)

PRIMARY

Calvin Bedient. *Eight Contemporary Poets.* New York: Oxford University Press, 1975. Pp. x, 198.

P. 185, primary books. Place, publisher, date, names of editors and illustrators.

GENERAL

Temple & Tucker; Vinson-Poets; Stratford.

SMITH, SYDNEY GOODSIR (1915-1975)

Daiches; Temple & Tucker, Vinson-Poets; NCBEL, IV, 351-352.

SNAITH, JOHN COLLIS (1876-1936)

NCBEL, IV, 736-737.

SNAITH, STANLEY (1903-)

NCBEL, IV, 352.

SNOW, CHARLES PERCY, LORD SNOW (1905-)

PRIMARY

Robert Greacen. *The World of C. P. Snow.* Lowestoft: Scorpion Press, 1962. Pp. 64.

Pp. 41-64, bibliography compiled by Bernard Stone. Primary, secondary selected. Form arrangement. Books: publisher, place, date, list of all editions and reprints, translations listed with name of translator; occasional notes. Pp. 51-59, periodical contributions and other writings: dates, occasionally volume and pages. Pp. 59-63, secondary bibliography.

A good checklist, although its value is decreased by the omission of such details as page numbers.

Jerome Thale. *C. P. Snow.* Edinburgh: Oliver and Boyd (Writers and Critics Series), 1964. Pp. 112.

Pp. 108-112, bibliography. Primary first editions, British and American; secondary selected. Form arrangement. Primary books: place, publisher, date. Periods: date, pages, volume. Pp. 110-112, secondary bibliography.

David Shusterman. *C. P. Snow.* Boston: Twayne Publishers, G. K. Hall and Co. (TEAS 179), 1975. Pp. 161.

Pp. 155-156, select primary bibliography. Form and genre arrangement.

Books: place, publisher, date. Period: volume, date, pages. Pp. 156-158, also pp. 148-153, select secondary bibliography.

[For collaborations with Pamela Hansford Johnson, see above, JOHNSON, PAMELA HANSFORD.]

SECONDARY

Above, Greacen, pp. 59-63; Thale, pp. 110-112; Shusterman, pp. 156-158, pp. 148-153.

GENERAL

Daiches; Temple & Tucker; Adelman & Dworkin (Novel); Vinson-Novelists; Drescher & Kahrmann; NCBEL, IV, 737-739; Bufkin.

SOMERVILLE, EDITH ANNA ŒNONE (1858-1949)

Including collaborations with Martin Ross, pseudonym of Violet Florence Martin (1862-1915).

PRIMARY

Elizabeth Hudson. *A Bibliography of the First Editions of the Works of E. Œ. Somerville and Martin Ross.* New York: The Sporting Gallery and Bookshop, Inc., 1942. Pp. 79. 300 copies.

Primary first editions. Form arrangement. Books: transcribed TP, full collation, pagination, price, binding, number of copies, British Museum Pressmark, extensive notes by Somerville. Periods: dates. Also sections on Collected Editions, Selected Criticism, Picture Books, Awards.

Geraldine Cummins. *Dr. E. Œ. Sommerville: A Biography.* London: Andrew Dakers Ltd., 1952. Pp. 271.

Pp. 245-271, "The First Editions of Edith Œnone Somerville and Violet Florence Martin. A Bibliography compiled by Robert Vaughan." Primary books. Chronological arrangement. Transcribed TP, full collation, pagination, binding, price, number of copies, full bibliographical notes include information on American first editions.

Maurice Collis. *Somerville and Ross. A Biography.* London: Faber and Faber, 1968. Pp. 286.

Pp. 13-15, 279-280, location and description of manuscripts. Hudson, Vaughan, and Collis together provide a fairly complete primary bibliography.

SECONDARY

Above, Hudson.

GENERAL

Batho & Dobrée, NCBEL, IV, 739-740.

SOMMERVILLE, FRANKFORT: *see* STORY, A. M. SOMMERVILLE.

SORLEY, CHARLES HAMILTON (1895-1915)

PRIMARY

W. R. Sorley, ed. *The Letters of Charles Sorley.* Cambridge: Cambridge University Press, 1919. Pp. 320.

No bibliography, but much information about Sorley's writings, *passim.* Bound-in advertisement, pp. [321-322], for Marlborough includes quotations from critical comments.

SECONDARY

Larry K. Uffelman. "Charles Hamilton Sorley: An Annotated Checklist." *Serif* 10, iv (1973): 3-17.

Primary writings, pp. 3-5. Secondary, pp. 6-17. Books: place, publisher, date. Periods: volume, date, pages. Secondary items are fully annotated.

GENERAL

Longaker & Bolles; Temple & Tucker; NCBEL, IV, 353.

SOUTAR, WILLIAM (1898-1943)

PRIMARY

William Russell Aitken. "William Soutar: Bibliographical Notes and a Checklist." *Bibliotheck* (Glasgow), 1, ii (1957): 3-14.

Primary books, selected primary periodical contributions; secondary selected. Chronological arrangement. Books: place, publisher, date. Periods: volume, date, pages. The introduction, pp. 3-8, includes bibliographical notes and explains limitations of the checklist.

Alexander Scott. *William Soutar. 1898-1943. Still Life.* London: Chambers, 1958. Pp. 218.

P. 210, primary books. Place, publisher, date. Pp. 211-212, Principal Manuscript Sources: Autobiographical Writings, Correspondence, Verses, Miscellaneous Prose.

GENERAL

Daiches; NCBEL, IV, 353-354.

SOUTHWOLD, STEPHEN (1887-1964)

Pseudonym used: Neil Bell.

NCBEL, IV, 523-524.

SOWERBY, KATHERINE GITHA (-1970)

(Mrs. John Kendall).

NCBEL, IV, 982.

SPARK, MURIEL SARAH (1918-)

PRIMARY

Thomas T. Tominaga and Wilma Schneidermeyer. *Iris Murdoch and Muriel Spark: A Bibliography.* Metuchen, N. J.: Scarecrow Press, Inc., 1976. Pp. xvi, 237.

Pp. 99-146, primary bibliography. Form and genre arrangement, alphabetical arrangement within each division. Books (all first editions and translations): place, publisher, date, reviews of the book, and translators: Periods: volume, date, pages. Reviews by Miss Spark include title and author of book reviewed. Occasional annotations. Pp. 147-192, secondary bibliography arranged under seven headings, including list of dissertations. Pp. 193-237, indices of authors, titles, and subjects (Murdoch and

Spark listed together). Pp. xiv-xvi, biographical and publications chronology.

SECONDARY

Above, Tominaga and Schneidermeyer, pp. 99-146, reviews of primary books; pp. 147-192, other critical writings.

GENERAL

Temple & Tucker; Adelman & Dworkin (Novel); Vinson-Poets; Vinson-Novelists; Drescher & Kahrmann; Bufkin.

SPENCER, CHARLES BERNARD (1909-1962)

Temple & Tucker; NCBEL, IV, 354.

SPENCER, COLIN (1933-)

Vinson-Dramatists.

SPENDER, STEPHEN HAROLD (1909-)

PRIMARY

A. Trevor Tolley. *The Early Published Poems of Stephen Spender.* Ottawa: Carleton University, 1967. Pp. [ii], [18]. Reproduced from typescript.

Pp. 1-6, general bibliographical information. Pp. [7]-[18], chronological list of poems, 1926-1934. Each entry provides title, first line, date of composition, and identifies first and subsequent publications. Books: place, publisher, date, pages. Periods: volume, date. pages.

Hemant Balvantrao Kulkarni. *Stephen Spender. An Annotated Bibliography*. New York and London: Garland Publishing, Inc., 1976. Pp. x, 264.

Primary, secondary selected. Form arrangement. Books (all editions): transcribed TP, part collation, binding, price, contents, date, textual and bibliographical notes. Periods: volume, date, pages, genre of contribution. Reviews by Spender include title and author of book reviewed. Includes description of manuscripts and recordings. Pp. 214-240, secondary bibliography, including selected book reviews listed under title of book reviewed. Pp. 243-264, index.

SECONDARY

Above, Kulkarni, pp. 214-240.

GENERAL

Millett; Daiches; Longaker & Bolles; Temple & Tucker; Breed & Sniderman; Vinson-Poets; NCBEL, IV, 355-357; Stratford.

SPRIGG, CHRISTOPHER ST. JOHN (1907-1937)

Pseudonym used: Christopher Caudwell.

Temple & Tucker.

SPRING, ROBERT HOWARD (1889-1965)

NCBEL, IV, 741.

SQUIRE, SIR JOHN COLLINGS (1884-1958)

PRIMARY

Iolo A. Williams. *Bibliographies of Modern Authors. No. 4 J. C. Squire and James Stephens.* London: Leslie Chaundy and Co., 1922. Pp. 13.

Pp. 1-9, bibliography of Squire. Primary books, English first editions. Genre arrangement. Part collation, publisher, date, binding, occasional notes. Includes checklist of books edited, selected, or introduced by Squire.

Patrick J. F. Howarth. *Squire: 'Most Generous of Men.'* London: Hutchinson, 1963. Pp. 308.

Pp. 289-297, "A Partial Bibliography of the Works of Sir John Collings Squire," by B. S. Benedikz. Part I, pp. 289-292, books partly or completely by Squire, arranged under type of authorship. Title, part collation, publisher, place, year, later editions. Part II, pp. 294-297, Squire's contributions to the *London Mercury,* arranged by genre. Volume, pages.

The text shows tht much of Squire's journalism has been omitted: this is indeed a partial bibliography.

GENERAL

Millett; Longaker & Bolles; Batho & Dobrée; Daiches; Temple & Tucker; NCBEL, IV, 357-359.

STALLWORTHY, JON HOWIE (1935-)

Vinson-Poets.

STANDISH, ROBERT (1898-)

Pseudonym of Digby George Gerahty.

Temple & Tucker.

STANFORD, DEREK (1918-)

Temple & Tucker.

STAPLEDON, WILLIAM OLAF (1886-1950)

NCBEL, IV, 741-742.

STARK, DAME FREYA MADELINE (1893-)

(Mrs. Stewart Perowne).

Daiches; Temple & Tucker; NCBEL, IV, 1324-1325.

STARKEY, JAMES SULLIVAN: *see* O'SULLIVAN, SEUMAS.

STEPHENS, JAMES (1882-1950)

PRIMARY

Birgit Bramsbäck. *James Stephens A Literary and Bibliographical Study.* Upsala: Irish Institute of Upsala University (Upsala Irish Studies, No. 4), 1959. Pp. 209.

Pp. 57-209, primary and secondary bibliography. Form and genre arrangement, with primary material divided Manuscript (pp. 57-112) and Printed Sources (pp. 115-169). MSS: complete identification, précis or abstract, description, location; includes letters written to or about Stephens. Primary books: date, publisher, place, occasionally format and binding, reprints; contents with page numbers and information concerning previous publication; occasionally number of copies; extensive notes. Other books: date, publisher, place. Periods: volume, pages, date, reprintings, notes. P. 199, list of BBC recordings by Stephens. Index.

The authoritative bibliography, although not complete.

Patricia McFate. "The Publication of James Stephen's Short Stories in 'The Nation.' " *Papers of the Bibliographical Society of America* 58 (1964): 476-477.

Corrections and additions to Bramsbäck.

"The James Stephens Papers [at Kent State University Library]: A Catalogue." *Serif* 2, ii (1965): 29-32.

Not seen.

Richard J. Finneran. *Letters of James Stephens.* London and New York: Macmillan, 1974.

Bibliography provides information supplementary to Bramsbäck.

Geoffrey Blum. "Some Notes for Stephens Bibliophiles." *Journal of Irish Literature* 4 (September 1975): 193-198.

Additions to Bramsbäck and Finneran.

SECONDARY

Above, Bramsbäck, pp. 170-191.

Richard Cary. "James Stephens at Colby College." *Colby Library Quarterly* 5, ix (March, 1961): 242-252.

Important association material.

Hilary Pyle. *James Stephens. His Work and an Account of His Life.* London: Routledge and Kegan Paul, 1965. Pp. [xii], 196.

Pp. 190-191, general secondary bibliography. (Also pp. 183-190, primary bibliography: inferior to that in Bramsbäck).

GENERAL

Millett; Longaker & Bolles; Batho & Dobrée; Daiches; Temple & Tucker; NCBEL, IV, 360-362; Bufkin.

STERN, GLADYS BERTHA (1890-1973)

(Mrs. Geoffrey L. Holdsworth).

Millett; Temple & Tucker; NCBEL, IV, 742-743.

STERN, JAMES ANDREW (1904-)

Vinson-Novelists.

STEVENSON, ROBERT LOUIS (1850-1894)

PRIMARY

W. F. Prideaux. *A Bibliography of the Works of Robert Louis Stevenson,* edited and supplemented by Mrs. Luther S. Livingston. London: Frank Hollings, 1917. Pp. 401.

Primary complete, secondary selected. Form and genre arrangement. Books: transcribed TP, part collation, pages, price, binding, contents with details of previous publication, subsequent editions, notes. Periods: volume, pages, date; details of subsequent publication in book form. Includes details of the collected editions. Pp. 313-382, secondary bibliography. Index.

A lucid, easy-to-use, and authoritative account of the publications to 1917.

George L. McKay. *A Stevenson Library. Catalogue of a Collection of Writings by and about Robert Louis Stevenson formed by Edwin J. Beinecke.* New Haven: Yale University Press, 1951-1964. 6 volumes. 500 copies of each volume.

I (1965): 1-370; II (1952): 373-526, 793-802, primary published writings, form arrangement. Books: transcribed TP, pagination, full collation, binding, date, contents, extensive notes; includes translations. Periods: volume, date, pages, notes. II: 529-762, secondary bibliography. Also includes: II: 765-790, books from Stevenson's library; II: 805-859, indices; III (1956): 861-1180, autograph letters by the Stevensons; IV (1958): 1197-1694, letters to and about Stevenson; V (1961): Manuscripts by Stevenson and others; VI (1964): 2221-2670, addenda, corrigenda, indices.

McKay's account of Stevenson's literary work is so complete as to be almost self-defeating. Thus Prideaux is the easy-to-use, authoritative bibliography; McKay is the more complicated final word; and all other bibliographical work is derivative—or merely a supplement necessitated by the passage of time. The beginning student will probably do well to turn to the selected primary and secondary bibliographies provided by Irving Saposnik. *Robert Louis Stevenson.* New York: Twayne Publishers, Inc. (TEAS 167), 1974. Pp. 155-156, selected primary; pp. 156-160, also pp. 137-153, selected secondary.

SECONDARY

Above, Prideaux, pp. 313-382; McKay, II, 529-762; Saposnik, pp. 156-160.

GENERAL

Batho & Dobrée; NCBEL, III, 1004-1014.

STEWART, JOHN INNES MACKINTOSH (1906-)

Pseudonym used: Michael Innes.

Daiches; Vinson-Novelists; NCBEL, IV, 617-618.

STIRLING, MONICA (1916-)

Vinson-Novelists.

STOKER, ABRAHAM (BRAM) (1847-1912)

PRIMARY

Daniel Farson. *The Man Who Wrote Dracula. A Biography of Bram Stoker.* London: Michael Joseph, 1975. Pp. 240.

Although there is no bibliography, many important details are given in the text of this chatty biography.

STOPPARD, TOM (1937-)

Breed & Sniderman; Vinson-Dramatists; Temple & Tucker.

STOREY, DAVID (1933-)

PRIMARY

John Russell Taylor. *David Storey.* Harlow: Longman Group Ltd. (WTW 239), 1974. Pp. 30.

P. 29, primary books: place, date, genre. Pp. 29-30, secondary.

GENERAL

Adelman & Dworkin (Novel); Vinson-Novelists; Vinson-Dramatists; Drescher & Kahrmann; Temple & Tucker; Bufkin.

STORM, LESLEY (1903-)

Née Mabel Margaret Cowie (Mrs. J. D. Clark).

NCBEL, IV, 982.

STRACHEY, GILES LYTTON (1880-1932)

PRIMARY

R. A. Scott-James. *Lytton Strachey.* London: Longmans, Green and Co. (WTW 65), 1955. Pp. [40] .

Pp. 33-34, primary books: date, genre. Pp. 35-39, alphabetical by title list of primary essays with titles of the volumes in which they are collected. A useful addition to Sanders' authoritative checklist (below).

Charles R. Sanders. *Lytton Strachey. His Mind and Art.* New Haven: Yale University Press; London: Oxford University Press, 1957. Pp. [xii], [382].

Pp. 355-366, primary bibliography. One chronological list. Books: British and American first editions only: place, publisher, date, details if any of serial publication. Periods: volume, pages, date, details of reprinting in collections. Reviews by Strachey include author and the title of book reviewed. Includes unsigned and pseudonymous writings, also unpublished writings. A complete list of Strachey's writings.

SECONDARY

Martin Kallich. "Lytton Strachey: An Annotated Bibliography of Writings about Him." *English Fiction in Transition* 5, iii (1962): 1-77.

Alphabetical by author. Books: place, publisher, date. Periods: volume, pages, dates. Annotations. Subsequent issues of *English Fiction* (later *English Literature*) *in Transition* provide additions to this basic list.

GENERAL

Millett; Longaker & Bolles; Daiches; Temple & Tucker; NCBEL, IV, 1215-1218.

STREATFEILD, NOEL (?1899-)

PRIMARY

Eugene Wendy Atie. *Noel Streatfeild: A Bibliography.* Johannesburg: University of the Witwatersrand, 1972. Pp. 21 (mimeographed sheets).

Pp. 1-16, primary bibliography. Form arrangement. Books: place, publisher, date, subsequent editions, selected reviews of the book. Periods: volume, date, pages.

SECONDARY

Above, Atie, pp. 17-19, and *passim.*

GENERAL

NCBEL, IV, 803-804.

STRODE, WARREN CHETHAM (1897-)

NCBEL, IV, 982-983.

STRONG, LEONARD ALFRED GEORGE (1896-1958)

PRIMARY

John Gawsworth. *Ten Contemporaries. Notes Toward their Definitive Bibliography. (Second Series).* London: Joiner and Steele Ltd., 1933. Pp. 240. 1000 copies.

Pp. 219-234, bibliography of Strong, 1919-1932. Primary first editions, books. Chronological arrangement. Transcribed TP, full collation, pagination, binding, date, bibliographical notes.

R. L. Mégroz. *Five Novelist Poets.* London: Joiner and Steele Ltd., 1933.

Pp. 243-244, bibliography of Strong, 1921-1932. Primary books. Chronological arrangement. Publisher, place, date, pages.

GENERAL

Millett; Longaker & Bolles; Daiches; Temple & Tucker; NCBEL, IV, 744-746; Bufkin.

STUART, HENRY FRANCIS (1902-)

Pseudonym used: H. Sauart.

PRIMARY

J. H. Natterstad. "Francis Stuart: A Checklist." *Journal of Irish Literature* 5 (January 1976): 39-45.

Primary writings, arranged by genre, including manuscripts and letters. Books (all editions and translations): place, publisher, date, translator. Periods: date, pages. P. 45, secondary bibliography.

GENERAL

Millett; Temple & Tucker.

STURT, GEORGE (1863-1927)

Pseudonym used: George Bourn.

PRIMARY

E. D. Mackerness. "George Sturt and the English Humanitarian Tradition" in *Essays and Studies* 1969 (NS 22), ed. Francis Berry for The English Association. London: John Murray, 1969. Pp. 105-122.

A survey of Sturt's literary work providing many titles and dates.

GENERAL

Batho & Dobrée; NCBEL, IV, 1312.

SUMMERS, MONTAGUE (1880-1948)

PRIMARY

Timothy d'Arch Smith. *A Bibliography of the Works of Montague Summers.* London: Nicholas Vane Ltd., 1964. Pp. 164.

Primary. Form arrangement. Books: transcribed TP, full collation, pagination, binding, date, price, contents, illustrations, later editions and impressions described fully. Lengthy notes. Periods: volume, pages, date, notes. Includes section on untraced, unpublished, and projected works, and a list of programme notes written by Summers for theatrical societies. Pp. 137-148, chronological list of published writings. Index.

Cecil Woolf, *Book Collector* 14 (1965): 106: "in every way this is an excellent piece of bibliographical work." Smith describes one additional primary title in "Note 359. Montague Summers: An Addition to the Bibliography." *Book Collector* 21 (1972), 558-559.

Joseph Jerome. *Montague Summers. A Memoir.* London: Cecil and Amelia Woolf, 1965. Pp. 105.

Pp. 91-94, "Bibliographical Checklist," by T. d'A. Smith. Primary. Form and subject arrangement. Publisher, date, place, reprints.

Drawn from Smith's work above, this checklist is particularly complete, while its arrangement helps to guide one through Summer's writings.

GENERAL

NCBEL, IV, 1122-1124.

SUTCLIFF, ROSEMARY (1920-)

PRIMARY

Susan Elizabeth McMurray. *Rosemary Sutcliffe: A Bibliography.* Johannesburg: University of the Witwatersrand, 1972. Pp. 33 (Mimeographed sheets).

Pp. 4-30, primary bibliography. Topical and form arrangement. Books, including reprints and translations: place, publisher, date, translator, reviews of the book. Periods: volume, date, pages. Annotations for each entry.

SECONDARY

Above, McMurray, pp. 30-33, and *passim.*

SUTHERLAND, ROBERT GARIOCH: *see* GARIOCH, ROBERT

SUTRO, ALFRED (1863-1933)

Millett; Temple & Tucker; NCBEL, IV, 983-984.

SWINGLER, RANDALL CARLINE (1909-1967)

NCBEL, IV, 362.

SWINNERTON, FRANK ARTHUR (1884-)

PRIMARY

Jesse F. McCartney. "The Frank Arthur Swinnerton Collection: A Special Literary Collection at the University of Arkansas." *English Literature in Transition* 18 (1975): 248-253.

A description of this important gathering of primary and secondary material, gained for Arkansas by Professor H. Blair Rouse, the Swinnerton authority.

GENERAL

Millett; Longaker & Bolles; Batho & Dobrée; Daiches; Temple & Tucker; Vinson-Novelists; NCBEL, IV, 746-747; Bufkin.

SYLVAINE, VERNON (1897-1957)

NCBEL, IV, 984-985.

SYMONS, ALPHONSE JAMES ALBERT (1900-1941)

PRIMARY

Julian Symons. *A. J. A. Symons. His Life and Speculations.* London: Eyre and Spottiswoode, 1950. Pp. 283.

This biography by Symon's brother is the beginning point of any bibliographical investigation, although it does not provide an actual bibliography.

SYMONS, ARTHUR (1865-1945)

PRIMARY

Henry Danielson. *Bibliographies of Modern Authors.* London: Bookman's Journal, 1921. Pp. [xii], [212].

Pp. 175-194, primary books and pamphlets, 1886-1920. Chronological arrangement. Transcribed TP, part collation, pagination, binding, variants, miscellaneous bibliographical notes.

Thomas Earle Welby. *Arthur Symons. A Critical Study.* London: Philpot, 1925. Pp. 148.

Pp. 141-148, bibliography. Primary books, secondary selected. Arrangement according to Symons's part in the books, including translations by, works edited or introduced by, and anthologies edited by. Titles and dates, only.

Roger Llombreaud. *Arthur Symons. A Critical Biography.* London: Unicorn Press, 1963. Pp. 333.

Pp. 325-326, checklist of primary books, British and American first editions. Chronological arrangement. Date, place, publisher.

SECONDARY

Above, Welby, pp. 147-148.

Carol Simpson Stern. "Arthur Symons: An Annotated Bibliography of Writings about Him." *English Literature in Transition* 17 (1974): 77-133.

Arranged alphabetically by author. Books: place, publisher, date, relevant pages. Periods: volume, date, pages.

GENERAL

Millett; Longaker & Bolles; Batho & Dobrée; Temple & Tucker; NCBEL, III, 649-651.

SYMONS, JULIAN GUSTAVE (1912-)

Longaker & Bolles; Temple & Tucker; Vinson-Novelists; NCBEL, IV, 362-363.

SYNGE, JOHN MILLINGTON (1871-1909)

PRIMARY

Maurice Bourgeois. *John Millington Synge and the Irish Theatre.* London: Constable and Co., 1913. Photographic reprint, New York: Blom, 1965. Pp. xiv, [338].

Pp. 251-314, bibliography. Primary secondary. Form arrangement. Books: place, publisher, date, part collation, price, annotations, reprints and subsequent editions (information not consistently given). Translations of Synge listed separately. Periodicals arranged alphabetically by title: date, pages, annotations. Secondary bibliography, pp. 265-296.

Annotated. Appendices: List of the best-known portraits of Synge; Bibliographical note on the exegesis and the non-dramatic versions of the Deirdre Saga; First performances of Synge's plays in various countries and places. The earliest bibliography which gives information not elsewhere available.

Ian MacPhail and M. Pollard. *John Millington Synge 1871-1909: A Catalogue of an Exhibition Held at Trinity College Library Dublin on the Occasion of the Fiftieth Anniversary of his Death.* Dublin: Dolmen Press, 1959. Pp. 38.

Primary. Form arrangement. Books: transcribed TP, part collation, bibliographical notes, reprints and subsequent editions. Pp. 30-32, annotated list of periodical contributions: volume, pages, date. Pp. 32-34, list of MSS.

In "John Millington Synge: Some Bibliographical Notes," *Irish Book*, I (1960), 3-10, MacPhail reports his work on the above *Catalogue* and surveys the bibliographical problems connected with Synge.

David H. Greene and E. M. Stephens. *John Millington Synge.* New York: Macmillan and Co., 1959. Pp. 321.

Pp. 308-310, "A List of the Published Writings of Synge": place, publisher, date, brief notes. Pp. 309-310, Synge's contributions to periodicals: alphabetical list of periodicals with dates and page numbers.

A convenient checklist in an important critical study.

Donna Gerstenberger. *John Millington Synge.* New York: Twayne Publishers, Inc. (TEAS 12), 1964. Pp. 157.

Pp. 142-147, primary bibliography. Form and genre arrangement. Books, first editions: place, publisher, date, bibliographical notes. Periods: dates, pages. Contents of collected editions. Pp. 147-152, secondary bibliography. Annotated.

There is no single, complete primary bibliography; one must refer to the four volumes listed above and to the bibliographies listed in them.

SECONDARY

Above, Bourgeois, pp. 265-296; Gerstenberger, pp. 147-152.

Paul M. Levitt. *J. M. Synge: A Bibliography of Published Crit-*

icism. Dublin: Irish University Press; New York: Barnes and Noble, 1974. Pp. [xii], [228].

Pp. 11-116: books and periodicals listed under such headings as Bibliography, Biography, General Dramatic Criticism, and under the title of the primary work being discussed. Pp. 119-210: newspaper references, arranged under title of newspaper, the newspapers being listed under city of publication, alphabetically arranged. Pp. 211-224: Index. Books: place, publisher, date. Periods: volume, date, pages.

Weldon Thornton, *Journal of Irish Literature* 3, iii (1974): 51-55, while very critical of the eccentric arrangement of this work, points to its all-inclusive nature: "contain[s] . . .almost everything of value written about Synge through 1969."

Edward Halim Mikhail. *J. M. Synge. A Bibliography of Criticism.* Foreword by Robin Skelton. London: Macmillan; Totowa, New Jersey: Rowman and Littlefield, 1975. Pp. [xiv], 214.

Arranged: Bibliographies, Reviews of Primary Books, Books, Periodicals, Reviews of Play Productions, Unpublished Material, Recordings, Background. Indices. Books: place, publisher, date. Periods: volume, date, pages.

Weldon Thornton, *Journal of Irish Literature* 5 (May, 1976): 131-135, compares Levitt and Mikhail, pointing out that Mikhail's cut-off date is 1971 and preferring Levitt to Mikhail. The conscientious student will use both bibliographies to find the most complete listing of material about Synge.

GENERAL

Longaker & Bolles; Batho & Dobrée; Temple & Tucker; Coleman & Tyler; Adelman & Dworkin; Salem; Palmer & Dyson; NCBEL, III, 1934-1938; Breed & Sniderman.

TABORI, GEORGE (1914-)

Salem; Vinson-Dramatists.

TAGORE, RABINDRANATH (1861-1941)

[Ravindranatha Thakura].

PRIMARY

Virgil Cândea. *Tagore en Roumanie.* Bucharest: UNESCO, 1961. Pp. 38.

List of primary writings translated into Roumanian; also includes secondary bibliography, especially relating to Tagore's visit to Roumania in 1926. Publisher, date, place. Index. (In French).

Odette Aslan, ed. *Rabindranath Tagore.* Paris: Editions Pierre Seghers (Poètes d'Aujourd'hui No. 80), 1961. Pp. 207.

Pp. 202-204, list of primary books published in French: title, translator, publisher (no dates). Arranged by genre.

Rabindranath Tagore, 1861-1961. Paris: Bibliothèque Nationale, 1961. Pp. 152.

Catalogue of an exhibition arranged to illustrate Tagore's life and career. Includes much peripheral material, but amplifies details given by Sen and Bhaumik (below). Arranged: Chronologie de la Vie et des Œuvres de Tagore; Le Cadre Familial et Social; La Pensée et la Religion du Poète; L'Œuvre Littéraire; L'Œuvre Musicale; L'Œuvre Pédagogique; Apôtre du Rapprochement Orient-Occident; Artisan de la Libération de L'Inde--Tagore et Ghandi; L'Œuvre Picturale; Hommages à Tagore. Usually title, publisher, place, date, part collation, annotations.

A Centenary Volume. Rabindranath Tagore, 1861-1961. New Delhi: Sahitya Akademi, 1961. Pp. 531.

Pulinbihari Sen and Jagadindra Bhaumik, "Works of Tagore. A Bibliography," pp. 504-519. Pp. 504-511, writings in Bengali: title, date, genre. Pp. 512-518, writings in English: title, place, publisher, date, translator, genre.

This checklist, along with the Bibliothèque Nationale catalogue (above), provides a fairly complete list of the primary writings.

SECONDARY

Above, Cândea, pp. 20-24, and Bibliothèque Nationale Catalogue.

Ethel M. Kitch. "Rabindranath Tagore–A Bibliography." *Bulletin of Bibliography* 11 (1921): 80-84.

Pp. 81-84, secondary selected bibliography. Topic arrangement; includes reviews of primary writings. Books: place, publisher, date. Periods: dates.

GENERAL

Adelman & Dworkin; Breed & Sniderman.

TARN, NATHANIEL (1928-)

Vinson-Poets.

TAYLOR, CECIL PHILIP (1929-)

Vinson-Dramatists.

TAYLOR, ELIZABETH (1912-)

(Mrs. J. W. K. Taylor).

Bufkin; Adelman & Dworkin (Novel); Vinson-Novelists; Drescher & Kahrmann.

TAYLOR, RACHEL ANNAND (1876-1960)

NCBEL, IV, 363.

TEMPLE, JOAN (-1965)

NCBEL, IV, 985.

TENNYSON, SIR CHARLES BRUCE LOCKER (1879-1977)

PRIMARY

Lionel Madden. *Sir Charles Tennyson. An Annotated Bibliography of his Published Writings.* Lincoln: The Tennyson Society, Research Centre (Tennyson Society Monographs No. 6), 1973. Pp. [40].

Pp. 13-37, chronological list of writings. Books: place, publisher, date, pages, list of contents. Periods: volume, date, pages, brief description of contents; for reviews by Sir Charles, title and author of book reviewed. Each item numbered in one sequence (total, 194 items).

TERSON, PETER (1932-)

Pseudonym of Peter Patterson.

Vinson-Dramatists.

TESSIMOND, ARTHUR SEYMOUR JOHN (1902-1962)

NCBEL, IV, 364.

THIRKELL, ANGELA MARGARET (1890-1961)

(Mrs. G. L. Thirkell).

Longaker & Bolles; Temple & Tucker; Adelman & Dworkin (Novel); NCBEL, IV, 747-748.

THOMAS, DONALD MICHAEL (1935-)

Vinson-Poets.

THOMAS, DYLAN MARLAIS (1914-1953)

PRIMARY

Elder Olson. *The Poetry of Dylan Thomas.* Chicago: University of Chicago Press, 1954. Pp. 164.

Pp. 102-146, "Bibliography" by William H. Huff. Primary, secondary. Chronological arrangement, subdivided by genre. Books: place, publisher, date, reprints, reviews. Periods: volume, date, pages. Reviews by Thomas include title and author of book reviewed. Includes BBC broadcasts by Thomas. Pp. 127-146, secondary bibliography.

J. Alexander Rolph. *Dylan Thomas. A Bibliography.* London: Dent and Co.; New York: New Directions, 1956. Pp. 108.

Primary. Genre and form arrangement. Books: transcribed TP, part collation, pagination, binding, price, number of copies, contents, extensive notes. Periods: volume, date, pages. Pp. 1-38, chronological list of Thomas's poems: for each, details of its publication and of textual variants. Includes translations and recordings. Indexed.

The authoritative bibliography: additions and corrections to it are made by: William B. Todd. "The Bibliography of Dylan Thomas." *Book Collector* 6 (1957): 71-73; Timothy d'Arch Smith. "Note 227. The Second Edition of Dylan Thomas's *18 Poems.*" *Book Collector* 13 (1964): 351-352; William White. "Dylan Thomas, Mr. Rolph, and 'John O'London's Weekly'." *Papers of the Bibliographical Society of America* 60 (1966): 370-372.

Hélène Bokanowski and Marc Alyn. *Dylan Thomas.* Paris: Editions Pierre Seghers (Poètes d'Aujourd'hui 92), 1962. Pp. 222.

Pp. 216-217, French translations of Thomas. Title, publisher, place, date, translator.

Roberto Sanesi. *Dylan Thomas.* Milan: Lerici Editori, 1960. Pp. 200.

Pp. 185-186, list of translations of Thomas into Italian, French, German, Swedish, and Danish.

Ralph Maud, assisted by Albert Glover. *Dylan Thomas in Print. A Bibliographical History.* Pittsburgh: University of Pittsburgh Press, 1970. Pp. [xii], 261.

Primary complete, secondary complete (to 1968-1969). Five sections: Books, anthologies, theses (arranged chronologically); Welsh periodicals and newspapers; London, etc., periodicals and newspapers; United States and Canadian periodicals and newspapers (entries listed under title of publication); Foreign-language publications (arranged according to language). Books: place, publisher, date, relevant pages, contents of new primary editions, extensive textual and bibliographical notes. Periods: volume, pages, date, notes and quotations. Pp. 229-261, index.

While Rolph remains the standard bibliography, Maud offers a wealth of supplementary information about the primary writings, and his annotations to them and the secondary bibliography make this book an indispensable aid to the student, who should always begin with the Index in order to overcome the idiosyncrasies of the presentation.

SECONDARY

Above, Olson, pp. 127-146; Maud, *passim.*

Sister Lois Theisen. "Dylan Thomas. A Bibliography of Secondary Criticism." *Bulletin of Bibliography* 26 (1969): 9-28, 32, 36, 59-60.

Topic and form arrangement. Includes list of previous bibliographies. Books: place, publisher, date, pages. Periods: volume, date, pages. Each entry numbered. Although providing less information than Maud, the simpler arrangement makes this an easier starting point for work with the secondary bibliography.

GENERAL

Longaker& Bolles; Daiches; Temple & Tucker; Stratford; Coleman & Tyler; Adelman & Dworkin; Salem; Palmer & Dyson; Breed & Sniderman; Vinson-Poets; NCBEL, IV, 220-230.

THOMAS, GWYN (1913-)

Vinson-Dramatists.

THOMAS, PHILLIP EDWARD (1878-1917)

PRIMARY

Gwendolen Murphy. "Bibliographies of Modern Authors, No. 2. Edward Thomas." *London Mercury* 16 (1927): 71-75, 193-198, 525-530; 17 (1928): 76.

Primary books and periodical contributions other than reviews. Form and genre arrangement. Books: transcribed TP, full collation, pagination, binding, price. Pp. 529-530, periodical contributions listed under title of period: date, pages.

One of the 1920 bibliographies aimed at the collector of "firsts"--less complete than Eckert (below), but still useful.

Robert P. Eckert. *Edward Thomas: A Biography and a Bibliography.* London: J. M. Dent and Sons, 1937. Pp. 328.

Pp. 185-289, bibliography. Primary, secondary selected. Form arrangement. Books: transcribed TP, partial collation, binding, date, previous publication of contents noted, bibliographical notes. Periods: volume, date, pages; notes on the reprinting of individual items; reviews by Thomas include title and author of book reviewed. Pp. 278-289, secondary bibliography: alphabetical by author, annotated. The standard bibliography, to which Cooke (below) provides additional information.

William Cooke. *Edward Thomas. A Critical Biography 1878-1917.* London: Faber and Faber, 1970. Pp. 292.

Pp. 279-282, primary books: place, publisher, date. Pp. 282-283, location of unpublished correspondence and manuscripts. Pp. 283-287, selected secondary bibliography.

SECONDARY

Above, Eckert, pp. 278-289; Cooke, pp. 284-287.

GENERAL

Longaker & Bolles; Batho & Dobrée; Temple & Tucker, NCBEL, IV, 364-367.

THOMAS, RONALD STUART (1913-)

PRIMARY

Calvin Bedient. *Eight Contemporary Poets.* New York: Oxford University Press, 1975. Pp. x, 198.

Pp. 185-186, primary books. Place, publisher, date, names of editors and illustrators.

Titles of periodicals to which Thomas contributed (but no bibliographical details) are provided by R. G. Thomas, *Ronald Stuart Thomas.* London: Longmans, Green and Co. (WTW 166), 1964, p. 43.

GENERAL

Temple & Tucker; Vinson-Poets; NCBEL, IV, 368.

THOMPSON, FRANCIS JOSEPH (1859-1907)

PRIMARY

C. A. and H. W. Stonehill. *Bibliographies of Modern Authors* (Second Series). London: John Castle, 1925. Pp. [xiv], 162. 750 copies.

Pp. 143-162, primary books; also incomplete other writings. Form arrangement. Transcribed TP, full collation, pagination, binding, price, number of copies, variants, bibliographical notes.

A collector's bibliography, concentrating upon the physical form of the book, rather than upon its contents.

Myrtle Pihlman Pope. "A Critical Bibliography of Works by and about Francis Thompson." *Bulletin of the New York Public Library* 62 (1958): 571-576; 63 (1959): 40-49, 155-161, 195-204.

P. 157, critical essays by Thompson; pp. 157-160, chronological list of Thompson's literary criticism; pp. 160-161, 195-196, other primary writings; pp. 196-203, chronological list of Thompson's poems; pp. 203-204, separate printings of "The Hound of Heaven." Pp. 48-49, list of 13 primary and secondary bibliographies; pp. 155-156, secondary bibliography.

A useful checklist of titles; the list of Thompson's unreprinted journalism is supplemented by Terence L. Connolly, "A Revised Essay toward a Bibliography of Francis Thompson's Book Reviews and Literary Criticism Contributed to Periodicals" in Francis Thompson, *The Real Robert Louis Stevenson and Other Critical Essays.* New York: University Publishers, Inc., for Boston College, 1959. Pp. xiv, 409. Pp. 353-398, primary, unsigned writings. Alphabetical list of periodicals with contributions listed chronologically under each. Dates. Author and title of books reviewed. For an account of MSS collections, see below, Danchin.

Peter Butter. *Francis Thompson.* London: Longmans, Green and Co. (WTW 141), 1961. Pp. 38.

Pp. 37-38, primary books: place, date, with notes on editors and revisions. Note also the list of bibliographies.

SECONDARY

Above, Pope, pp. 48-49, 155-156; Butter, p. 38.

Pierre Danchin. *Francis Thompson. La Vie et L'Œuvre d'un Poète.* Paris: A.-G. Nizet, 1959. Pp. 554.

Pp. 524-544, secondary bibliography. Form and genre arrangement. Annotations. Pp. 526-527, list of MSS collections and descriptions of catalogues of them. (In French).

The most comprehensive study of Thompson, with an important secondary bibliography.

J. C. Reid. *Francis Thompson. Man and Poet.* London: Routledge and Kegan Paul, 1959. Pp. [xii], 232.

Pp. 218-219, primary books. Pp. 219-224, secondary bibliography.

GENERAL

Longaker & Bolles; Batho & Dobrée, NCBEL, III, 597-601.

THOMPSON, SYLVIA ELIZABETH (1902-1968)

(Mrs. Peter Luling).

Millett; Temple & Tucker.

THOMSON, DERICK SMITH (1921-)

Vinson-Poets.

THOMSON, HUGH (1860-1920)

PRIMARY

Marion H. Spielmann and Walter Jerrold. *Hugh Thomson: His Art, His Letters, His Humour and His Charm.* London: A. and C. Black, Ltd., 1931. Pp. 269.

Pp. 237-254, bibliography of printed work. Primary, secondary selected. Form arrangement. Books: author, title, publisher, date. Periods: date, title of work illustrated. Pp. 251-252, index of authors illustrated by Thomson.

SECONDARY

Above, Speilmann and Jerrold, pp. 250-251.

THORNTON, A. G. (-)

NCBEL, IV, 748.

THWAITE, ANTHONY SIMON (1930-)

Vinson-Poets; Stratford.

TILLER, TERENCE ROGERS (1916-)

Daiches; Temple & Tucker; Vinson-Poets; NCBEL, IV, 368.

TINDALL, GILLIAN ELIZABETH (1938-)

Vinson-Novelists.

TODD, RUTHVEN (1914-)

Temple & Tucker; Vinson-Poets, NCBEL, IV, 368-369.

TOLKIEN, JOHN RONALD REUEL (1892-1973)

PRIMARY

Richard C. West. *Tolkien Criticism. An Annotated Checklist.* Kent: Kent State University Press (Serif Series, 11), 1970. Pp. [xvi], 73.

Pp. 1-8, primary bibliography. Chronological arrangement. Books: place, publisher, date, selected subsequent editions. Periods: volume, date, pages, reprintings. Annotations. Pp. 9-64, secondary bibliography, annotated. Reviews of Tolkien's books listed under title of books. Index of secondary titles. Pp. viii-xi, list of periodicals devoted to or largely concerned with Tolkien.

Bonniejean McGuire Christensen. "J. R. R. Tolkien: A Bibliography." *Bulletin of Bibliography* 27 (1970): 61-67.

Primary, secondary. Genre and topic arrangement with particular emphasis on separation of scholarly and popular writings. Books: place, publisher, date, all editions, reprints, occasionally textual notes. Periods: volume, pages, date. Reviews of Tolkien listed under title of primary work being reviewed.

West and Christensen together provide a formidable amount of information about Tolkien. For translations of his works one should turn to Susan Barbara Melmed. *Tolkien: A Bibliography.* Johannesburg: University of Witwatersrand, 1972. Pp. iv, 31 [mimeographed sheets]. Translations are listed under the language with place, date, and publisher, pp. 25-28. There is also a list of the journals devoted to Tolkien with editors and addresses, p. 31.

Humphrey Carpenter. *Tolkien. A Biography.* London: Allen and Unwin; Boston: Houghton Mifflin Co., 1977. Pp. [xii], 287.

Pp. 268-275, chronological list of primary writings. Books: place, publisher, date, translations. Periods: volume, date, pages. Extensive notes. See text, *passim,* for important bibliographical notes and references to unpublished writings.

SECONDARY

Above, West, pp. 9-64, Christensen, pp. 62-67.

GENERAL

Temple & Tucker; Adelman & Dworkin (Novel); Vinson-Novelists; NCBEL, IV, 748-749; Bufkin.

TOMLINSON, ALFRED CHARLES (1927-)

PRIMARY

Calvin Bedient. *Eight Contemporary Poets.* New York: Oxford University Press, 1975. Pp. x, 198.

P. 186, primary books. Place, publisher, date, names of editors.

GENERAL

Temple & Tucker; Vinson-Poets; Stratford.

TOMLINSON, HENRY MAJOR (1873-1958)

PRIMARY

Howard S. Mott, Jr. "H. M. Tomlinson. A Checklist Bibliography." *Reading and Collecting* 1, iii (February, 1937): 25.

Primary books, including books with contributions by Tomlinson. Chronological arrangement. Place, date, binding, bibliographical notes usually concerned with "points," all editions.

Apparently this is the only available bibliography, although in the *Book Collector* 11 (Summer, 1962): 219, Peter R. Haack asked for information for a bibliography he was preparing.

GENERAL

Millett; Daiches; Longaker & Bolles; Temple & Tucker; NCBEL, IV, 749-750; Bufkin.

TONKS, ROSEMARY (-)

Vinson-Poets, Vinson-Novelists.

TOYNBEE, THEODORE PHILIP (1916-)

Daiches; Temple & Tucker; Vinson-Poets; Vinson-Novelists; Drescher & Kahrmann; NCBEL, IV, 750-751; Bufkin.

TRACY, HONOR LILBUSH WINGFIELD (1913-)

Vinson-Novelists; Bufkin.

TRAVERS, BEN (1886-)

Vinson-Dramatists; NCBEL, IV, 985-986.

TREASE, ROBERT GEOFFREY (1909-)

PRIMARY

Eleanor Margaret Lechmere-Oertel. *Geoffrey Trease--38 Years: A Bibliography.* Johannesburg: University of the Witwatersrand, 1972. Pp. viii, 29. (mimeographed sheets).

Pp. 1-25, primary bibliography, secondary selected. Form and topic arrangement. Books, including later editions, translations, and broadcasts: place, publisher, date, translator, reviews of the book. Periods: volume, date, pages.

SECONDARY

Above, Lechmere-Oertel, pp. 1-25, *passim;* p. 23.

GENERAL

NCBEL, IV, 810.

TREECE, HENRY (1911-1966)

Daiches; Longaker & Bolles; Temple & Tucker; NCBEL, IV, 369-370; Bufkin.

TREMAYNE, SYDNEY DURWARD (1912-)

Vinson-Poets.

TRENCH, FREDERICK HERBERT (1865-1923)

PRIMARY

"Bibliographies of Modern Authors. Frederick Herbert Trench." *London Mercury* 4 (1921): 87.

Primary books, 1901-1919. Chronological arrangement. Publisher, year, brief notes.

GENERAL

Batho & Dobrée; Temple & Tucker; NCBEL, III, 1911.

TRESSELL, ROBERT: *see* NOONAN, ROBERT.

TREVELYAN, ROBERT CALVERLEY (1872-1951)

NCBEL, IV, 370-371.

TREVOR, WILLIAM (1928-)

Pseudonym of William Trevor Cox.

Vinson-Novelists; Drescher & Kahrmann; Temple & Tucker; Bufkin.

TRICKETT, MABEL RACHEL (1923-)

Vinson-Novelists.

TRIPP, JOHN (1927-)

Vinson-Poets.

TROCCHI, ALEXANDER (1925-)

Vinson-Novelists.

TUOHY, JOHN FRANCIS [FRANK] (1925-)

Vinson-Novelists; Bufkin.

TURNBULL, GAEL LUNDIN (1928-)

Vinson-Poets.

TURNER, JAMES ERNEST (1909-)

Temple & Tucker.

TURNER, REGINALD (1867?-1938)

PRIMARY

Stanley Weintraub. *Reggie. A Portrait of Reginald Turner.* New York: George Braziller, 1965. Pp. [x], 293.

Bibliographical information, both primary and secondary, in text, *passim,* and in notes, pp. [281]-288. Index.

TURNER, WALTER JAMES REDFERN (1889-1946)

Millett; Longaker & Bolles; Daiches; Temple & Tucker; NCBEL, IV, 371-372.

TURNER, WILLIAM PRICE (1927-)

Vinson-Poets.

TYNAN, KATHARINE (1861-1931)

(Mrs. Henry Albert Hinkson)

PRIMARY

Marilyn Gaddis Rose. *Katharine Tynan.* Lewisburg: Bucknell University Press (Irish Writers Series), 1974. Pp. 97.

Pp. 94-97, selected primary and secondary books. Place, publisher, date.

GENERAL

Millett; Longaker & Bolles; Temple & Tucker; Dictionary of National Biography, 1931-1940; NCBEL, III, 1910-1911.

TYNAN, KENNETH PEACOCK (1927-)

Temple & Tucker.

UNDERHILL, EVELYN (1875-1941)

(Mrs. Hubert Stuart Moore).

PRIMARY

Evelyn Underhill. London: Ernest Benn Ltd. (Augustan Books of Poetry), 1932. Pp. 32.

P. [31], primary books. Publisher, price.

Margaret Cropper. *Evelyn Underhill.* London: Longmans, Green and Co., 1958. Pp. 244.

While there is no bibliography, this authorized biography gives a full account of Underhill's literary work.

GENERAL

Millett; NCBEL, IV, 1301-1302.

UPWARD, EDWARD FALAISE (1903-)

Vinson-Novelists; NCBEL, IV, 751-752.

URQUHART, FRED (1912-)

Vinson-Novelists.

USTINOV, PETER ALEXANDER (1921-)

PRIMARY

Geoffrey Williams. *Peter Ustinov.* London: Peter Owens Ltd., 1957. Pp. 180.

P. 180, "Summary." Plays by Ustinov (theatre and date of production); films by Ustinov, and also those in which he appeared; books by Ustinov (publisher, date). Other works by Ustinov mentioned in text, *passim.*

GENERAL

Daiches; Temple & Tucker; Coleman & Tyler; Adelman & Dworkin; Salem; Palmer & Dyson; Breed & Sniderman; Vinson-Dramatists; NCBEL, IV, 986.

UTTLEY, ALISON (1884-1976)

NCBEL, IV, 797-798.

VACHELL, HORACE ANNESLEY (1861-1955)

Temple & Tucker; NCBEL, IV, 752-754.

VAN DRUTEN, JOHN WILLIAM (1901-1957)

Daiches; Temple &Tucker; Adelman & Dworkin; Breed & Sniderman; NCBEL, IV, 986-988.

VANE, VANE HUNT SUTTON (1888-1963)

Coleman & Tyler; Salem; Palmer & Dyson; NCBEL, IV, 988.

VAUGHAN, HILDA (1892-)

(Mrs. Charles Morgan).

PRIMARY

G. F. Adam. *Three Contemporary Anglo-Welsh Novelists: Jack*

Jones, Rhys Davies, and Hilda Vaughan. Bern: A. Francke A. G. (University of Bern Monograph), [1950]. Pp. 109.

P. 108, bibliography. Primary books. Genre arrangement. Publisher, date.

VOSPER, FRANK (1899-1937)

NCBEL, IV, 988.

VULLIAMY, COLWYN EDWARD (1886-1971)

Temple & Tucker.

WADDELL, HELEN JANE (1889-1965)

Daiches; Longaker & Bolles; NCBEL, IV, 799, 1127-1128.

WADDELL, SAMUEL: *see* MAYNE, RUTHERFORD.

WAIN, JOHN BARRINGTON (1925-)

Temple & Tucker; Adelman & Dworkin (Novel); Vinson-Poets; Vinson-Novelists; Drescher & Kahrmann; Bufkin.

WAITE, ARTHUR EDWARD (1857-1942)

PRIMARY

Robert Galbreath. "Arthur Edward Waite. Occult Scholar and Christian Mystic. A Chronological Bibliography." *Bulletin of Bibliography* 30 (1973): 55-61.

Primary books. Chronological arrangement. Place, publisher, date, annotations.

The limitations of this checklist are described on pp. 55-56.

WALEY, ARTHUR DAVID (1889-1966)

PRIMARY

Francis A. Johns. *A Bibliography of Arthur Waley* [English title: *The Strategist: A Bibliography of Arthur Waley*]. New Brunswick, New Jersey: Rutgers University Press; London: George Allen and Unwin, 1968. Pp. xii, 188.

Primary, secondary selected. Form and genre arrangement. Books: transcribed TP, part collation, binding, date, price, number of copies, printer, contents with cross-references to previous publications, subsequent impressions and editions, translations (date, publisher, number of copies). Extensive bibliographical and textual notes. Periods: date, pages, occasionally volume; reviews by Waley include title and author of book reviewed. Index.

Lawrence S. Thompson, *Papers of the Bibliographical Society of America* 63 (1969): 354: "a carefully detailed record of Waley's work."

SECONDARY

Above, Johns, pp. 173-174.

GENERAL

Daiches; NCBEL, IV, 372-374.

WALKER, EDWARD JOSEPH (1934-)

Vinson-Poets.

WALL, MERVYN (1908-)

PRIMARY

Robert Hogan. *Mervyn Wall.* Lewisburg: Bucknell University Press (Irish Writers Series), 1972. Pp. 75.

Pp. 74-75, selected primary bibliography. Books: place, publisher, date. Selected periodical contributions: volume, date, pages. Brief note naming periodicals and newspapers to which Wall has contributed.

WALLACE, RICHARD HORATIO EDGAR (1875-1932)

PRIMARY

William Oliver Guillemont Lofts and Derek Adley. *The British Bibliography of Edgar Wallace.* London: Howard Baker, 1969. Pp. [xvi], 246.

Primary. Form and genre arrangement. Variously arranged lists of titles with cross-references, the most important being an alphabetical by title list of primary books: publisher, date, format, pages, dedication (pp. 15-35); the same list with contents of each book listed with place of first publication (pp. 36-143); alphabetical by title list of periodicals, Wallace's contributions listed under each title: date, occasionally volume or pages, cross-reference to primary book in which collected (pp. 155-246). Many notes and much miscellaneous bibliographical information.

Not an easy book to use, but immensely informative about the British publications (no others are considered).

GENERAL

Temple & Tucker; NCBEL, IV, 754-758.

WALPOLE, SIR HUGH SEYMOUR (1884-1941)

PRIMARY

Henry Danielson. *Bibliographies of Modern Authors.* London: Bookman's Journal, 1921. Pp. [xii], [212].

Pp. 201-208, primary books, 1909-1921. Chronological arrangement. Transcribed TP, part collation, pagination, binding, variants, miscellaneous bibliographical notes.

Jean Marty. "Hugh Walpole Bibliography." *Reading and Collecting* 2 (February-March, 1938): 26.

Primary books. Chronological arrangement. Place, date, occasionally collector's "points," subsequent editions. Includes books with contributions by Walpole and books about Walpole.

Rupert Hart-Davis. *Hugh Walpole A Biography.* New York: Macmillan, 1952. Pp. xiv, 503.

Pp. 481-483, primary books, 1909-1948. Chronological arrangement. Date. Contents listed for collections.

Elizabeth Steele. *Hugh Walpole.* New York: Twayne Publishers, Inc. (TEAS 120), 1972. Pp. 178.

Pp. 162-166, selected primary bibliography, mainly useful for its lists of periodical contributions and of unpublished MSS at the University of Texas. Pp. 166-170, secondary bibliography, annotated. Additional critical material cited in Notes, pp. 153-161.

SECONDARY

Above, Marty, Steele.

Elizabeth Steele. "Hugh Walpole: An Annotated Bibliography of Writings about Him." *English Literature in Transition* 19 (1976): 150-233.

Alphabetical by author arrangement. Books: place, publisher, date. Periods: volume, date, pages. Précis of each entry.

GENERAL

Millett; Daiches; Batho & Dobrée; Temple & Tucker; Bufkin; NCBEL, IV, 758-761.

WALSH, MAURICE (1879-1964)

PRIMARY

Joanne L. Henderson. "Checklist of Four Kerry Writers: . . . Maurice Walsh . . ." *Journal of Irish Literature* 1 (May 1972): 104-111.

Primary, secondary. Form arrangement. Books: place, publisher, date; all English language editions; reviews of each book. Periods: volume, date, pages.

WALTON, JOHN: *see* CONWAY, OLIVE.

WARD, MARY AUGUSTA (1851-1920)

Née Arnold (Mrs. Humphry Ward).

Batho & Dobrée; Longaker & Bolles; NCBEL, III, 1081-1082.

WARLOCK, PETER: *see* HESELTINE, PHILIP.

WARNER, FRANCIS (1937-)

Vinson-Potes.

WARNER, REGINALD (REX) ERNEST (1905-)

PRIMARY

A. L. McLeod. *Rex Warner: Writer. An Introductory Essay.* Sydney, N. S. W.: Westworth Press, 1964. Pp. vi, 50.

Pp. 46-50, "A Select Bibliography." Primary. Genre and form arrangement. Books: place, publisher, date. Periods: date, pages. Includes list of unpublished radio and TV talks.

Pp. 49-50, selected secondary bibliography.

SECONDARY

Above, McLeod, pp. 49-50.

GENERAL

Daiches; Temple & Tucker; Adelman & Dworkin (Novel); Vinson-Poets; Vinson-Novelists; NCBEL, IV, 761-762; Bufkin.

WARNER, SYLVIA TOWNSEND (1893-)

Millett; Longaker & Bolles; Daiches; Temple & Tucker; Vinson-Novelists; NCBEL, IV, 762-763; Bufkin.

WATERHOUSE, KEITH SPENCER (1929-)

Breed & Sniderman; Adelman & Dworkin (Novel); Temple & Tucker; Vinson-Novelists; Vinson-Dramatists; Drescher & Kahrmann; Bufkin.

WATKINS, VERNON PHILLIPS (1906-1967)

PRIMARY

Brynmor Jones. *Vernon Watkins 1906-1967.* Welsh Arts Council (Bibliographies of Anglo-Welsh Literature, 5), 1968.

Not seen.

Jane McCormick. "Vernon Watkins: A Bibliography." *West Coast Review* 4, i (Spring, 1969): 42-48.

Primary, secondary selected. Form arrangement. Books: place, publisher, date, subsequent editions. Periods: volume, pages, date. Includes selected translations by Watkins and selected anthologies in which his poems appear; also recordings by Watkins. Pp. 46-48, secondary bibliography. Alphabetical-by-author arrangement; annotated.

GENERAL

Longaker & Bolles; Temple & Tucker; Vinson-Poets; NCBEL, IV, 374-375; Stratford.

WATSON, SIR WILLIAM (1858-1935)

PRIMARY

Cecil Woolf. "Some Uncollected Authors. XII: Sir William Watson." *Book Collector* 5 (Winter), 1956): 375-380.

Primary books. Chronological arrangement. Place, publisher, date, format, binding and variants, limitations of edition, miscellaneous notes.

Norman Colbeck. "Sir William Watson: Additions and Corrections." *Book Collector* 6 (Spring, 1957): 66-67. Walter E. Swayze. "Sir William Watson: Additions and Corrections." *Book Collector* 6 (Autumn, 1957): 285-286; (Winter, 1957): 402.

These several entries together provide a fairly complete list of Watson's books.

SECONDARY

James G. Nelson. *Sir William Watson.* New York: Twayne Publishers, Inc. (TEAS 45), 1966. Pp. 193.

Pp. 183-185, secondary bibliography, annotated. Other secondary material in Notes, pp. 164-180.

GENERAL

Millett; Longaker & Bolles; Temple & Tucker; NCBEL, III, 653-654.

WAUGH, ALEXANDER [ALEC] RABAN (1898-)

Millett; Daiches; Longaker & Bolles; Temple & Tucker; NCBEL, IV, 763-764; Bufkin.

WAUGH, AUBERON ALEXANDER (1939-)

Vinson-Novelists.

WAUGH, EVELYN ARTHUR ST. JOHN (1903-1966)

PRIMARY

Robert Murray Davis, Paul A. Doyle, Heinz Kosok, Charles E. Linck, Jr. *Evelyn Waugh: A Checklist of Primary and Secondary Material.* Troy, New York: Whitston Publishing Co., 1972.

Pp. iv, 211.

Primary (pp. [1]-82); secondary. Form arrangement. Books: place, publisher, date for British, American, and revised editions; for translations, title, date, and country. Periods: volume, date, pages. Includes uncollected writings, drawings, ephemera. Secondary bibliography includes list of previous bibliographies; also books and monographs, dissertations, general commentary, articles on and reviews of individual works by Waugh. Index.

This volume incorporates all previously published bibliographical information and, although lacking collations and other bibliographical descriptions, is the beginning point for study of Waugh. For supplementary information one should turn to *The Evelyn Waugh Newsletter* (1967-to date), an indispensable aid to the student of Waugh. Additional information is provided by Alain Blayac in two essays: "Evelyn Waugh's Drawings." *Library Chronicle of the University of Texas at Austin* NS 7 (Spring, 1974): 43-57. Listing and description of Waugh's sketches and drawings in the University of Texas collection; "Evelyn Waugh. A Supplementary Bibliography." *Book Collector* 25 (1976): 53-62. Eighty-two additional items with an appendix listing Waugh's thirteen broadcasts.

SECONDARY

Above, Davis, *et al,* pp. 83-188.

GENERAL

Millett; Daiches; Longaker & Bolles; Temple & Tucker; NCBEL, IV, 764-768; Adelman & Dworkin (Novel); Bufkin.

WEBB, MARY GLADYS MEREDITH (1881-1927)

PRIMARY

"Checklist Bibliographies of Modern Authors: Mary Webb." *Book Trade Journal,* No. 61 (10 July, 1936), p. 30.

Primary books. Chronological arrangement. Publisher, date, binding and binding variants.

Charles Sanders. "Mary Webb: An Introduction." *English Literature in Transition* 9 (1966): 115-118.

An essay in which the primary books are mentioned with date and genre.

SECONDARY

Charles Sanders. "Mary Webb: An Annotated Bibliography of Works about Her." *English Literature in Transition* 9 (1966): 119-136.

Alphabetical by author. Books: place, publisher, date. Periods: volume, pages, date. Annotations. Continued in subsequent issues, especially 11 (1968): 56.

GENERAL

Millett; Temple & Tucker; NCBEL, IV, 768-769; Bufkin.

WELCH, MAURICE DENTON (1917-1948)

PRIMARY

Robert Phillips. *Denton Welch.* New York: Twayne Publishers (TEAS 163), 1974. Pp. 189.

P. 177, primary books: place, publisher, date. Pp. 177-184, secondary bibliography. Arranged: alphabetical by author. Periods: volume, date, pages. Each entry annotated. Other secondary references in notes, pp. 169-176.

An essay description of an important collection of manuscripts, books, and related material is given by Jean-Louis Chevalier, "The Denton Welch Collection at Austin," *Texas Quarterly* 15 (Summer, 1972, part 2): 7-23.

SECONDARY

Above, Phillips.

GENERAL

Temple & Tucker; NCBEL, IV, 769-770; Bufkin.

WELDON, JOHN (1890-1963)

Pseudonym used: Brinsley MacNamara

PRIMARY

Michael McDonnell. "Brinsley MacNamara (1890-1963). A Checklist." *Journal of Irish Literature* 4, ii (1975): 79-88.

Primary bibliography. Genre arrangement. Books: place, publisher, date. Periods: dates. Also includes (pp. 86-88) the MSS and TSS (with title and genre) in the University of Texas (Austin) Library.

GENERAL

NCBEL, IV, 965; Breed & Sniderman.

WELLESLEY, DOROTHY VIOLET ASHTON (1889-1956)

(Duchess of Wellington).

Longaker & Bolles; Daiches; Temple & Tucker; NCBEL, IV, 375-376.

WELLS, HERBERT GEORGE (1866-1946)

PRIMARY

Geoffrey H. Wells. *The Works of H. G. Wells, 1887-1925, A Bibliography, Dictionary and Subject Index.* London: George Routledge and Sons, Ltd.; New York: H. W. Wilson Co., 1926. Pp. [xxvi], 274.

Primary. Form arrangement: books and pamphlets, pp. xxiii-xxiv, 1-65; books with contributions by Wells, pp. 66-72; unreprinted primary writings, pp. 73-79; letters to the press, pp. 80-81. Books: transcribed TP, full collation, pagination, printer, binding, variants, brief account of previous serial publication, occasional textual or bibliographical notes. Periods: date. [Pp. 89-251, the dictionary; pp. 255-274, subject index] .

Costa (below), p. 168: "no Wells scholar should be without it" The authoritative bibliography for the years covered.

Gordon N. Ray. "H. G. Wells' Contribution to the *Saturday Review.*" *Library* (5th Series) 16 (1961): 29-36.

Pp. 29-32, introductory essay; pp. 32-36, primary writings, signed and unsigned. Chronological arrangement. Volume, date, pages. Reviews by Wells include author and title of books reviewed.

Ingvald Raknem. *H. G. Wells and his Critics.* Oslo and Bergen. Universitatsforlaget (Scandinavian University Books), 1962. Pp. [iv] , 475.

Pp. 432-434, unreprinted primary writings. Chronological arrangement. Volume, pages, date. Pp. 435-440, general secondary books and books about Wells: place, publisher, date. Pp. 446-459, reviews of primary books listed under title of book reviewed: volume, pages, date. Pp. 460-471, general studies in periodicals. P. 472, obituary notices.

[H. G. Wells Society] . *H. G. Wells. A Comprehensive Bibliography.* London: H. G. Wells Society, 1968. Pp. vi, 70.

Pp. 1-45, primary books. Chronological arrangement. Place, publisher, date, pages, annotations, brief bibliographical notes. Pp. 46-50, short stories listed with periodical and date in which originally published. Pp. 51-57, other primary writings. Pp. 57-63, secondary bibliography. Chronological arrangement. Pp. 64-66, stage and film adaptations of Wells' writings.

Kenneth Young. *H. G. Wells.* Harlow: Longman Group (WTW 233), 1974. Pp. [60] .

Pp. 49-56, primary books, chronologically arranged. Date, genre, details of previous serial publication.

Perhaps the best bibliography for the beginning student.

J. R. Hammond. *Herbert George Wells. An Annotated Bibliography of His Works.* New York and London: Garland Publishing, Inc., 1977. Pp. xvi, 257.

Primary. Genre and form arrangement. Books: transcribed TP, full collation, pagination, binding, date, reprints, contents, extensive textual and bibliographical notes, including first periodical publication of contents. Pp. 235-257, index of titles.

The *Works of Wells,* the inaccurately-named *Comprehensive Bibliography,* and Hammond together supply an almost complete bibliography of this most prolific writer.

SECONDARY

Above, Raknem, pp. 435-472; [H. G. Wells Society], pp. 57-63; Mackenzie, pp. 473-474; Young, pp. 56-58.

Robert P. Weeks. "H. G. Wells." *English Fiction* (later *English Literature*) *in Transition* 1 (Fall-Winter, 1957): 37-42.

Annotated secondary bibliography. Note references to previous compilations, the contents of which are not here relisted. This bibliography is continued by various writers in subsequent issues, particularly 1, ii, 35; 4, ii (1961): 59-64; 5, ii (1962): 36-43; 6, ii (1963): 119-123, etc. The Annotated Secondary Bibliography Series on English Literature in Transition, Northern Illinois University Press, is to include a volume on Wells.

Richard Hauer Costa. *H. G. Wells.* New York: Twayne Publishers, Inc. (TEAS 43), 1967. Pp. 181.

Pp. 165-167, primary books (fiction complete, other genres selected). Chronological arrangement. Place, publisher, and date of either English or American first edition. Pp. 167-173, secondary bibliography. Annotated. Additional items in notes, pp. 151-164.

By examining the bibliographies in each of the books listed above, one begins to locate some of the references to Wells: there is no single, comprehensive listing.

GENERAL

Millett; Longaker & Bolles; Batho & Dobrée; Temple & Tucker; NCBEL, IV, 417-428; Bufkin.

WESKER, ARNOLD (1932-)

PRIMARY

Harold U. Ribalow. *Arnold Wesker.* New York: Twayne Publishers, Inc. (TEAS 28), 1965. Pp. 154.

Pp. 137-138, primary bibliography. Chronological arrangement. Books: place, publisher, date, British and American editions, revisions and reprints. Periods: date, pages. Pp. 138-150, secondary bibliography. Alphabetical by author under divisions Criticism and Background Material. Information as for primary writings, with extensive annotations. Additional secondary material on pp. [11]-[13] and 123-136. One of the better bibliographies in this series.

Glenda Leeming and Simon Trussler. *The Plays of Arnold Wesker.* London: Gollancz, 1971. Pp. 222.

Pp. 217-222, primary and secondary bibliography. Genre arrangement. Books: publisher, date, all editions. Periods: date, pages. Pp. 209-216, details of first production of each play: cast, place, date, director, designer.

Glenda Leeming. *Arnold Wesker.* Harlow, Essex: The Longman Group (WTW 225), 1972. Pp. 30.

Pp. 29-30, selected primary and secondary bibliography. Books: place, date. Periods: volume, date, pages.

SECONDARY

Above, Ribalow, pp. [11]-[13], 123-136, 138-150; Leeming and Trussler, pp. 219-222; Leeming, pp. 29-30.

GENERAL

Temple & Tucker; Coleman & Tyler; Adelman & Dworkin; Salem; Breed & Sniderman; Vinson-Dramatists.

WEST, ANTHONY PANTHER (1914-)

Temple & Tucker; Vinson-Novelists, NCBEL, IV, 770; Bufkin.

WEST, MORRIS LANGLO (1916-)

Pseudonym used: Michael East.

Temple & Tucker; Bufkin.

WEST, DAME REBECCA (1892-)

Pseudonym of Cicily Isabel Fairfield.

(Mrs. Henry M. Andrews).

PRIMARY

G. Evelyn Hutchinson. *A Preliminary List of the Writings of Rebecca West, 1912-1951.* New Haven: Yale University Library, 1957. Pp. 102.

Primary first editions, British and American. Form and genre arrangement. Books: transcribed TP, part collation, binding, date, price, contents and cross-references to earlier publication, occasional notes on limitations of issue, reprints, presence of advertisements, and variants. Periods: volume, pages, date, reviews by West include title and author of book reviewed. Separate list of translations of primary books with information as for first editions. Also lists of dramatisations, of works announced but not published, and of spurious titles.

The author disclaims completeness, particularly in the list of contributions to newspapers and periodicals. Additional titles, including post-1951 writings and a list of periodicals to which Dame Rebecca contributed (with some dates) are provided by Verena Elsbeth Wolfer. *Rebecca West. Kunsttheorie und Romanschaffen.* Bern: Francke Verlag (Schweizer Anglistische Arbeiten 66), 1972. Pp. 171. Primary bibliography, pp. 159-162; secondary, pp. 163-169. Additional secondary material is found in the notes (pp. 149-159) to Peter Wolfe. *Rebecca West. Artist and Thinker.* Carbondale: Southern Illinois University Press, 1971. Pp. [xiv], 166.

GENERAL

Millett; Daiches; Temple & Tucker; Adelman & Dworkin (Novel); Vinson-Novelists; NCBEL, IV, 770-771; Bufkin.

WHEELER, HUGH (1916-)

Salem.

WHIGHAM, PETER GEORGE (1925-)

Vinson-Poets.

WHISTLER, ALAN CHARLES LAURENCE (1912-)

Vinson-Poets; NCBEL, IV, 376.

WHISTLER, REGINALD JOHN [REX] (1905-1944)

PRIMARY

Laurence Whistler and Ronald Fuller. *The Work of Rex Whistler.* London: Batsford, 1960. Pp. [lxxxvi], 122.

Pp. 1-113, Catalogue. Arranged by topic and genre. "A Note," p. [lxxv] explains details provided. Index, pp. 115-122.

SECONDARY

Whistler and Fuller, above, p. 114, "Bibliography of the principal books and articles on Rex Whistler, and printed references to him."

Includes more specialized bibliographies.

WHITE, ANTONIA (1899-)

Daiches; Vinson-Novelists; Bufkin.

WHITE, JON MANCHIP (1924-)

Vinson-Novelists.

WHITE, KENNETH (1936-)

Vinson-Poets.

WHITE, TERENCE HANBURY (1906-1964)

PRIMARY

Sylvia Townsend Warner. *T. H. White.* New York: Viking Press; London: Jonathan Cape, 1968. Pp. 352.

Pp. 346-348, bibliography. Primary books. Chronological arrangement. Place, publisher, date. Also list of unpublished writings and titles of short stories. See text for references to primary periodical contributions.

GENERAL

Temple & Tucker; NCBEL, IV, 771-772; Bufkin.

WHITEING, RICHARD (1840-1928)

PRIMARY

Vincent Brome. *Four Realist Novelists.* London: Longmans, Green and Co. (WTW 183), 1965. Pp. 36.

P. 34, bibliography. Primary books. Chronological arrangement. Place, date, genre.

SECONDARY

Wendell V. Harris. "A Selective Annotated Bibliography of Writings about Richard Whiteing." *English Literature in Transition* 8 (1965): 44-48.

GENERAL

Batho & Dobrée.

WHITING, JOHN (1917-1963)

PRIMARY

Ronald Hayman, ed. *The Collected Plays of John Whiting.* London: Heinemann, 1969. Two volumes.

This edition includes all of the primary plays, while the Introductory Note to each play gives selected secondary references. I, vi: acknowledgement of bibliographical aid to G. S. Robinson's unpublished London Ph. D. thesis. II, 273-275: Bibliography of Whiting's Other Writings. Genre arrangement. Films (date, producer); Translations by Whiting; Interviews; Periodical Contributions (dates; not complete, but names periodicals for which Whiting wrote).

GENERAL

Adelman & Dworkin; Breed & Sniderman; Temple & Tucker.

WICKHAM, ANNA (1884-1947)

Pseudonym of Edith Alice Mary Harper Hepburn.

Millett; Longaker & Bolles; Daiches; NCBEL, IV, 377.

WILDE, OSCAR FINGAL O'FLAHERTIE WILLS (1856-1900)

PRIMARY

Stuart Mason [pseudonym of Christopher Millard] . *Bibliography of Oscar Wilde.* London: T. W. Laurie, 1914. Reprinted with introduction by Timothy d'Arch Smith, London: Bertram Rota, 1967. [3 unnumbered leaves] , xxxix, 605.

Primary bibliography, arranged: Periodical contributions listed under title of periodical; books; collected editions; pirated editions; selections. Transcribed TP, full collation, bibliographical and textual notes. Information is not consistently given, but this is the single most important source of bibliographical information. It incorporates much of the information in Stuart Mason. *A Bibliography of the Poems of Oscar Wilde.* London: E. Grant Richards, 1907. Pp. [xii] , 148. 475 copies, although this volume is still valuable for its account of textual variants. Mason is the standard bibliography for Wilde up to 1914.

Owen Dudley Evans, *Book Collector* 16 (1967): 530-534: lists errors in this unchanged reprint of the 1914 edition, pointing out that it is not to be used without the cautions he has put forward; "a totally new bibliography is overdue."

Robert Ernest Cowan, William Andrews Clark, Jr., Cora Edgerton Sanders, Harrison Post. *The Library of William Andrews Clark, Jr. Wilde and Wildeiana.* San Francisco: John Henry Nash, 1922-1931. 5 volumes. 100 copies of each, privately circulated.

Primary and secondary bibliography. Generally genre arrangement, with exceptions. Description of unique copies in the Clarke collection. Transcribed TP, binding, pagination, full collation, date, extensive historical, bibliographical and textual notes. Includes translations of Wilde. Annotations. Exclusively secondary bibliographies are found in I (1922): 67-93; II (1922): 85-99; III (1924): 107-144; V (1931): 39-112. Other secondary references, *passim.*

Although Mason (1914) is the presiding genius, this catalogue of an important collection (since 1934 in the Clark Memorial Library, Los Angeles) supplements and corrects Mason; it contains numerous indices; and it should be used in conjunction with Mason.

John Charles Finzi. *Oscar Wilde and his Literary Circle. A Catalogue of manuscripts and letters in the William Andrews Clark Memorial Library.* Berkeley: University of California Press, 1957. Pp. [xviii] ; unnumbered pages containing reproductions of 2892 file cards; indices on pp. xix-xxxiv.

Preface, pp. [vii-viii] , describes the unique collection, including sections of it not herein catalogued. Cards arranged alphabetically by writer of manuscript or letter: each gives brief physical description, place of publication if published, and Clark pressmark. No details of contents of manuscripts.

James Laver. *Oscar Wilde.* London: Longmans, Green and Co. (WTW 53, revised edition), 1963. Pp. 32.

Pp. 27-30, primary books. Chronologically arranged. Genre, date. Pp. 30-32, secondary books and periodical articles. Chronologically arranged. Author, title, date.

The student who wants only a list of the primary titles may find Laver easier to use than the preceding works, while the secondary bibliography in Laver is particularly complete within its limits.

SECONDARY

Above, Mason, pp. 565-582, and *passim;* Cowan (as noted above); Laver, pp. 30-32. Many of the books described in these lists (as well as those named below) themselves contain secondary bibliographies which should be consulted.

Peter Funke. *Oscar Wilde in Selbstzeugnissen und Bilddokumenten.* Hamburg: Rowohlt Taschenbuch Verlag (Rowohlt Monographien Series), 1969. Pp. [186].

Pp. 177-[186], secondary bibliography by Helmut Riege. Books and periodicals, including many Continental writings.

Karl Beckson, ed. *Oscar Wilde. The Critical Heritage.* London: Routledge and Kegan Paul, 1970. Pp. xiv, 434.

Chronological list (1881-1927) of secondary criticism with extensive quotations and bibliographical annotations; additional references are given in Introduction, pp. 1-32, *passim.*

GENERAL

Longaker & Bolles; Coleman & Tyler; Adelman & Dworkin; Salem; Palmer & Dyson; NCBEL, III, 1182-1188.

WILKINSON, LOUIS UMFREVILLE: *see* MARLOW, LOUIS.

WILLIAMS, CHARLES WALTER STANSBY (1886-1945)

PRIMARY

Lawrence R. Dawson, Jr. "Checklist of Reviews by Charles Williams." *Papers of the Bibliographical Society of America* 55 (1961): 100-117.

Pp. 100-112, reviews by Williams, chronologically arranged. Periods: volume, pages, date; title and author of book reviewed. P. 112, index of periodicals; pp. 113-117, index of authors reviewed.

Mary McDermott Shideler. *The Theology of Romantic Love. A Study in the Writings of Charles Williams.* Grand Rapids, Michigan: William B. Eerdmans Publishing Co., 1966. Pp. [xii], 243.

Pp. 223-234, selected primary bibliography, arranged in one list alphabetically by title. Books: place, publisher, date. Periods: volume, date, pages. Reviews by Williams include title and author of book reviewed.

Mary McDermott Shideler. *Charles Williams. A Critical Essay.* Grand Rapids, Michigan: William B. Eerdmans Publishing Co. (Contemporary Writers in Christian Perspective Series), 1966. Pp. 48.

Pp. 46-48, selected primary and secondary bibliography. Books: place, publisher, date. Periods: volume, date, pages. The beginning student will find the selected list of critical studies of Williams particularly useful.

Lois Glenn. *Charles W. S. Williams. A Checklist.* Kent: Kent State University Press (Serif Series 33), 1975. Pp. viii, 128.

Not seen. *PBSA* 71 (1977): 133: "records all of the writer's published works and works about him, including dissertations and reviews of single works."

SECONDARY

Above, Shideler, *Charles Williams,* pp. 47-48; Glenn.

GENERAL

Daiches; Temple & Tucker; Coleman & Tyler; Breed & Sniderman; NCBEL, IV, 772-774; Bufkin.

WILLIAMS, DAVID GWYN (1904-)

Vinson-Poets.

WILLIAMS, GEORGE EMLYN (1905-)

Longaker & Bolles; Temple & Tucker; Coleman & Tyler; Adelman & Dworkin; Salem; Palmer & Dyson; Breed & Sniderman; Vinson-Dramatists; NCBEL, IV, 989.

WILLIAMS, HUGO (1942-)

Vinson-Poets.

WILLIAMS, PEGGY EILEEN ARABELLA (1909-1958)

Pseudonym used: Margiad Evans.

NCBEL, IV, 567.

WILLIAMS, RAYMOND HENRY (1921-)

Temple & Tucker; Vinson-Novelists; Drescher & Kahrmann.

WILLIAMSON, HENRY (1895-)

PRIMARY

I. Waveney Girvan. *A Bibliography and a Critical Survey of the Works of Henry Williamson.* Chipping Campden, Glos.: Alcuin Press, 1931. Pp. 56. 420 copies.

Pp. 17-56, primary books. Chronological arrangement. Transcribed TP, part collation, pagination, binding, date, price, number of copies in limited editions, contents, extensive textual notes.

Book Collector's Quarterly, No. 5 (March, 1932), p. 111: "the bibliographer . . . has made the most (in two senses of the word) of Mr. Williamson's not very extensive output."

GENERAL

Millett; Longaker & Bolles; Temple & Tucker; Vinson-Novelists; NCBEL, IV, 774-776; Bufkin.

WILLIAMSON, HUGH ROSS (1901-)

Temple & Tucker; NCBEL, IV, 990.

WILLIS, GEORGE ANTHONY ARMSTRONG (1897-)

Pseudonym used: Anthony Armstrong.

NCBEL, IV, 906-908.

WILLY, MARGARET ELIZABETH (1919-)

Vinson-Poets.

WILSON, ANGUS FRANK JOHNSTONE (1913-)

PRIMARY

Jay L. Halio. *Angus Wilson.* Edinburgh: Oliver and Boyd (Writers and Critics Series), 1964. Pp. [viii] , 120.

Pp. 117-120, bibliography. Primary selected, secondary selected. Genre arrangement. Books: place, publisher, date (English editions only). Periods: volume, date, pages. Includes selected periodical contributions by Wilson, 1951-1963.

K. W. Gransden. *Angus Wilson.* London: Longmans, Green and Co. (WW 208), 1969. Pp. 31.

P. 31, "A Select Bibliography." Primary books, 1949-1967, plus four primary periodical contributions. Date, place, genre. Three secondary items from periodicals: volume, date.

While Halio and Gransden provide lists of book titles to 1967, there is no complete record of Wilson's extensive journalism or of his periodical contributions.

SECONDARY

Above, Halio and Gransden.

GENERAL

Daiches; Temple & Tucker; Adelman & Dworkin (Novel); Vinson-Novelists; Drescher & Kahrmann; NCBEL, IV, 776-777; Bufkin.

WILSON, COLIN (1931-)

PRIMARY

John A. Weigel. *Colin Wilson.* Boston: Twayne Publishers, G. K.

Hall and Co. (TEAS 181), 1975. Pp. 157.

Pp. 145-147, primary books. Chronological arrangement. British and American editions including reprints; place, publisher, date. Pp. 147-149, selected secondary criticism, annotated. Additional secondary criticism is given in the notes, pp. 137-144.

There is no complete list of Wilson's journalism, and this list of books extends only through 1974. Additional bibliographical information about primary books and unpublished writings is given by R. H. W. Dillard, "Books by Colin Wilson," *Hollins Critic* 4 (October, 1967): 6-7, and by Sidney R. Campion, *The World of Colin Wilson.* London: Frederick Muller, 1962 [not seen] . There is no complete list of the secondary criticism.

SECONDARY

Above, Weigel.

GENERAL

Temple & Tucker; Adelman & Dworkin (Novel); Vinson-Novelists; Drescher & Kahrmann.

WILSON, JOHN BURGESS: *see* BURGESS, ANTHONY.

WILSON, ROMER (1891-1930)

Pseudonym of Florence Roma Muir Wilson.

Millett; NCBEL, IV, 777; Bufkin.

WINCH, JOHN: *see* LONG, GABRIELLE.

WINGFIELD, SHEILA CLAUDE (1906-)

Vinson-Poets; NCBEL, IV, 377.

WINTER, JOHN KEITH (1906-)

Salem; NCBEL, IV, 990-991.

WODEHOUSE, SIR PELHAM GREVILLE (1881-1975)

PRIMARY

David A. Jasen. *A Bibliography and Reader's Guide to the First Editions of P. G. Wodehouse.* Hamden, Connecticut: Archon Books, 1970. Pp. [x] , 290.

Primary books. Chronological arrangement. Date, place, publisher, pages, binding, and contents for both British and American first editions. Also list of places and of characters with descriptions for each title. Various indices, including one of publishers of the primary books.

The most complete list of primary books, 1901-1970.

David A. Jasen. *P. G. Wodehouse: A Portrait of a Master.* New York: Mason and Lipscomb Publishers, 1974. Pp. [xxii] , 294.

Pp. 258-261, primary books (British and American editions): publisher, date. Pp. 264-271, published short stories (British and American): periodical, date, title of volume in which collected. Pp. 274-275, plays with details of British and American productions: theatre, date, number of performances. Pp. 278-285, musicals and song lyrics: details as for plays with titles of lyrics by Wodehouse. Each section chronologically arranged. Pp. 254-256, secondary bibliography.

The most accessible listing of Wodehouse's writings.

SECONDARY

Above, Jasen (1974), pp. 254-256.

GENERAL

Daiches; Temple & Tucker; Vinson-Novelists; NCBEL, IV, 778-781.

WOLFE, HUMBERT (1885-1940)

Millett; Daiches; Temple & Tucker; NCBEL, IV, 377-379.

WOOD, CHARLES (1933-)

Vinson-Dramatists.

WOOD, MARGARET LOUISA BRADLEY (1856-1945)

(Mrs. H. G. Woods).

NCBEL, III, 1083.

WOOLF, LEONARD SIDNEY (1880-1969)

PRIMARY

Lelia M. J. Luedeking. "Bibliography of Works by Leonard Sidney Woolf (1880-1969)." *Virginia Woolf Quarterly* 1 (Fall 1972): 124-140.

Primary books. Original writings and editings arranged alphabetically by title; translations arranged alphabetically by author. Place, publisher, date, reprints, pages. Pp. 120-124, omissions are described and suggestions are made concerning the location of Woolf's other writings.

GENERAL

Millett; Daiches; Temple & Tucker; NCBEL, IV, 1239-1240.

WOOLF, ADELINE VIRGINIA STEPHEN (1882-1941)

(Mrs. Leonard Sidney Woolf).

PRIMARY

Brownlee Jean Kirkpatrick. *A Bibliography of Virginia Woolf.* London: Rupert Hart-Davis (Soho Bibliography 9, Revised Edition), 1967. Pp. xii, 212.

Primary. Arrangement: Books and Pamphlets; Contributions to Books and Translations by Woolf; Contributions to Periodicals and Newspapers by Woolf; Translations of Woolf; Foreign Editions of Woolf; Books and Articles containing letters by Woolf; MSS and Autograph letters; Index. First editions of books: transcribed TP, part collation, pagination, binding, date, number of copies, price, contents, bibliographical notes; reprints and later editions (information about these editions is less complete). Periods: date, pages. Reviews by Woolf include title and author of books reviewed. Includes unsigned pieces and information about reprinting of periodical contributions.

The authoritative bibliography.

J. Howard Woolmer. *A Checklist of The Hogarth Press, 1917-1938.* With a Short History of the Press by Mary E. Gaither. Andes, N.Y.: Woolmer-Brotherson Ltd., 1976. Pp. [xii], 177.

Chronological listing of the 440 books published during Mrs. Woolf's association with the press. Extensive bibliographical notes, appendices, and indices.

SECONDARY

Maurice Beebe. "Criticism of Virginia Woolf: A Selected Checklist with an Index to Studies of Separate Works." *Modern Fiction Studies* 2 (February, 1956): 36-45; continued by Barbara Weiser, "Criticism of Virginia Woolf from 1956 to the Present: A Selected Checklist with an Index to Studies of Separate Works." *Modern Fiction Studies* 18 (1972): 477-486.

General criticism listed alphabetically by author. Studies of specific titles listed under those titles.

The beginning point for study of the criticism of Woolf.

Jean Guiget. *Virginia Woolf and Her Works,* translated by Jean Stewart. London: Hogarth Press, 1965. Pp. 488.

Pp. 466-482, secondary bibliography, arranged: Books on Woolf; Articles on Woolf; General studies.

This bibliography is more complete and more accurate than that in the original French edition (Paris: Didier, 1962).

Jane Novak: "Recent Criticism of Virginia Woolf: January 1970-June 1972. Abstracts of Published Criticism and Unpublished Dissertations." *Virginia Woolf Quarterly* 1 (Fall, 1972): 141-155.

Annotated secondary bibliography. Subsequent issues of this periodical should be examined for additional bibliographical material.

Robin Majumdar. *Virginia Woolf. An Annotated Bibliography of Criticism, 1915-1974.* New York and London: Garland Publishing, Inc., 1976. Pp. xxii, 118.

Not seen.

GENERAL

Millett; Daiches; Longaker & Bolles; Temple & Tucker; NCBEL, IV, 472-481; Bufkin.

WOOLL, EDWARD (1878-1970)

NCBEL, IV, 992.

YATES, DORNFORD (1885-1960)

Pseudonym of Major Cecil William Mercer.

PRIMARY

Richard Usborne. *Clubland Heroes.* London: Constable, 1953. Pp. 217.

Although there is no bibliography, details of the primary writings can be gathered from pp. 21-79.

GENERAL

NCBEL, IV, 781.

YATES, PETER (1914-)

NCBEL, IV, 992.

YEATS, JACK BUTLER (1871-1957)

PRIMARY

E. MacC[arvill]. "Jack B. Yeats. His Books." *Dublin Magazine* NS 20 (July-September, 1945): 47-52.

Primary books and broadsheets, 1901-1944, written and illustrated by Yeats. Chronological arrangement. Transcribed TP, full collation, pagination, illustrations, binding notes.

Hilary Pyle. *Jack B. Yeats. A Biography.* London: Routledge and Kegan Paul, 1970. Pp. xii, 228.

Pp. [175]-180, primary bibliography. Arranged: Books written and illustrated by Yeats; Contributions to periodicals; Books illustrated by Yeats; Magazine articles and stories illustrated by Yeats; Prints for Cuala Press. Books: place, publisher, date. Periods: date. Pp. 181-185, secondary bibliography. Pp. 187-201: portraits by Yeats; public collections of his works; his contributions to illustrated papers. Pp. 203-219, chronological list of Yeats' exhibitions.

An all-inclusive list. Additional items, including unsigned and pseudonymous writings, along with necessary bibliographical details, are listed by Martha Caldwell, "A Bibliography of the Published Writings of Jack B. Yeats" in Roger McHugh, ed., *Jack B. Yeats. A Centenary Gathering.* Dublin: Dolmen Press, 1971, pp. 110-114.

GENERAL

Breed & Sniderman; Hogan.

YEATS, WILLIAM BUTLER (1865-1939)

PRIMARY

Allan Wade. *A Bibliography of the Writings of W. B. Yeats.* London: Rupert Hart-Davis (Soho Bibliographies No. 1, Third Edition, Revised and Edited by Russell K. Alspach), 1968. Pp. 514.

Primary, secondary books. Form arrangement. Books: transcribed TP, part collation, pagination, binding, date, contents including details of earlier publication, limitations of edition, bibliographical and textual notes. Complete descriptions of later editions follow that of the first edition. Periods: date, brief bibliographical note includes titles of volumes in which later collected; reviews by Yeats include author and title of book reviewed. Translations of Yeats listed separately. Appendices include: pp. 451-457, list of books published by the Cuala (previously Dun Emer) Press, 1903-1938; pp. 458-466, short-title list of books about Yeats; pp. 467-477, details and descriptions of radio broadcasts by Yeats (by George Whalley). Pp. 479-514, Index.

The definitive primary bibliography. See pp. 9-10 for descriptions of earlier bibliographies, and pp. 9-15 for the history of this volume.

Klaus Peter S. Jochum. "Additions to the Yeats Bibliography." *Bulletin of Bibliography* 28 (1971): 129-135.

Important additions to Wade-Alspach (3rd edition).

SECONDARY

Above, Wade-Alspach, pp. 458-466.

Alice Thurston McGirr. "Reading List on William Butler Yeats." *Bulletin of Bibliography* 7 (1913): 82-83.

Valuable list of early reviews arranged under title of book reviewed. Annotated; other information.

(The following entries are cumulative: that is, items listed in these entries themselves include extensive secondary bibliographies).

George B. Saul. *Prolegomena to the Study of Yeats's Poems.* Philadelphia: University of Pennsylvania Press, 1957. Pp. 196. *Prolegomena to the Study of Yeats's Plays.* Philadelphia: University of Pennsylvania Press, 1958. Both reprinted, 1971.

Particularly useful because the critical writings are listed under the title of the Yeats work being studied.

Hazard Adams. "Yeats Scholarship and Criticism: A Review of Research." *Texas Studies in Literature and Language* 3 (Winter, 1962): 439-451.

An important essay-survey, with subject headings, of primary material and of secondary writings.

K. G. W. Cross. "The Fascination of What's Difficult: A Survey of Yeats Criticism and Research" in *In Excited Reverie: A Centenary Tribute to William Butler Yeats,* 1865-1939, ed. by A. Norman Jeffares and K. G. W. Cross. New York; London: Macmillan Co., 1965. Pp. viii, [354].

Pp. 315-337, an essay on the history of Yeats scholarship.

K. P. S. Jochum. *W. B. Yeats's Plays. An Annotated Checklist of Criticism.* Saarbrücken: Anglistisches Institut der Universitat des Saarlandes, 1966. Pp. 180.

Subject arrangement, including on pp. 35-38, bibliographies, reviews of research and concordances, and on pp. 113-156, chronological list of the plays, with criticism arranged under the appropriate title. Pp. 161-180, Index.

John E. Stoll. *The Great Deluge: A Yeats Bibliography.* Troy, New York: Whitston Publishing Co., 1971. Pp. [viii], 100.

Secondary bibliography arranged alphabetically by author under these headings: General Critical Background; Esoteric and Historical Background; Criticism and Biography: Books; Articles.

A helpful tool for the beginning student.

K. G. W. Cross and R. T. Dunlop. *A Bibliography of Yeats Criticism, 1887-1965.* With a foreword by A. Norman Jeffares. London and New York: Macmillan Company, 1971. Pp. xxvi, 341.

Secondary bibliography. Arranged: Bibliographies, Concordances, and Descriptions of Yeatsiana; Reviews listed under title of book reviewed; Books and Pamphlets on Yeats, including the reviews of these books; Special issues of Periodicals; Articles; Dissertations. Index. Books: place, publisher, date, pages. Periods: volume, date, pages. Occasional brief descriptions of material.

One of the most important secondary bibliographies. The research student will find the listing of other bibliographies on pp. 3-12 particularly useful. Five additional items are listed by George Monteiro. "Addenda to Cross and Dunlop's *Yeats Criticism 1887-1965.*" *Papers of the Bibliographical Society of America* 70 (1976): 278.

James Lovic Allen. "Charts for the Voyage to Byzantium. An Annotated Bibliography of Scholarship and Criticism on Yeats's Byzantium Poems, 1935-1970." *Bulletin of the New York Public Library* 77 (1973): 28-50.

Secondary bibliography of material relating to "Sailing to Byzantium" and "Byzantium." Arranged alphabetically by author. Annotated.

Klaus Peter S. Jochum. "W. B. Yeats: A Survey of Book Publications, 1966-1972." *Anglia* 92 (1974): 143-171.

An important survey and evaluation of secondary material in thirteen categories, including the genres, translations, editions of primary material, and bibliography.

GENERAL

Millett; Longaker & Bolles; Temple & Tucker; Coleman & Tyler; Adelman & Dworkin; Salem; Palmer & Dyson; NCBEL, III, 1915-1934; Breed & Sniderman; Hogan.

YORKE, HENRY: *see* GREEN, HENRY.

YOUNG, ANDREW JOHN (1885-1971)

PRIMARY

Andrew Young. *Collected Poems.* London: Rupert Hart-Davis, 1960. Pp. 219.

Pp. 13-22, bibliographical essay by Leonard Clark. Titles, publisher, date; complete information about contents and many references to textual changes between editions.

Leonard Clark. *Andrew Young.* London: Longmans, Green and Co., Ltd. (WTW 166), 1964. Pp. 43.

Pp. 25-26, primary books. Place, date, genre.

GENERAL

Daiches; NCBEL, IV, 379-380; Stratford.

YOUNG, DOUGLAS (1913-)

Daiches; Vinson-Poets.

YOUNG, EMILY HILDA (1880-1949)

(Mrs. J. A. H. Daniell).

Millett; NCBEL, IV, 781-782; Bufkin.

YOUNG, FRANCIS ERIC BRETT (1884-1954)

PRIMARY

Jessica Brett Young. *Francis Brett Young, A Biography.* London: Heinemann, 1962. Pp. 360.

No bibliography, but details concerning almost all the novels and references to much of the secondary criticism are given in the text, *passim.* Indexed, with titles of primary novels italicized.

SECONDARY

Above, Young.

GENERAL

Millett; Longaker & Bolles; Temple & Tucker; NCBEL, IV, 782-784; Bufkin.

ZANGWILL, ISRAEL (1864-1926)

PRIMARY

Annamarie Peterson. "Israel Zangwill (1864-1926): A Selected Bibliography." *Bulletin of Bibliography* 23 (1961): 136-140.

Primary selected. Form arrangement, principal divisions being Books and pamphlets; Published writings apparently not gathered into Zangwill's books; Unpublished plays. Books: place, publisher, date, British and American editions but no translations. Miscellaneous notes. Periods: volume, pages, date, genre, occasional notes. Important introductory note concerning Zangwill's periodical contributions.

A very comprehensive checklist.

Maurice Wohlgelernter. *Israel Zangwill A Study.* New York: Columbia University Press, 1964. Pp. 344.

Pp. 321-334, primary selected, secondary selected bibliography. Form arrangement. Books: place, publisher, date, translations. Periods: volume, pages, date.

Although a checklist of only the works referred to in the text, it gives additions to Peterson.

SECONDARY

Above, Wohlgelernter, pp. 327-334.

Elsie B. Adams. "Israel Zangwill: An Annotated Bibliography of Writings about Him." *English Literature in Transition* 13 (1970): 209-244.

Secondary selected. Books: place, publisher, date. Periods: volume, pages, date. Complete annotations for each entry.

The beginning point for study of the criticism of Zangwill.

GENERAL

NCBEL, III, 1084; Breed & Sniderman.

INDEX OF NAMES

excluding

the names of principal entries and the names of authors of the general bibliographies listed on pp. ix-xiv.

A Descriptive Catalogue
of the Bibliographies of Twentieth Century
British Poets, Novelists, and Dramatists

Composed in IBM Selectric Composer *Journal Roman* and printed offset, sewn and bound by Braun-Brumfield, Incorporated, Ann Arbor, Michigan. The paper on which the book is printed is Warren's "1854".

A Descriptive Catalogue is a Trenowyth Book, the scholarly publishing division of The Whitston Publishing Company.

This edition consists in 700 casebound copies.